A. B. GRAHAM

A. B. Graham, Superintendent of Agricultural Extension,
Ohio State University, 1911 *(Portrait Photo by Prof. Frank H. Haskett,
Photo Archives, The Ohio State University)*

A. B. GRAHAM
COUNTRY SCHOOLMASTER AND EXTENSION PIONEER

by
Virginia E. and Robert W. McCormick

Cottonwood Publications
Worthington, Ohio

Manufactured in the United States of America.

Typesetting and printing by Worthington Lithography.

Binding by Beck & Orr, Columbus, Ohio.

Library of Congress Cataloging in Publication Data
McCormick, Virginia Evans, 1934 —
   A. B. Graham: country schoolmaster and extension pioneer

   Bibliography: p.
   Includes index.
   1. Graham, Albert Belmont, 1868-1960. 2. Agricultural extension work — United States — History. 3. Education, Rural — Middle West — History. 4. 4-H clubs — United States — History. 5. Educators — United States — Biography. 6. United States. Dept. of Agriculture — Officials and employees — Biography. I. McCormick, Robert W. (Robert William), 1921-   . II. Title. III. Title: AB Graham, country schoolmaster and extension pioneer.

S417.G76M35   1984   630′.92′4 [B]   84-14242

ISBN 0-918887-02-X

Contents

Illustrations

Frontispiece: A. B. Graham, Superintendent of Agricultural Extension, Ohio State University, 1911 *(Portrait Photo by Prof. Frank H. Haskett, Photo Archives, The Ohio State University)*

Part I — between pages 26 and 31

1 Joseph A. Graham and Esther Reeder at time of marriage, 1867 *(Graham Family)*

2 Esther Reeder Graham with Albert and Lettie after fire destroyed home and killed Joseph A. Graham, 1879 *(Graham Family)*

3 Esther Graham home at Lena, Ohio where Albert lived from age eleven through the first year of his marriage *(Graham Family)*

4 Rev. Lauer's home at Conover, Ohio where Maud lived as a girl *(Graham Family)*

5 Albert B. Graham and Maud Keyte Lauer at the time of marriage, 1890 *(Graham Family)*

6 The home the Grahams built in 1909 at 168 Twelfth Ave., Columbus across from the O.S.U. Campus *(Graham Family)*

7 Supt. and Mrs. Graham leaving for New England business trip, 1912 *(Graham Family)*

8 Blair, Helen, Joseph, and Walter Graham at Amityville, New York home, 1914 *(Graham Family)*

Part II — between pages 62 and 71

9 Carmony School, Johnson Twp., Champaign Co., Ohio where Graham began teaching in 1885 *(Graham Family)*

10 First teaching certificate earned by sixteen-year-old Graham before completing his last year at Lena-Conover School *(Photo Archives, The Ohio State University)*

11 Lena-Conover School, Miami Co., Ohio; A. B. Graham, principal, April 1890 *(Ohio Historical Society)*

12 Auditorium at National Normal University, Lebanon, Ohio; seating capacity 1400 *(Ohio Historical Society)*

Part IV — between pages 175 and 182

Charts and Maps

To
Those Educators
past and present
who have walked in more than one world

Foreword

Education for youth and adults in America evolved, in considerable measure, from the philosophy, achievements and dedicated commitment of such men as A. B. Graham, about whom this book is written. This professional biography traces some of the significant educational changes through the eyes of an influential participant. It focuses particularly on the development of the agricultural extension organization, 4-H Club work and the rural schools in Ohio. Its evolution is examined from the background of one pioneer who helped to shape it. If Dr. Graham were alive today he would be extremely proud, yet humble, to realize the distinguished service he rendered as a country schoolmaster and extension pioneer as recorded by the authors.

In preparing this biography the authors have done extensive background research of personal correspondence, records of The Ohio State University Library Archives, the National Archives, Graham family records, official reports, many speeches and articles in professional journals. Featured heavily in this book are Graham's collections of original materials, as well as reconstructed data and remembrances written later in his professional life. Of particular interest is this renowned leader's influence as a one-room school teacher, as an innovative county superintendent of schools, as a spokesman for the Champaign County (Ohio) Teachers Asscoiation, as Superintendent of Agricultural Extension at The Ohio State University, and as "a teacher of teachers" in the Extension Service of the United States Department of Agriculture.

A. B. Graham: Country Schoolmaster and Extension Pioneer is a biography that challenges the reader's interest, intellect, educational philosophy, pioneering spirit, and skills as a teacher, leader and administrator. This publication should have wide acceptance with rural and adult educators, school administrators and Cooperative Extension personnel. If I were to return to training and development of Extension workers, this biography would definitely be required reading. Every person in a supervisory and administrative position in education could learn much from this authoritative record of a great humanitarian educator.

Robert C. Clark
Madison, Wisconsin

Acknowledgments

The A. B. Graham story is more than a chronicle of the accomplishments of this educational pioneer. These achievements occurred within the context of a rapidly developing rural society and a changing educational philosophy. It is essential to understand this context to set Graham's accomplishments in proper perspective.

Some of the sources which have been helpful to us are cited in the bibliographic notes, but we are deeply indebted to many persons whom we regret cannot be named individually. We do wish to express our gratitude to some who have given specific assistance during the preparation of this manuscript.

We deeply appreciate the cooperative support provided by Helen Graham Baker and Joseph R. Graham. They have generously shared their father's materials without imposing any constraints regarding their use, have patiently responded to our many queries, and have trusted us with valuable family treasures.

Our research in the Ohio State University Library Archives has been assisted by Raymond Goerler, University Archivist; Robert Bober, Assistant Archivist; Ruth Jones, Assistant for Photography; and by Dorothy Ross, whose title as Assistant for Manuscripts inadequately describes her supportive role in everything from providing space for research to extended searches for obscure files.

Numerous individuals at the Ohio Historical Society have aided our access to their excellent Graham manuscript and photograph collections. We remain especially indebted to Conrad Weitzel, Boyd Winans, Arlene Peterson and Kathleen Conway of the Archives/Library Division.

Many persons have assisted our research in various ways and places. Luke M. Schruben, retired Assistant Administrator, Federal Extension Service, U.S.D.A. provided a very helpful preview inventory of Extension Service records in the National Archives and Richard C. Crawford of the Scientific, Economic and Natural Resources Branch provided on site assistance. James T. Veeder, while he was Manager of the Resource Center of the National 4-H Council in Washington, D. C. helped us search photographs and correspondence of the former National 4-H Service Committee in Chicago. Floyd Barmann, Director of the Clark County Historical Society assisted us in finding the Graham materials in that collection. Sandra B. Neyman of the Dawes Memorial Library at Marietta College searched their records relating to honorary degrees. Mike Ludlow, Librarian at Graham High School located their collection of original materials relating to its dedication. Michael E. Haubner, County Extension Agent, Chairman and Janet Lannon, Secretary of the Clark County Extension office helped us search their files for materials relating to the Golden Jubilee and the dedication of the Graham Memorial Building.

Many persons who knew A. B. Graham in some capacity have generously shared insights from their perspectives regarding his contributions. We especially wish to thank Richard E. Putnam, retired principal, Miami East Junior High, formerly the Lena-Conover building where Graham was principal; Robert and Helen Grieser, president of the Clark County 4-H Council during the 1952 Golden Jubilee; Mary Lou Pfieffer Saunway, former Women's Director at Radio WRFD who made tapes preserving Graham's philosophy; Wilbur B. Wood, retired Director, Ohio Cooperative Extension Service; John T. Mount, Vice President Emeritus, The Ohio State University; Beatrice J. Cleveland and James W. Marquand, both retired members of the Ohio State 4-H Club staff. Their insights have contributed to our perception.

We are deeply indebted to four persons who reviewed the entire manuscript from a particular perspective: Robert C. Clark, formerly Director of the National Extension Center for Advanced Study at the University of Wisconsin and currently Executive Secretary of Epsilon Sigma Phi, Extension Honorary Fraternity; Luvern L. Cunningham, Novice G. Fawcett Professor of Educational Administration at The Ohio State University; Edwin L. Kirby, retired Administrator, Federal Extension Service, United States Department of Agriculture; and Charles W. Lifer, Assistant Director and State Leader, 4-H, Ohio Cooperative Extension Service. Their critical suggestions have been most helpful.

Finally, the authors extend their thanks posthumously to the subject of this biography, A. B. Graham for his careful preservation of records and materials which provided the primary documentation for this study.

We are sincerely grateful to many persons who have contributed to the accuracy of this manuscript. Any errors which may remain are the sole responsibility of the authors.

Virginia E. and Robert W. McCormick

Introduction

This is the story of a teacher who made a difference . . . one who had an educational philosophy based upon scientific inquiry, a zealous commitment to the implementation of those beliefs, enough courage to stand alone on matters of principle, and the humor to challenge the power of the status quo without malice. It is both a biography and the story of an educational movement, described through the experiences of a front line participant. It is a viewpoint which has not been expressed by educational leaders who wrote as administrators or professors, nor by local teachers who saw only small parts of the picture and rarely had avenues for mass communication. It is a story as relevant to the high tech explosion of the 1980s as to the country life movement of the early 1900s. There are principles to be applied whenever society lays its challenges at education's doorstep.

American democracy is firmly rooted in the belief that education is the avenue for upward social mobility and the source of knowledge and skills for productivity. Public education has successfully integrated foreign speaking immigrants and provided skills for traveling and working in space; yet our expectations are, and always have been, that education should do more and do it better. Our current environment creates an acute awareness that education is never terminal and we must seek effective models for continuous learning.

At the turn of the twentieth century rural America ranked high among education's priority problems. Agricultural production still required the largest labor force within the nation's economy and rural families were frequently socially and culturally deprived by their geographic isolation.

Education responded in some dramatic ways: consolidating schools for increased efficiency and broader curriculum; improving supervision through rural superintendents; incorporating course work in agriculture, domestic science and manual training; creating institutions for training and certifying specialized teachers; designing junior high schools to improve the transition from elementary to secondary education; and providing massive adult education through the extension programs of land-grant institutions.

This professional biography traces such changes through the eyes of an influential participant, focusing particularly on the development of the agricultural extension organization. Its evolution is examined from the background of one pioneer who helped to shape it; in the context of contemporary educational issues, the problems of agricultural production, and the disadvantages faced by rural families. This personal story reminds educators that educational institutions are molded by their times and cannot be successfully replicated or maintained without significant change in a different social context.

In an educational career spanning more than half a century, A.B. Graham's influence stretched from one-room schools to land-grant universities. Details of his family background and his boyhood community have been included only as they contributed to his professional development. The concept of indigenous leadership has been personalized to graphically illustrate such difficulties as supporting a family on the salary of a one-room school teacher. But this is not primarily a personal story, and data from personal correspondence and interviews have intentionally been limited. Ohio is described only as the arena in which Graham worked and the context for analysis, not as an example of typical public school or extension programs.

The A.B. Graham story can be reconstructed because a wealth of original material is available. From an early age he was a curious and intelligent observer of his environment, an appreciative collector of information, and a careful keeper of everything.

Researchers are provided a luxurious choice including handwritten correspondence, examination questions from early teacher examinations, notes collected for speeches and articles, photographs taken to illustrate reports and brochures, and journal notations for compiling monthly and annual reports. The authors have had unlimited access to Graham family materials in the possession of his daughter Helen Graham Baker and son Joseph R. Graham, manuscript and photograph collections at the Ohio Historical Society, the Graham collection in the Ohio State University Library Archives, memorabilia in the Clark County Historical Society relating to the Graham agricultural club, Graham correspondence and reports in the Extension Service records in the National Archives, and some private holdings. Specific references are identified in the bibliographic notes and sources.

One who questions why the Graham story is not already widely known must consider his background as the son and grandson of farmers, a Normal School graduate, and a teacher rising from a decade of one-room school experience. He became a leading pioneer in the agricultural extension movement, but was never quite accepted by the agriculturists because of his education background and never fully recognized by educators because of his agricultural affiliations.

If it were not for the agricultural experiment club he organized while a township superintendent at Springfield, Ohio Graham's name and accomplishments would not have been preserved. This club, however, was a forerunner of the 4-H program now known worldwide, and the spotlight thrown on this accomplishment has drawn attention to one small portion of a fascinating educational career. The broader story deserves telling. Many educational specialists who today identify themselves as extension educators, adult educators, agricultural educators, educational administrators, 4-H leaders, child development specialists, or educational psychologists may find inspiration in A.B. Graham's goals and accomplishments.

As in many stories, one must resolve conflicting data, and perhaps at times tread heavily on some of the legends which arise around a local hero. But the facts of this story need no embellishment, and rich collections of contemporary data speak eloquently of Graham's beliefs and accomplishments.

Realizing that anyone who selects a biographical subject already possesses sufficient information to have developed a bias, this venture began with the commitment to avoid claims that any Graham accomplishment was the first, best, or largest of its kind. Such subjective judgments cannot be documented in an evolving social movement. It was surprising, however, to discover the breadth of this educator's concepts and the consistency of his commitment to certain issues over a fifty year career spanning local, state and national positions. Graham's genius as an early adopter of educational practices was deeply rooted in his background as a common man. He was an expert translator of educational theory into practical applications. If one were to select a prototype of the extension concept of interpreting research into useful practice, one would be hard pressed to match this career as a source of examples.

The Graham collections contain original materials as well as reconstructed data and remembrances written late in life. When possible, the authors have relied upon materials written at or near the time the event occurred, but certain materials such as Graham's remembrances of his parents and his boyhood are valuable for their perceptions. In many instances it was possible to compare public records such as published reports with private records such as interoffice memoranda. This was particularly valuable for the 1900 to 1904 period when Graham's daily journal and much original correspondence could be compared with his annual reports and with contemporary news articles and later memorial tributes. Newspaper articles are among the most variable sources in regard to accuracy. Late in life when Graham was receiving numerous honors, inaccuracies were sometimes obvious enough to be embarrassing, but Graham seems to have taken it in stride, noting on one article he filed away, "Contains some very erroneous statements. Truth and jazzing up news stories are not always compatible."[1]

One rich source of material is the vast amount of published information in which Graham was not identified as the author. As a fourteen year old boy Graham wrote his first letter to the editor of the local paper under a pseudonym, a common practice in the 19th century, but an interesting portent of his professional career. During the 1890s he wrote an outstanding but anonymous collection of editorial columns on educational issues as the spokesman for the Champaign County Teachers Association. Both at the Ohio State University and in the U.S. Department of Agriculture he frequently outlined concepts for presentations by his superiors or prepared drafts for a politician's presentation. The total scope of these contributions can never be known, but enough evidence exists in memoranda to attribute many ideas to Graham much earlier than they were publicly expressed.

Careful readers may be disturbed by apparent inconsistencies within this manuscript in the use of organization titles. It is quite true that A.B. Graham's role as Superintendent of Agricultural Extension at the Ohio State University is essentially the same role now known as the Director of the Cooperative Extension Service. However, it is the authors' belief that readers are better served by the use of contemporary terms and referred to a glossary for notations regarding title changes and abbreviations.

Viewing an array of problems from the perspective of time permits some realistic evaluation of educational efforts. The positive balance between success and failure as educators addressed the problems of rural America, provides an encouraging view of education's potential for addressing current needs. Some ambivalence may be appropriate in observing the confidence many early educators seemed to feel regarding the "rightness" of their position and their missionary zeal in promoting that position. This educator's experiences raise some thought provoking questions. Was the turn of the century a simpler time or was education charged with less of the total responsibility for solving social problems? Were educational leaders of the past more willing to take a stand and be held accountable or is that a constant characteristic which can be attributed only to a courageous few?

The increasing speed of social change can be expected to place ever larger expectations on our educational insitiutions. Our nation's highest court has affirmed that, " . . . education is perhaps the most important function of state and local government."[2] The challenge to educators is whether professional maturity can keep pace with social change and exert confident leadership. This biography suggests that some of the answers will be found among the ranks of conscientious practitioners.

PART I
Graham Family and Lena-Conover Boyhood

Archibald Graham (1759-1823) m. Hannah Johnson (1767-1830)

Jane (Harvey)
Achsah (Slack)
Joseph (1795-1872) m. Maria Duer (-1864)

John
Hulda (Boyd)
William
Mary (Davis)

Ann T. (Wolcott)
James. d. inf.
Louisa B. (Roberts)
George D.
Eleanor J. (Short)
Joseph A. (1839-1879) m. Esther P. Reeder (1845-1912)

John S. Reeder m. Letitia Pownall

Margery A.
Esther P.

Martha R.
Ellen K.
Miles P.
Eliza J.
William H.
Mary E.
John E.
George W.

James D. Lauer m. 1)

William H.
Elizabeth H.
Mary B.
Walter S. d. inf.
Clara B.

m. 2) Elizabeth Keyte

Alvaretta (Dodd)
Minerva (Stephenson)
J. Quinn
Maud K.

Albert B.

Letitia M. (Love)

Walter S. d. inf.
Harrie J. d. inf.

ALBERT BELMONT GRAHAM (1868-1960) m. 1890 **MAUD KEYTE LAUER** (1870-1950)

Rettie E.
d. inf.

Walter S.
m. Alene Pollock
— Walter S.

Helen E.
m. Robert Baker
— Robert A.
— Barbara

Joseph R.
m. Cecelia McGolrick
— Stanley R.
— James A.
— Marilyn A.

E. Blair
m. Ruth Grau
— Martha J.

Chapter 1
A Boy in the
Lena-Conover Community

"He showed me how to locate a swarm of bees in a
bee-tree, how to make willow and leather-wood whistles
in the springtime, how to make elder pop guns, water
wheels from corn stalks, siphons from jimson stalk
forks, how to support a tumbler of water upside down,
how to make leaves of long blades of grass squeal...."[1]

For a family dependent on each other for simple pleasures, Sunday, February 2, 1879 began tragically. Just before dawn, fire
started in the living area and spread rapidly through the frame
two-story farmhouse just east of the Miami-Champaign County,
Ohio line. The force of the blaze and smoke knocked the father
unconscious as he opened the door from the downstairs bedroom,
and the mother was seriously burned as she managed to escape
through the kitchen. The son, sharing their room because he was
ill, cut his hands and feet as he broke the bedroom window to
escape into the yard. An uncle, a hired man, and the young
daughter sleeping upstairs fled through a window to the porch
roof from which the men jumped as the mother caught the
daughter.

Sam Hughes, the strongly built young farmhand managed to
reach through the broken bedroom window and pull out the
unconscious father, the uncle carried the daughter in his arms to
the village of Lena about sixty rods west. Neighbors who rushed
to help were too late to save home or belongings, but the burned
and cut family members were quickly laid on wagons and taken
to Lena where doctors could attend them. Joseph A. Graham, the
father whose lungs had been burned and eyes blinded by the
flames, was taken to the home of William and Louise Roberts, his
sister and brother-in-law. Dr. Frank Gabriel of Piqua, a respected
former resident and Civil War surgeon was called to assist local

doctors, but the damage was too severe. On Monday morning, eight days later, the tolling of the Methodist Church bell told the community of his death.

The son's cuts and burns were first treated by Dr. W.S. Cox, the same physician who had attended the boy's birth. Albert Belmont Graham had been born in that farmhouse Friday the 13th of March, 1868. As his scars gradually healed, the eleven-year-old boy's world changed dramatically. Boarding temporarily with Dr. Asa Brecourt, he spent his convalescence reading anatomy books. Neighbors had quickly raised more than $400 to help the family rebuild their home, but these plans changed with Joseph Graham's death. The farm was sold to pay off mortgages Joseph had assumed when he agreed to purchase the interests of the other heirs after his father's death six years earlier. Esther Reeder Graham, a widow at thirty-three, used the community's help to build a small frame home in Lena for herself and the two children. Contributions of miscellaneous furniture and clothing were helpful, but Albert long remembered the humiliation of an eleven- year- old boy whose only hat and coat were much too large men's garments.

Albert's teacher Daniel Death, who had also taught his father at one-room Carmony School, headed a collection effort to replace the boy's most cherished possession, his 1800 page *Webster's Dictionary*. A year earlier Albert had emptied his red tin bank of nearly $9 savings to purchase the wonderful book he had seen at a spelling match in Piqua. Years later Graham could remember all ten of the books his parents had treasured in that farm home: the family Bible, Fleetwood's *Life of Christ, Life of Fred Douglas* (a free Negro), Dr. Chase's *Recipe Book,* Dr. Gunn's *Family Medicine,* Howe's *History of Ohio, A History of the Civil War,* Burns' *Poems,* Mitchell's *Geography and Atlas,* and *Illustrated Proverbs.*

The Graham farm, like many others in that part of the state, was an eighty acre half section. In Albert's boyhood a twenty acre woodlot survived, but the remainder had been cleared and was planted to wheat, rye, and corn in nearly equal proportions. Livestock were kept for farm work and family use, but not for commercial sale. In 1870, these included four milk cows, four horses, three beef cattle, and five pigs. The family butchered its own meat, churned its butter, made its molasses, and raised a garden to provide its own fruits and vegetables.[2]

The farm home was a humble one where father and mother had only a common school education but where curiosity was encouraged and learning was appreciated. Albert learned his alphabet from the large letters used in advertisements of the *Cincinnati Enquirer* his parents regularly received. Work, play and learning were intermingled as the parents and children contributed to family needs. Large flocks of passenger pigeons, attracted by the acorns and beechnuts in the woodlot, were still common in the area in the 1870s. Albert could recall his father standing in the barnyard and bringing down three or four of the steel blue birds with a single shotgun blast. Children also contributed to the family food supply, collecting berries from the nearby fields or fishing with a willow branch pole. Lost Creek crossed the Graham farm south of the road and provided a good source of sunfish, shiners, catfish or chub.

Like farm youngsters everywhere Albert and his sister Lettie, a year and a half younger, had regular chores such as gathering eggs and hoeing the garden. From an early age each was given the responsibility of raising a baby pig or calf. The small profit from the sale of Albert's first baby pig was his first "earned" money, and became part of the savings he used for the dictionary. By the time he was ten, Albert was considered responsible enough to ride one of the team of horses to harrow a six acre field for planting, but working with horses was disagreeable and frightening to the boy and he decided early that he wanted to be a school teacher not a farmer when he grew up.

The improved gravel road past the house became free to the public in 1872 after being built as a turnpike fifty years earlier and operating with five toll gates on the twenty-six mile stretch between Urbana and Piqua. In Albert's boyhood vagrants frequently sought handouts at the Graham kitchen or slept the night in the barn. The summer he was seven that pike brought Albert's first circus, a couple of horse drawn wagons and an elephant to help erect a tent at the edge of Lena. Everyone gathered on the few blue benches in the tent lighted by coal oil lamps to see the animal acts, clowns, acrobats and dancers. In Albert's mind it didn't measure up to the exaggerated yellow and black show bills, but it was nevertheless a special treat for the small village.

Inside the home Esther Graham carefully preserved on the kitchen door her son's crayon drawn maps of the eastern and western hemispheres. She was an accomplished seamstress who taught this skill to both her son and daughter. Albert was only nine when he proudly pieced his first quilt top for his mother to quilt. After Joseph's death, widow and children used this skill to support themselves. For years the most treasured possession in their Lena home was an ash sewing table, 23 inches by 44 inches with drawers on each side, built by the Conover furniture factory. As a space for cutting out garments, sewing, and preparing lessons it was the center of family activity.

The village of Lena had about 150 residents by the time Esther Graham and the two children moved into town. Workers digging the cellar for their home on Lot 27 in the spring of 1879, discovered remnants of bricks and brick bats apparently used in building the Predestinarian Baptist church a quarter mile north about 1830. At that time, "Allen's Post Office" had just been established on the turnpike, but it was two years before a village was surveyed and christened "Elizabethtown." It was soon discovered that another village already had that name so by the 1840 census it had become known as Lena and so it continued.

To catch the passenger train, Lena residents went a mile southwest to Conover, a village of about 100 persons which had developed after the Pittsburg, Cincinnati and St. Louis Railroad went through in 1856. As a boy, Albert stood on the farmhouse porch and watched the trains go by to the southwest, but he was twelve years old and living in Lena before he took his first ride. His uncle paid the 55 cent round trip fare so he could accompany him on the nine mile, thirty minute ride to Piqua. Years later he recalled, "As I settled down at a window on the red plush seat, how I wanted to be a train man and ride forever. How I envied the newsboy who could ride that train every day."[3] It was a trip long discussed and much envied among his friends.

For special shopping trips, Lena residents were more likely to go to Piqua than to the county seat towns of Troy or Urbana where they went for courthouse business. Some residents regularly did business in Fletcher, a village of nearly 400 persons four miles west, or in St. Paris, a town of more than 1000 persons three and a half miles east. But many met most of their needs in Lena.

In the early 1880s John Hamilton's confectionery marked the corner where the Bellefontaine road intersected the Urbana-Piqua turnpike, but J.F. Colvin & S.G. Frazier's General Store was the heart of the village. Cracker and sugar barrels, some locally made by Evan Davis, combined with nail kegs to provide enough seats to make this a village club room on winter evenings. Merchandise included all the expected 19th century items from bolts of calico to patent medicines, but the ever observant Albert was impressed by the tub containing a lemon tree which bore fruit and flowers at the same time, and the Webster's Dictionary within convenient reach for settling arguments.

Lena boasted two milliners and several seamstresses like Esther Graham who could fashion the bustle skirts so popular in the early 1880s. For tailoring, men went to David Jones, whose shop on occasion served as the village voting place, and on Saturdays became the barbershop of Lucian Carey, a Negro from St. Paris. George Cox, the doctor's son, was a blacksmith who sometimes had odd jobs for young Albert Graham as did his uncle William Roberts, a wheelright and wagon maker. Several nearby farmers specialized as carpenters, plasterers, and painters making the village of Graham's boyhood a very typical, self-sufficient 19th century village. In fact, in the 1880s it was becoming quite modern with Carmony's Grocery offering bread baked in St. Paris and Josiah Boyd blowing his cornet to announce the weekly arrival of his fresh meat wagon.

Albert was large for his age and able to find a variety of jobs to help support the little family. With the gift of a saw and sawbuck from his uncle William Roberts he cut stove wood for village families at 50 cents a cord. John McCarthy would pay 5 cents for cleaning his blacksmith shop and give the boy a chance to practice his German in the process. Farmers were often in need of extra hands for 50 to 75 cents a day during haymaking and threshing seasons. The dirtiest, dustiest, and most disliked of all jobs was "tailing" the threshing machine. Albert knew it well. In the fall, pay for cutting corn was seven or eight cents per shock and for husking $1 per day plus two meals.

Graham ancestors were Presbyterian and the Reeders Hicksite Quaker, but neither had a congregation in Lena. Albert's grandparents, Joseph and Maria Graham, had joined in forming the Methodist Episcopal Church. Albert attended Sunday School in the congregation's second structure, a frame building with two front doors and a pew-high partition through the center, although the custom of separating men and women worshippers was largely ignored by Albert's boyhood. Before the Grahams moved into town coal had replaced wood in the two heating stoves, kerosene lamps had replaced candles, and a reed organ and hymnals had eliminated the need for a leader to "line out" the hymns for the congregation[4].

Sunday School was based on "Golden Texts" for reading and discussing a Bible passage with the goal of covering the entire Bible in seven years. In later years A. B. Graham wrote, "The general idea in such a lesson plan was uniformity, but in the opinion of the writer it did as much to deaden interest as it did to establish uniformity. System for the sake of the system."[5] The boy was absorbing ideas which influenced the educator which he was to become. During the winter, revival sevices were a social highlight, with everyone joining in favorite hymns such as "Ninety and Nine," "I Need Thee Every Hour," "What a Friend We Have in Jesus," and "In the Sweet Bye and Bye."

Sunday School was especially gala at Christmas time. The native cedar trees common a little farther south were rare around Lena and few families had a Christmas tree at home, but one was always found and decorated for the Sunday School celebration. At home stockings were hung and usually filled with a hand knitted item such as a cap or mittens, a few pieces of candy, and a small china toy, whistle or horn. A special treat was a package of firecrackers, which in the Graham home made their appearance only at Christmas.

Other winter treats at one of the churches or Masonic Lodge were the oyster suppers featuring shipments from Baltimore packed in ice. Subscription singing schools were taught each year by a succession of teachers, and "magic lantern" shows were occasionally featured at the school. The most memorable snow of Graham's boyhood actually occurred not in the winter but on May 21, 1883, when a freak storm dropped eighteen inches. A young man north of town caused quite a stir by driving his sleigh into the village, but he was rewarded with muddy slush for much of the ride home.

Memorial Days were celebrated with much ceremony at Fletcher Cemetery where soldiers' graves were decorated and Civil War veterans of the 94th Ohio Volunteer Infantry, like Albert's uncle George, were honored. On such occasions the Lena Cornet Band in their dark blue uniforms and white plumed "chapeaux" played proudly. Independence Day was likely to be celebrated locally with picnics and speeches at Merritt's woods south of town, but the nation's centennial July 4, 1876 was a big event in Piqua long remembered by all in spite of the rain. For some boys,

Halloween was the most clebrated holiday of the year, but Graham remembered so much "senseless deviltry" he was not allowed to go out on October 31st. The example most often recounted in Lena occurred in 1880 when local youth took apart a spring wagon and carefully reassembled it on the roof of William Robert's wagon shop.

The Graham family farm in Champaign County and later their home in the village of Lena exposed young Albert to rural schools in both Miami and Champaign Counties. Union or "Carmony" School in District #3, Johnson Township, Champaign County, which Albert was attending when the family home burned, was a single-room frame building completed two years earlier and graded only informally by the McGuffey Reader each student was using.Albert and Lettie walked the half mile from their home daily on the mud and gravel road.

After moving into Lena they attended Allen's School in District #6, Brown Township, Miami County. This double brick building had a primary room built in 1851 and a room for advanced students added in 1870 as the population increased with the coming of the railroad. The advanced room had factory made desks which each accommodated two students. Each room was heated by a wood burning stove and the "blackboard" was a coating of plaster mixed with lampblack. Misbehavior was commonly punished by requiring the student to stand in the corner or the aisle or to stay inside during recess. For serious miscreants, Mr. Allen's nearly apple orchard supplied a ready source of whips.

Around the old oak tree in the schoolyard games were more active than quiet. Winter set the stage for fox and geese or snow forts with snowball fights. Spring brought out marbles and occasionally a clandestine game of the forbidden "Keeps."[6] See-saws were made from borrowed fence rails and groups formed for "Blackman," Prisoner's Base" or "Three Deep." "Swing Tail" was banned after Minta Frazee died of injuries received when the end of the crack-the-whip line crashed against the school foundation.

When the teacher's handbell rang for classes, Albert studied U.S. history, Harvey's *Grammar,* Ray's *Higher Arithmetic,* and, of course, advanced McGuffey *Readers* for literature. Teachers were poorly paid and frequent changes exposed students to a variety of teaching styles. Graham recalled one who required orization whether or not the meaning was understood. "Never was he much of a teacher, but he was a quiz master and driller." George Snyder, his first college educated teacher was remembered fondly for his homemade bookcase with books Albert was free to use. "(He) awakened me to the possibilities of becoming an educated young man."[7]

By 1884 Allen's School was crowded and in need of repair. Led by the blacksmith of German ancestry, the community created a special district high school so students did not have to travel to Piqua or St. Paris. That fall a handsome three-room brick building known as "Heidelberg" School was opened at a cost of $5000. A.T. Moore, a graduate of National Normal School at Lebanon, Ohio, became superintendent and high school teacher for $70 per month. Two elementary teachers each received $45 per month and student Graham was paid $5 per month as janitor. One of his final duties was tolling the 400 pound bell in its steeple to announce the death of President U.S. Grant to the community in the summer of 1885.

June 19, 1885 this new Lena-Conover School graduated its first class: Albert B. Graham, Minnie S. Lauer, and G. Rosseau Wilgus. All three had taken the examinations and been certified to teach in Miami County. In the absence of an accredited high school curriculum, teacher certification was the accepted form of competency testing, and Albert had taken the examinations a year earlier. The most dreaded subject was the arithmetic, but Albert like other candidates had practiced the sample teacher examination questions regularly published in local newspapers. "How many cords of wood in a pile 13 ft. long, 4 ft., 2 in. wide and 3 ft. 6 in. high?" "What is the present value of a note of $1300, due in two years, 8 mos. at 7 per cent, true discount?" "Solve a problem in long division and explain the process as you would to a class."[8] What a relief when the envelope containing a one year certificate arrived from the county examiners. Failures in Miami County were mailed in an envelopes with the stamp upside down, which certainly publicized the bad news, since everyone in the community had to go to the post office to collect their mail.

Sixteen year old Albert chose to go back another year to attend the new "high school," but the days of the schoolboy were about to merge gently, as they often did in rural 19th century Ohio, into the days of the rural schoolmaster. Boyhood on the farm and in the village of Lena had offered pleasures as well as tragedy, few material possessions but numerous opportunities to assume responsibilities and measure one's accomplishments. The seeds had been planted and nurtured for curiosity about his environment, unusually detailed memories of people and events, and an unspoken sensitivity toward paucity of educational opportunity. Perhaps the influence of the Lena-Conover boyhood can be measured by realizing the man who lived it devoted almost a decade in retirement to collecting and recording the community's history.

Chapter 2
Graham Family
Ancestors and Descendants

"A person that gains a good name within his own
neighborhood and acts well, he will be respected by his
fellows as the person who has gained a worldwide reputation is respected by the nations of the world."[1]

As a seventeen-year-old high school graduate and for a decade
thereafter, Albert B. Graham's world was defined by an extended
family which simultaneously supported and confined him. This
particular family network traced to the westward migration of his
grandparents and their siblings.

Bits of stories passed down through the Graham family offer
only a tantalizing glimpse of JOSEPH and MARIA DUER GRA-
HAM'S journey to Ohio in the spring of 1834. Albert's aunt Louisa
Roberts was a favorite with her nephew for her sugar cookies and
rich rice puddings, and she could remember the journey as an
eleven-year-old girl traveling with her parents, thirteen-year-old
sister Anna and five-year-old brother George. It was a twenty-five
day journey from eastern Pennsylvania to western Ohio with a
horse drawn wagon and the family milk cow tied behind. No one
recorded the exact route and overnight stops, but the Ohio portion
of the journey undoubtedly utilized the new National Road which
that year was completed as far west as Springfield.

The most carefully guarded possession in the farm wagon
was a sack in which Joseph was carrying 1800 silver half dollars
in expectation of purchasing an eighty acre half section in western Ohio. This he did on June 10th, 1834 paying Jonathan and
Rachel Printz $900 for the west half of the northwest quarter of
section thirty-six in township three of range eleven between the
Miami Rivers.[2] Adjustment of the survey line actually included
eighty-seven acres in this farm, but Joseph Graham was paying
more than $10 per acre when government lands in Ohio were still
available to the north and west for $2 per acre. For this price he

was buying partial improvements including a log house and barn and partially cleared acreage which was cultivated around some remaining tree stumps. But most important, Joseph and Maria Graham were settling in a community of "kinfolk" from Bucks County, Pennsylvania.

After their mother's death four years earlier Joseph's sister and brother-in-law Achsah and Cornelius Slack had purchased a farm just one mile north of this site and sister Jane's husband, Abner Harvey, purchased a 160 acre quarter section about two miles south in Lost Creek township of Miami County. Brother William had migrated west in 1832 and was practicing his black-smith trade in Miami County near Allen's post office.

Of ARCHIBALD and HANNAH JOHNSON GRAHAM'S grown children only John remained in Pennsylvania. Six migrated west after their parents' deaths, and settled within five miles of each other on both sides of the Champaign-Miami county line in what was to become known as the Lena-Conover community. There were already a variety of Graham, Johnson, Duer and Anderson relatives in this part of western Ohio and the opportunity to purchase land at an affordable price was a magnet for westward movement in the 1830s. The frontier period with its dangers of Indian raids was past in this part of the country. The National Road was moving westward a few miles to the south, the Miami and Erie Canal had recently reached nearby Piqua, and the Urbana to Piqua turnpike crossed the new Graham purchase. Joseph and Maria were settling in a farming community poised for agricultural development.

The circumstances had been surprisingly similar for the Graham immigrants who came to eastern Pennsylvania. Archibald Graham's parents came to America from Scotland shortly before his birth in 1759. This placed them among the early settlers but not the frontier pioneers of eastern Pennsylvania. Archibald was born and died in Bucks County, north of Philadelphia, just across the Delaware River from Trenton, New Jersey. During the American Revolution this part of Pennsylvania was repeatedly crossed by troops and became best known for General Washington's stormy crossing of the Delaware River on Christmas Eve of 1776. In August of 1775, at sixteen, Archibald had been old enough to join the Pennsylvania militia unit in Warwick Township. The following spring his name appeared among the 1500 men enrolled in Col. Samuel Miles rifle regiment which moved to join Gen.

Mercer in July and participated in the Battle of Long Island on August 27, 1776. Archibald Graham was in Capt. James Long's Company of Col. Samuel Atlee's Musket Battalion. Col. Atlee was captured by the British during this battle and exchanged two years later. Archibald Graham was among a large number listed as missing on muster rolls after the battle and still missing in September.[3] It is not clear when and how he worked his way back to Bucks County, but it is likely that any further service was confined to local militia duty.

September 2, 1790 at the Newtown, Pennsylvania Presbyterian church were she had been baptized, Archibald Graham married Hannah Johnson, daughter of Joseph and Hannah Johnson. They made their home and raised their family on a farm in Upper Makefield Township near Dolington. Here Joseph, their third child and first son, was born March 29, 1795. Like his father, he was old enough to be in the local militia when the colonies fought the British, this time as the United States of America in the War of 1812. But the war which burned the young nation's capitol and caused such fear from Britain's Indian allies on the western frontier did not actively involve the Bucks County militia.

Joseph married Maria Duer on December 17, 1818 and farmed in Bucks County for fifteen years before making the decision to migrate west with their three living children. Several Duer relatives had also been in the Bucks County group migrating to Ohio in 1830 and their letters were most encouraging. One cousin wrote, "We are more comfortably fixed than we could possibly have been if we had stayed in Bucks County."[4] After the Joseph Graham's arrival, that same cousin wrote, "Cousin Maria Graham and family are well and appear to be very much pleased with the place."[5]

Two additional children were born to Joseph and Maria while they were living in the log house on the south side of the Urbana-Piqua turnpike, Eleanor J. in 1835 and Joseph A. on November 30, 1839. Joseph and Maria were in Ohio almost twenty years before they built a new home with clapboard siding on the north side of the road, the same house which burned so tragically in 1879. They joined several families in the neighborhood in the Mt. Vernon Methodist Church and young Joseph A. began school at the age of five in the nearby "Mt. Vernon" School.

By the time the Civil War disrupted the community, the Graham daughters were married, Ann to a prosperous farmer near

Lena, Louisa to a wagon maker at Lena, and Eleanor had migrated to Missouri. George, past his thirtieth birthday and still single, enlisted as a private in the 94th Ohio Volunteer Infantry August 5, 1862.[6] The regiment was mustered in at Camp Piqua August 23rd and "with three rounds of cartridge to the man . . . without uniform or camp equipage, and never having drilled as a regiment,"[7] was ordered to march to Kentucky to assist in repelling Confederate General Kirby Smith's threat to Cincinnati. Lexington was filled with stragglers and wounded when the 94th O.V.I. arrived late in the evening of August 31st. There were no arrangements for their accommodations or rations before they were ordered to march fifteen miles east to Tate's Ford the next day. As the hot and exhausted troops reached the creek in late afternoon and fell out to drink and rest, Rebel scouts fired on them from ambush. In the brief skirmish several were wounded and more than sixty were taken prisoner, including George D. Graham and twenty-eight others from Company C. He was carried to Richmond, Virginia, paroled several months later, and spent most of the war on guard duty, being mustered out in July 1865 in St. Paul, Minnesota.

Such incidents seldom make the history books but they are known to the enlisted men of every war and when shared with the home community are perhaps as significant as patriotic idealism in affecting local recruitment and community loyalty. When Ohio began conscripting men to fill its quotas, Joseph A. Graham remained on the farm, his father paying $300 for a substitute so that he could remain to do the farm work and take care of his aging parents. It was a difficult decision in a community sharply divided in its sentiments. The Methodist church removed Joseph A.'s name from the roll and he suffered many a gibe from his contemporaries.

Early in 1864 at the age of sixty-three Maria Graham died and was one of the first to be buried in the new cemetery at Fletcher where Joseph and his brother-in-law, Cornelius Slack, had bought adjoining lots. When George returned from the war he farmed some with his father and brother, but his heart was never in it and he worked most of his life as a traveling book agent.

After Maria Graham's death Esther Reeder was hired to take care of the household for Joseph and his sons Joseph A. and George. Esther was the second of John Saxton Reeder and Letitia Pownall Reeder's ten children and had been born September 3,

1845 at Lumberville in Bucks County, Pennsylvania. Her parents were Hicksite Quakers who had moved to Ohio and settled on a farm northeast of Fletcher when Esther was six years old. Esther attended "Lake" School until she was fourteen and when she was eighteen joined the "Brush" Christian Church which her family attended. She began working as a hired girl for $1 per day when she was fourteen, working for at least four other families in the Lena-Conover area before coming to the Graham household.

On October 7, 1867 JOSEPH ARCHIBALD GRAHAM and ESTHER POWNALL REEDER were married by Rev. Overholser of Lena. Joseph A. continued to farm and they made a home for his father until his death five years later. Joseph's will written June 25, 1872 compensated Joseph A. for staying home on the farm by giving him $1000, a clock, desk, sled, sleigh, and windmill.[8] The remaining real estate and personal property was to be divided equally among his five living children, including Joseph A. Son-in-law John Wolcott was designated executor and he led the other heirs to appeal this distribution as unfair. Joseph A. mortgaged the farm to buy out his brother and three sisters for $5600.[9]

Albert remembered his father as a good bass singer "but true to the general make up of the family of Grahams was not much to offer for beauty." As an adult Joseph A. wore chin whiskers and a mustache. Friends were welcome in the Graham home for an evening of checkers, charades or cards. The church disapproved of dancing and Esther of drinking, but taffy and popcorn were treats as much fun to make as to eat. All of the Graham men; Joseph A., his brother George, and their cousin William, were active in the Masonic Lodge at Lena which had been chartered in 1852.

Joseph had not been able to pay off the farm mortgage before his death so Esther had little choice but to sell the farm and equipment to pay creditors and settle the estate. Since the household goods had burned, the items to be sold were just the livestock, equipment and a little grain. The sale bill March 4, 1879 included a bay mare for $100, a bay horse for $25, a white horse for $30, twelve hogs for $68, two cows for $35, three bull calves at $21, nine acres of wheat for $50, 457 bushels of corn for $119, a spring wagon for $40, a farm wagon for $35, a reaping machine for $35, a set of buggy harness for $10, a saddle for $5, a plow for $4 and a few small tools. The final total was $772.24.

The farm was appraised at $44.33 per acre and sold to William A. Jones for $50 an acre, considerably less than the $70 per acre Joseph had paid his brother and sisters six years earlier. After paying creditors and estate administration costs Esther Graham received $1021.75 to begin life as a widow with two children in the village of Lena.[10] Prices may have been low because the widow was forced to make a quick sale, but it seems a meager accumulation for nearly a half century of hard physical labor by father and son.

Census records suggest the Graham family were so nearly average one might well have chosen them to typify a rural community in western Ohio. Their example underlines the importance of extended family groups migrating westward together so they might support each other in times of need. Relatives and neighbors contributed about $400 to help Esther Graham build a new home, and gifts of hand-me-down clothing embarrassed the children but made it possible for them to re-enter school as soon as they were well enough. It was a community debt Albert never forgot.

Esther Graham worked steadily as a dressmaker; at Lena from 1879 to 1893, then in the Fletcher community, and when Lettie's husband left her with a small son to raise, she moved to Piqua and made her home with her daughter and grandson until her death in 1912. She visited her son frequently, touring the Clark County Fair exhibits in Springfield during his tenure there, and marveling at the 600 loads of fill dirt needed (at ten cents per load) when his family was building their home on 12th Avenue in Columbus. Esther Graham played an extremely important role in shaping the man her son was to become and she lived long enough to take pride in the result.

Quoting Lincoln's tribute to his mother, A.B. Graham often indicated that he, too, owed his success to his mother's encouragement. It was his mother who supported his wish to obtain a high school certificate and pursue a teaching career. It was his maternal grandmother who loaned him money to attend college and her Quaker admonishment, "Thee keep still," ingrained throughout childhood which influenced him to resign a job he deeply wanted to keep rather than fight his superior. It was his mother's brother-in-law who rescued him with a teaching position when a nervous breakdown threatened to doom his early career. Graham learned early that the elected school directors might be men, but women significantly influenced education in the community. In later years he wrote a colleague, "As a rule the women of a community are inclined to look closely into educational matters, and it is their united effort many times which changes the entire educational policy of the school."[11]

Perhaps the woman who made the most significant contribution to his professional accomplishments was his wife of nearly sixty years. After her death, ALBERT GRAHAM vividly described the first time he saw MAUD KEYTE LAUER; a nine-year-old girl in a bright dress, with a red dinner bucket, crossing the road on her way to Allen's School. Born January 2, 1870 at Eaton, Ohio while her father was serving as minister of the Christian Church, she became a classmate and best friend of Lettie Graham when the latter moved to Lena.

Maud Lauer was the youngest of James D. and Elizabeth Keyte Lauer's four children, and the baby adored by two older half sisters. From the age of two until her marriage, her home was the five room bungalow in Conover facing the railroad tracks where the Lauers moved after Rev. Lauer became minister of the Universalist Church. Like the Grahams, the Lauers had migrated from Bucks County, Pennsylvania where J.D.'s father had founded the Christian Church of Carversville. The 1870s were a period of growth for the Universalist Church, but James Lauer's reputation as a healer also attracted attention and much of his later years was devoted to treating cancer patients, many of whom came from some distance.

Maud's sister, Minnie, graduated with Albert and it would be far more accurate to describe the Lauer and Graham children as best friends than to consider Albert and Maud childhood sweethearts. Their "first date" in June 1886, after Albert had been teaching school for a year, actually occurred when he called at the Lauer home and found Minnie entertaining another young man, so Maud was called to entertain Albert. He continued to call off and on, enjoying a game of cards or dominoes or the Lauer sisters' singing,until he went to National Normal School. While he was at Lebanon, Albert often wrote Minnie one week and Maud the next, or occasionally sent both sisters a letter in the same envelope. It was an innocent time in which letters were addressed "Dear Friend" and signed "your true friend" and contained long newsy accounts of each others' friends and activities.

Albert's letter to Maud, February 12, 1888, remarks "It seems as natural as an old shoe to write letters to you." The following week Maud asked if he received any valentines and noted that nobody sent her any.

Maud, like her sisters, acquired a teaching certificate as a prerequisite for graduating from the Lena-Conover School in 1887, but she had no desire to teach and began studying dressmaking with Mrs. Mary Young, receiving 50 cents per day as her helper. When Albert returned to teach at Carmony School their relationship became more serious and they wrote regularly the following year while he attended Ohio State. In June 1890, with the assurance of the principalship at Lena-Conover, he sought and received her mother's approval for their marriage, since her father had died two years previously. On August 14th he took the train to Troy to obtain the marriage license, met Maud at his sister Lettie's home in Piqua and went to the manse of the Presbyterian church where they were married by the Rev. Alex M. Carson. Their wedding trip was the train ride back to St. Paris where the groom splurged to hire a horse and buggy for the ride to his mother's home in Lena.

During their first year of marriage, the couple lived with Esther Graham where Maud helped her mother-in-law with dressmaking and learned to cook, a skill she had not been taught at home because food was too limited for "experimenting." Housekeeping on their own began the following year near Brush School in a small house on a dirt road rented for $12 for six months. They borrowed money to buy a few dishes, a gasoline stove for cooking and a wood burning "box stove" for heating, a table and some cane chairs, a bedroom suite and some carpet. The biggest items were a $75 buggy and $90 for a horse named "Bill."

When their rental agreement expired in March, Maud was pregnant and their isolated location on a very muddy road was becoming too much of a struggle. Part of their debts had been repaid and they were able to borrow enough to purchase their first home, a little house in Conover two doors north of brother-in-law John Dodds store, for which they paid $367.50 as part of an estate settlement.[12] Here their son Blair was born on the Saturday before Graham began teaching at New Hope School. Maud was within walking distance of her mother and sisters, but two and a half years later when Albert accepted a better paying position in

Champaign County they sold this home with the stable Albert had built for $500.[13]

For the next thirteen years "home" was a series of rented houses as Graham changed teaching positions. The birth of daughter Rettie was celebrated with joy in a rented home near Rosewood February 25th, 1896, but the young parents were crushed by her death eleven months later from complications related to whooping cough. In April 1899 while the Grahams were living at Terre Haute, "Bill" was killed by lightning when he stuck his head out of the stable during a violent thunderstorm. The buggy was sold to pay bills and from then on the Grahams walked, rode trains, interurban or city cars; or on rare occasions hired a horse and buggy. They never owned an automobile, perhaps because by the time they could afford it they had become accustomed to public transportation.

Rent in Springfield, their first urban residence, was $12 per month for a modest house on Rice Street accessible to the city cars. But finances were always tight and Maud's sewing skills created not only her own wardrobe but everything for her two sons from underwear to dress suits. For household linens, Wren's offered unbleached muslin at 35 cents per yard or bleached for 50 cents, and Murphy and Brother advertised fine silk for ladies' waists for $1. Men could find the latest "Grand Duke" hats at Bancrofts for $2 and Starkey's in the Arcade advertised ladies' or mens' work oxfords for 75 cents to $1.25 or dress shoes from 95 cents to $1.95.[14]

Wherever the Grahams lived they planted a large garden and Maud canned quantities of produce for winter use. At that time potatoes were 60 to 70 cents per bushel, cabbage 5 to 10 cents per head, apples 30 to 50 cents per peck, oranges 25 to 50 cents per dozen, butter 15 to 25 cents per pound, and eggs 15 to 25 cents per dozen depending on the season.

During the Springfield years when Graham earned $750 to $900 annually the family had few luxuries, but local prices permit evaluation of the buying power of such a salary for a family of four. Flanery's offered pianos for $150 to $675 while P. Slack & Sons sold bicycles for $7.50 to $50. The Central Union Telephone charged $1 per month for residential installations and *The Press-Republic* charged 7 cents per week or 30 cents per month for subscriptions to its eight page daily and Sunday edition. Springfield was a railroad center which provided round trips to Cincinnati for $1.25 or excursions to the 1901 Pan American Exposition in Buffalo for $7.35. When the local opera house presented a traveling company in "Nell Gwynne" seats were 25 cents to $1. Lots in Springfield's new "Melrose" subdivision cost $100 to $250. Real estate agents advertised homes from $500 to $7000 depending on their location, and farmland for about $80 to $150 per acre. Graham had been a rural teacher for twenty years without earning $1000 annually, but local papers carried advertisements for salesmen at $936 per year or machinists at $2.75 to $3.25 per ten hour day.

What a luxury the $1500 salary seemed when Graham accepted a position at Ohio State University. Paying $20 per month to rent a six room house on West Lane Avenue, the Grahams in 1905 experienced the joys of their first inside toilet accommodations and bath tub. They immediately began depositing $40 from each month's $125 salary in the building and loan, acquiring enough by 1909 to buy a lot at 168 12th Avenue and to finance the construction of a $5000 home. It was a sturdy brick house without architectural distinction but within walking distance of the Ohio State University campus and the High Street cars. Father could walk to the office and the boys could skate on Mirror Lake. Most of all, there was room for baby Helen, born about the time construction began, and for Joseph nineteen months later.

The Graham family always lived frugally, enjoying nature walks in nearby parks, visits to museums or on rare occasions a special outing to the theater. His daughter does not believe that her father ever took a vacation, but professional meetings took him throughout the country, and on three special occasions his wife shared these travels. About 1912, Maud's sister, Minnie Stephenson, stayed with the children while Maud made a trip with her husband to New England. During his years at the U.S.D.A. she accompanied him once on a business trip of a month or more through the western states. She also shared Graham's most unique U.S.D.A. trip, a voyage to Puerto Rico. Enroute, he tested his memory of his National Normal School astronomy nearly fifty years earlier by plotting the ship's course from the stars, and was pleased when the captain confirmed that his chart was very nearly accurate.

With the notable exception of his fraternal lodges and professional memberships, A. B. Graham was not an organization man.

Shortly after his twenty-first birthday he joined the Masonic and I.O.O.F. Lodges at Lena and the Knights of Pythias at St. Paris. Graham men had been active in the F. & A. M. #217 since its founding in 1852 and Albert's membership may have been the local equivalent of manhood rites. It was a commitment he took seriously, even changing from Wittenberg College to Ohio State University to continue active participation, but it seems curiously inconsistent with his posture on religious affiliation.

In religion and politics, A. B. Graham carefully avoided denominational or party labels. Explaining his reasons, he once wrote, "I think I have been able to serve helpfully in directing the interests of some, without having them feel that I was making a defense from the standpoint of a denomination to which I may belong."[15] He aspired to a religious philosophy Ralph Waldo Emerson categorized a "Christian Theist." Graham described his beliefs as "unlimited tolerance for any belief that gives man an idea of his proper relation to his fellow man and to an ever living, omniscient, omnipresent ruling power called 'God' in our language."[16] He collected various translations of the Bible and enjoyed reading varied theological treatises, not just Protestant and Catholic theologians, but parts of the Koran and discussions of the Islamic faith. When possible the Grahams attended the services of various congregations. During one six month period his journal recorded participating in the services of six different Protestant denominations as well as a Jewish synagogue.[17] In later years he regularly listened to radio sermons and enjoyed corresponding on philosophical issues with Rev. Lance Webb, Minister of North Broadway United Methodist in Columbus. Rev. Webb quoted from some of these letters in conducting Graham's memorial service.

Family ties were always close for both of the Grahams. During the years they lived in the east, Maud and the children came back to Ohio for part of each summer to visit relatives, and Graham's business trips often brought him back through Ohio with a stop to check on sister Lettie or son Blair. The Grahams' hearts were always in Ohio and it was not until 1919, five years after he left Ohio State that they sold the home they had built on 12th Avenue so that they might buy a home in Hyattsville, Maryland within commuting distance of the United States Department of Agriculture. Here Graham and some helpers did most of the necessary remodeling and hauled in loads of manure to bring the clay soil up to the standards he expected of his garden. Wherever the Grahams lived, a large garden was important and this one included fruit trees, a grape arbor, raspberry and currant bushes, as well as a variety of vegetables. In the Clintonville area of Columbus where the Grahams retired, a surprised neighbor questioned why the eighty-year-old was planting fruit trees in his backyard, and was told he expected to live to eat their fruit but if he did not someone else would enjoy it.

Graham's personal life reflected his priorities as an educator. It was 1894 before the Grahams could afford their first bookcase, but books were always important and in retirement his library of approximately 1000 volumes included an extensive collection of late nineteenth century schoolbooks. In 1894 he also purchased the rolltop desk he used throughout his Springfield and Columbus superintendencies. He became an accomplished amatuer photographer, justifying the purchase of a camera and learning to process his film because photographs enhanced his writings about school conditions. One of the family's highest priorities was to make it possible for the children to acquire as much education as each desired. While their father never dictated this, his influence on the four who lived to maturity is quite evident.

EMERSON BLAIR GRAHAM, born September 3, 1892 at Conover, began his schooling in Mad River Township where his father was high school teacher and superintendent, spent most of his elementary years in Springfield, and his high school days in Columbus. After graduating from North High School in 1911 he enrolled in the College of Agriculture at Ohio State University, but soon withdrew to take a business course. After working as a stenographer for Adams Express Co. and occasionally helping to carry heavy trunks up flights of stairs, college looked better. Blair enrolled in the Ohio State University College of Education and graduated in June 1917. He reported to Camp Sherman as a private in Co. M, 329th Infantry in January 1918, attended Officer Candidate School that spring, and was commisssioned a 2nd Lt. with the 40th Infantry June 1st, but was discharged in December 1918 without serving overseas.[18]

In 1919 he married Ruth Grau, and their daughter Martha Jean, born in 1924, made Albert and Maud Graham delighted, although long distance, grandparents. Blair began his teaching career at Bowling Green, Ohio but returned to Columbus as a science teacher at Highland Elementary, then West Junior High and North High Schools. He became principal of John Burroughs Elementary on the west side in 1935 and earned his Master of Science in Education from Ohio State two years later. After serving seventeen years at John Burroughs he transferred in 1952 to Indianola Elementary where he was serving as principal at his untimely death in 1955.

WALTER SCOTT GRAHAM, born April 5, 1898 while his father was teaching at Terre Haute, completed most of his schooling in Columbus but graduated from Central High School in Washington, D.C. Attending the University of Maryland while living at home, he studied military science along with his major in plant pathology, but the World War ended before he was called to serve. Married in 1924 to Alene Pollock, their son Walter born two years later was a special joy to his grandfather because A.B. was the only descendant of Archibald Graham with male heirs to carry on the Graham surname. March 13, 1928, on his father's birthday and less than a month short of his own thirtieth birthday, Walter Graham died of appendicitis complications. It was a tragic blow to his parents and they contributed furnishings for a modern hospital room as a living memorial to him. The death of this young man in the prime of life reinforced Albert Graham's memories of his own father's death and made the grief doubly difficult.

HELEN ESTHER GRAHAM, born April 9, 1909 in Columbus was the delight of a mother who loved babies and had lost her first daughter when she was less than a year old. Helen was in the fourth grade when the family moved to Hyattsville, Maryland which had a very limited high school curriculum. Her father arranged for her to transfer in the ninth grade to the District of Columbia and attend Central High School, which children of government employees could do without paying tuition. It may have been a better education but it was a spartan social life for a teenager who had to ride street cars into town in the morning and home again every evening. As graduation approached her father asked if she would like to go to college and she responded enthusiastically. He thought perhaps a small college would be best to allow her more of the social life she had missed in high school so they sat down and he described many of the small colleges in Ohio, both taking it for granted that she would go back to Ohio. Helen narrowed the choice to Miami, Ohio Wesleyan or Wittenberg and then chose Wittenberg because it was located closest to her brother Blair in Columbus, her aunt Lettie in Piqua, and her aunt Minnie in Rosewood. The fact that her family had lived for five years in Springfield had no particular meaning to her since that was before her birth. It was some time after she became a student before she learned her father had briefly been enrolled there in the fall of 1889. Both he and she simply considered it a good school in an ideal location. He encouraged her to get a general education so she earned a Bachelor of Arts degree with enough summer courses to acquire a secondary teaching certificate.

Married in 1930 to Robert C. Baker, a fellow student at Wittenberg, she taught English and social studies in Middletown, Ohio junior high schools. Later she earned a Bachelor of Science degree in elementary education at Miami University and taught 4th and 5th grade before becoming a counselor and curriculum specialist. Their son Robert and daughter Barbara, born after their grandparents had retired to Columbus, became a chemist and an elementary teacher.

JOSEPH R. GRAHAM was born Sunday morning, November 20, 1910 at his parents' new home on 12th Avenue. Except for three years at Hyattsville, he attended schools in Washington, D.C. and graduated from Central High School in 1930. He lived with his brother Blair part of the four years he attended Ohio State University majoring in metalurgical engineering. For two years he worked for the U.S. Geodetic Survey and then in 1936 he joined Armco Steel Corporation in Middletown, Ohio where his brother-in-law was employed. Severe burns in 1945 forced him to transfer from the open hearth department to industrial engineering where he worked until his retirement in 1971.

Married in 1934 to Cecilia H. McGolrick they became the parents of four children: Stanley R., James A., Marilyn A. and Richard E. Living at Trenton in Butler County, Ohio James and Marilyn Graham became members of the 4-H club program which made their grandfather so well known, and James later served it as a volunteer leader.

Graham family ties were traditional and close. It is quite evident that wherever they might be living, Ohio was "home." Education was important and the children were encouraged to obtain as much as they could. The parents helped financially as much as possible, but each child had considerable freedom to choose the subjects of his or her own interest. The resulting emphasis on science and education reflects home environment, sometimes consciously resisted and then subconsciously chosen.

The matriarchal influence of the Reeder, Lauer, and Graham grandmothers maintained family ties which influenced A.B. Graham's choices at many points. There are surprising similarities between the deprivations of his rural boyhood and those of inner city families a century later. Utilizing education, a traditional ladder for upward mobility, Graham's achievements as a rural educator typify what sociologists currently describe as indigenous leadership. Family heritage and boyhood environment developed a man capable of translating theory into practice as a country schoolmaster.

1 Joseph A. Graham and Esther Reeder at time of marriage, 1867

2 Esther Reeder Graham with Albert and Lettie after fire destroyed home and killed Joseph A. Graham, 1879

3 Esther Graham home at Lena, Ohio, where Albert lived from age eleven through the first year of his marriage

4 Rev. Lauer's home at Conover, Ohio, where Maud lived as a girl

5   Albert B. Graham and Maud Keyte Lauer at the time of marriage 1890

6   The home the Grahams built in 1909 at 168 Twelfth Ave., Columbus,
across from the O.S.U. campus

7   Supt. and Mrs. Graham leaving for New England business trip, 1912

8   Blair, Helen, Joseph and Walter Graham on steps of Amityville, N.Y. home, 1914

PART II
Country Schoolmaster to
Innovative Superintendent

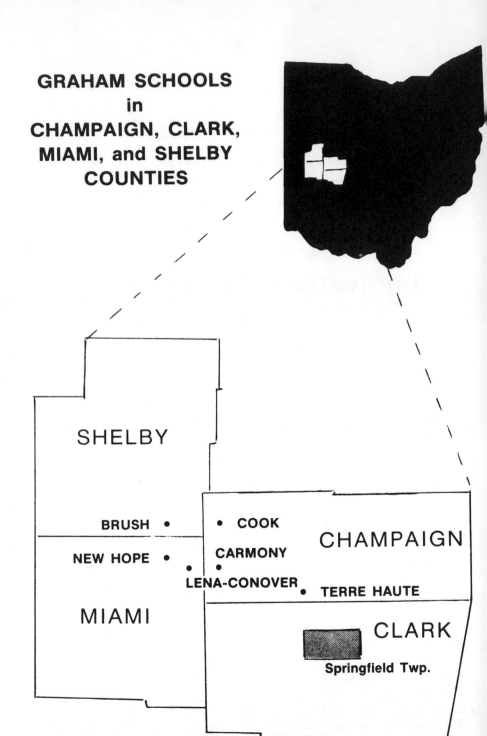

GRAHAM SCHOOLS in CHAMPAIGN, CLARK, MIAMI, and SHELBY COUNTIES

SHELBY

CHAMPAIGN

BRUSH •

• COOK

NEW HOPE •

CARMONY
•

• LENA-CONOVER

• TERRE HAUTE

MIAMI

CLARK

Springfield Twp.

Chapter 3
One-Room Schools and Normal School Study

> "Why should children be compelled to be sur-
> rounded with bare walls not always completely covered
> with plastering? Why should most of their wakeful
> hours during the school year be spent where a red
> rusted stove and festoons of cobwebs, the checked and
> scaled blackboard, and intense sunshine through an
> unshaded window are the only things to break the
> monotony of the brush streaked wall?"[1]

The one-room country school so often remembered with nostalgia today bears little resemblance to the daily reality experienced by many teachers and pupils a century ago. But the
immediate aspirations of the seventeen-year-old high school
graduate who wanted to teach were quite modest, and local
opportunities were actually above average. In May of 1885
Albert Graham had high hopes for obtaining a teaching position
within walking distance of home.

At that time in rural Ohio, schools were built and maintained and teachers and textbooks were chosen by locally elected
school directors responsible for a township subdistrict about two
miles square. Ephraim Servis, a local director, had confided to
Albert at Colvin and Frazier's store in Lena a few weeks earlier
that the directors of District #3 in Johnson Township were thinking of making a change at Carmony School. Would Albert be
interested? He would indeed, but since he did not have a Champaign County certificate he would have to take the next
examination.

The fact that his Miami County certificate had no value in
the adjacent county was an excellent example of certification
conditions in Ohio in the late 19th century. County school examiners in the 1880s were under the jurisdiction of the county
probate court. They had great latitude to prepare their own questions within the eight subjects specified by the state legislature
for common school certification: spelling, reading, writing,

arithmetic, geography, grammar, U.S. history, and teaching theory and practice. Examinations were usually held in each county every four to six weeks, and candidates for the lowest level, a twelve month certificate, had to score at least 55% or better in each of these subjects.

By 1885 county examiners could award five classes of certificates, from one to five years. Ten year and life certificates were granted by state board examinations, but the applicants were required to have at least 45 months of teaching experience and good testimonials from "leading educators." The National Education Association had been revitalized the previous year and teaching was in the early stages of becoming a profession. The report of Ohio's Commissioner of Common Schools clearly shows, however, that the field was dominated by beginners. In 1885, of the 21,336 certificates granted state-wide, 15,993 were one year certificates, and 37% were awarded to persons under twenty years of age.[2]

Albert was told that applicants who lived outside Champaign County rarely passed the teaching examination until they completed the four week normal school offered each summer by A.C. Deuel. Mr. Deuel, Superintendent of Urbana City schools, was the key to certification because he was the clerk of the county board of school examiners, but Graham had no money to attend his institute that summer. He borrowed an English grammar text written by Deuel to bone up on his favorite terminology and did a little politicking among friends to remind the examiners that he had been born in Champaign County and lived there until the family farmhouse burned.

On June 27, 1885 he got up at 4:30 a.m. to walk to Conover and take the train to Urbana. It was the seventeen-year-old graduate's first trip to the town of Urbana, only seventeen miles away. Teacher examinations took all day, but Graham's combination of studying and politicking succeeded and he was among the 201 applicants who were granted teaching certificates in Champaign County that year.[3]

Graham lost no time in reporting his new certification to his friend Ephraim Servis, who met with the other two district directors Daniel Snapp and William Wheaton and unanimously awarded young Graham the Carmony School at $40 per month for eight months. Mr. Snapp, a thrifty German farmer, reportedly did question, "Don't you dink he es a leetle yoong?" But Mr.

Wheaton reminded, "My goodness Daniel, he may be young but he has a certificate, everyone has to have a first experience." This was evidently reasonable to Snapp, who indicated, "Yah, Yah, I vote for em."[4]

Forty-five pupils of school age were enumerated in District #3 (Carmony School) that year. Depending on the season, attendance of 60% to 80% on a daily basis was about average for rural disticts across the state. Thirty or more pupils studying at eight different levels must have been quite a challenge for a serious minded seventeen-year-old who had been on their side of the desk only the year before.

Meager as his $320 annual salary sounds, it was actually above average for Ohio rural teachers in 1885-86. Nearly 6000 teachers in township district schools had an average school term of 29 weeks with men receiving an average monthly salary of $37 and women $27.[5] Rural areas of Champaign and Miami Counties had better farm land and tax rates above the state average. For a first-year country teacher young Graham was doing well.

During the summer of 1886 he was able to attend Supt. Deuel's normal school and his Champaign County certificate and his teaching contract with District #3 were renewed. Pictures of Carmony School show an unadorned frame building with a few trees in the area where the children played; no better nor worse than many throughout the midwest. The directors paid the young schoolmaster an extra $2 per month to serve as janitor and he undoubtedly arrived early to start the fire. Lessons were probably recited from the same books Graham had used a few years earlier: McGuffey *Readers*. Ray's *Arithmetic*, Harvey's *Grammar*.

Any beginner who aspired toward a career in education late in the 19th century soon realized that he needed higher education. During the Civil War women had begun to enter primary teaching in large numbers to replace men in military service and local boards were pleased to find they could be hired more cheaply than men. Men who expected to support a family by teaching found the pay better in city school districts, high schools, and positions such as district principals or superintendents which involved part-time supervision. It was the turn of the century before any significant number of full-time administrative or supervisory positions began to appear in Ohio.

For a widow's son teaching country school at $40 per month, four years of university education seemed an impossible dream, but normal school was a realistic challenge. Living at home and walking to his school, Graham saved for two years and enrolled in the autumn of 1887 at the National Normal University in Lebanon, Ohio. This was the largest such institution in southwestern Ohio and the alma mater of Albert Moore, Graham's most respected teacher. Its recent name change from Normal School to University reflected broadened aspirations rather than increased faculty.

National Normal University was the domain of the Holbrook family who had taken over the Lebanon Academy in 1855 with the blessings of the town and the Southwestern Ohio Normal School Association which had originated at Miami University. Professor Alfred Holbrook, the institution's president for fifty years, was born in New England and began his teaching career in northeastern Ohio. Although the curriculum was dominated by his courses and by those taught at various times by his first and second wives, children, and grandchildren, it was a broad curriculum. The Holbrooks were a brilliant family, although some considered them egotistical.

Graham attended the institution during its peak years when the enrollment annually exceeded 2000 students and 800 to 1000 attended each of the ten-week terms. Flushed with enthusiasm, Graham signed up for an entire year, fifty weeks at the bargain tuition of $40 (rather than $10 per ten-week term). The Teachers College had by far the largest enrollment, but Graham chose to be one of 154 students enrolled in the College of Science. There were also Colleges of Business, Engineering, Liberal Arts, Law, Medicine and Theology in addition to a Conservatory of Music and Schools of Fine Arts, Telegraphy, Phonography, Type-writing, Pharmacy, Modern Languages, and Photography.

In breadth of curriculum and size of enrollment National Normal University compared quite favorably with other institutions of higher education in the midwest at that time. In depth it failed to reach the goals President Holbrook envisioned. Much of the teaching load was carried by his son, R. Heber Holbrook, Ph.D., who lectured in subjects as diverse as history and natural science. Since lectures by experts were the accepted educational mode of the period, the auditorium of University Hall which seated 1000 on the main floor and 400 in the balcony was ideally designed to maximize the institution's few qualified faculty.

This imposing central building had been completed in 1883 with a dining hall in the basement, a library of 5000 volumes and several small recitation rooms on the first floor. The two story auditorium served for general exercises each morning, lectures throughout the day, and special events such as concerts and commencement. The school had some dormitory rooms available for 30 to 40 cents per week with an additional $1.25 to $1.50 for meals, but this was too expensive for Albert. He shared a room rented from the Corwin family on East Mulberry Street with a Miami County friend, J.E. Stuart. It was a simple second floor room furnished with a bed covered by a straw tick, a small coal stove, a washstand with a pitcher and bowl, a table for books and study, and a coal oil lamp. Textbooks were rented from local book dealers.

Candidates for a Bachelor of Science degree were required to complete a term of advanced rhetoric, advanced geometry, advanced tigonometry, Caesar, Ovid, Virgil, analytics, calculus, astronomy, algebra, botany, physiology, physics, chemistry, zoology, geology, Lowell's poems, Shakespeare, Kellogg's English literature, Boyd's Milton, letter writing, and drawing; write 3 essays in U.S. history, 3 essays in English history, 3 essays in English literature; compete in 4 debating sessions, and 4 public final examinations. Graham also elected to take terms of teaching methods and German, an asset in the predominantly Scots-Irish and German community of his boyhood.[6] By attending the summer preceding and the one following the regular school term, he completed sixty weeks of study. Years later, after National Normal University had been absorbed by Wilmington College, their registrar evaluated Graham's work at 2 7/9 semester hours credit for each of twenty-four courses, or a total of 66 2/3 semester credits, an above average load for a student completing two years in residence.[7]

It was a rigorous program, not to mention the general exercises which began each day at 8 a.m. with speakers on topics ranging from etiquette to Darwinian theory. It was probably his own preparation which influenced Graham's lifetime conviction that teachers should have thorough preparation in subject matter, not just teaching methods. August 17, 1888 Graham was among sixty-six students who received a Bachelor of Science degree and, with the exception of Latin, where his marks were only fair, his standing was good to excellent. He was one of ten selected by classmates to present a commencement oration, but Professor Heber Holbrook prevented this because of his average in Latin. However, A.B. Graham remained in good standing with his classmates, and in the 1940s organized a reunion and maintained a "round robin" letter among those who could be traced.

The year in Lebanon with its rigorous schedule and spartan living conditions took a toll on young Graham's health which played an important part in his subsequent career. It was far more common for students to alternate teaching and schooling over a period of several years, but Graham was a young man in a hurry in spite of his meager funds. In later years, the lack of a degree in either education or agriculture from an accredited university would be an insurmountable deficiency in the minds of some of his colleagues. The year at National Normal University, however, provided a base for a self-motivated individual committed to continued learning through observation, reading and experimentation. Graham's most memorable learning experience there was an astronomy class during the 1888 summer term in which each student plotted an expected lunar eclipse and then viewed the prophesied result. The majesty of such universal laws was a scientific and religious experience Graham never forgot.

It might have seemed meager in the halls of Yale or Princeton, but by midwestern standards in 1888, National Normal University and the town of Lebanon provided a stimulating intellectual environment for a country teacher who had never lived outside of Lena. An eyewitness account on the front page of *The Western Star* described the impressions of a visitor to the city at the time of Graham's graduation. "On reaching University and Court House squares, we found ourselves surrounded by half a thousand students of all descriptions and from nearly every state in the Union. On one hand some one might be divulging the horrors of some Arctic Expedition, while on the other the charms of some fascinating story of the tropical regions might be heard."[8] Even discounting the excesses of Victorian prose, one envisions a diverse gathering engaged in animated conversation.

Graham returned to teaching in the Carmony School and living in his mother's home during the 1888-89 school year to replenish his finances. On May 18th, 1889 he took and passed the Miami County teachers' examination for a three year primary and high school certificate with scores in all thirteen areas between 90 and 100%. He might have accepted a high school teaching position had one been available, but he was also anxious to acquire more education at the first opportunity, and chose that over a return to the one-room school.

That fall, with a loan from Grandmother Reeder, he was accepted at Wittenberg College in Springfield. After renting a room and moving to campus he and a friend discovered that they would not be allowed to leave campus to attend evening Masonic meetings in town. This seemed paternalistic to the twenty-one-year old who had managed his own life for the past four years, so he took a train to Columbus where he was interviewed by President Scott and accepted for the fall term at Ohio State University.

In the fall of 1889, Ohio State University had an enrollment of 428 students and a faculty of thirty. Graham took the required military drill and three 5 credit courses: German, algebra, and geometry. The second term he enrolled in algebra, German and comparative anatomy, but the winter courses were barely underway before he developed a severe case of "la grippe" which prevented him from attending classes for two weeks and eventually forced him to return to Lena to recuperate.

In mid-March after he had regained his health, a classmate from National Normal University who had been teaching and serving as principal of the Lena Conover School left to accept an engineering position and Graham was offered and accepted the opportunity to complete the two and a half month term. At the end of May the school directors offered Graham the position for the 1890-91 school year at $70 per month. It seemed an opportunity too good to pass up and Graham accepted. It was a salary on which one could hope to support a family and after Graham attended the annual Miami County Teachers' Institute at Covington, he and Maud Lauer were married.

The three room brick Lena-Conover School was one of the most elegant rural schools in that part of the state. Having been one of its frst graduates just five years before, Graham must have experienced both feelings of pride and trepidation becoming its high school teacher and principal. Surely he was eager to prove himself to his young wife, his proud mother, and all of the relatives and neighbors who had helped him reach this point. One of his most difficult assignments was teaching Latin, the subject which Graham had found most difficult at National Normal University, which was included in the curriculum for the first time.

Several students from nearby districts which did not have a high school paid tuition to attend Lena-Conover. The Philomathean Literary Society, organized when the school was built in 1884, gave older students an opportunity to practice parliamentary procedure and debating skills, and raised funds to contribute to the school library. Lizzie Hendershot taught the intermediate room and Lou C. Miller the primary room. While no specific records describe Graham's responsibilities as principal, these duties were probably confined to the preparation of attendance reports, supervision of building operations and maintenance, and bringing matters such as decisions about textbooks to the attention of school directors. Personnel decisions were the responsibility of the district board members and certification and teacher training were responsibilities of county examiners.

Whatever the pressures of this position, they became too much for young Graham. He managed to complete the school year but soon afterward suffered a "nervous breakdown," and spent most of the summer recuperating under a doctor's care. The board did not renew his contract and he was forced to seek another position. Uncle John Wiles, husband of his mother's younger sister Mary, drove to Lena to ask if he would take the Brush School across the Shelby County line northeast of Fletcher. The other members of the Greene Township, District #1 Board concurred and offered $50 per month for a nine month term. Since this was across the county line, Graham traveled to Sidney June 6th to take and pass the examinations for a three year teaching certificate in Shelby County, and gladly accepted the Brush School offer.

This school, about six miles from Lena, forced A.B. and Maud to rent their first home and buy a horse and buggy. Much of his $50 salary had to be applied to doctor bills from the previous summer and the money borrowed for furniture, horse and buggy. The isolated location was not good after Maud became pregnant and in the spring the young couple were able to purchase their first home in Conover. Graham completed the school term by driving seven miles each morning and evening, but began looking for a school closer to Conover for the next school year.

He was offered and accepted the New Hope School in Brown Township, District #2, about halfway between the Lena-Conover School and the village of Fletcher. This was a two mile drive and Graham began the school term two days after the birth of his first son. The pay was less, only $45 per month for nine months, but having his family in Conover was an advantage, since both Maud and baby Blair had serious illness during the next two years.

The following year he returned to Carmony School in Johnson Township of Champaign County because they offered $50 per month for a nine month year and it was still within driving distance of their Conover home. This was the 1893-94 school year and farmers were feeling the effects of a serious financial recession. In May the district board decided to cut the school term to eight months for the following year to save money. Graham looked for another school and was hired to teach at the Cook School in Adams Township, again at $50 per month for nine months. This was too far to drive daily from Conover, so the Grahams sold their home and rented a house near Rosewood. For the first time since their marriage Graham taught two successive years, 1894-95 and 1895-96, in the same school.

These five years in four one-room schools; Brush, New Hope, Carmony, and Cook, were typical of the times. Country teachers rarely taught more than two or three consecutive years in the same school, and a year or less was not uncommon. Many were young and quit to return to school or marry. For five dollars more per month Graham, like many others, considered it worthwhile to move. Many school directors felt that teachers had more enthusiasm and better discipline if they hired a different teacher every year or two. Since many of the pupils stayed in the same school for all of their schooling, directors often felt they received a better education if the teachers changed.

The meager school records kept by township clerks during this period have not survived for the districts where Graham taught, and he recorded very little about these early teaching experiences. Photographs show these particular schools to be quite typical of thousands of country schools in Ohio and throughout the midwest during the 1880s and 1890s. Whether brick or frame, their single rooms might hold fewer than ten or more than forty scholars from about five to nineteen years of age. It was a stark environment dominated by a heating stove, rarely enlivened by library books or pictures for classroom walls, often not even providing the privacy of sanitary outdoor toilets.

Graham probably was a conscientious teacher, for the most part using the same texts he had studied himself a few years earlier. He undoubtedly tried to make the lessons meaningful to students rather than memory drills. He learned a great deal about the meager opportunities for those who attended country schools and the educational aspirations parents held when they sent their children. He gradually recovered his physical strength and gained confidence in his teaching ability. As he became an active participant in Champaign County teachers' meetings, he became acutely conscious of the differences in opportunity for students in Urbana or St. Paris compared with the township district schools.

Somewhere and somehow during these years, Graham developed the commitment of a professional educator who could and would make a difference in the lives of rural people. In retrospect one can clearly see that he turned a corner professionally in the mid-1890s. The educator who emerged could not have matured in the same way without the teaching experiences of those one-room schools. If he had returned to Ohio State to finish a degree in science, he might have become influential or famous, but he might not have developed the inner fire which set him apart as a dedicated teacher.

Chapter 4
Terre Haute — The Emergence of a Professional Educator

> "Many times the schools or school premises do not
> have what they should because teachers are sometimes
> timid about asking for necessities. Talk them over with
> the director or board of education, teacher... Don't feel
> discouraged if first talks result in nothing. Agitation is
> the beginning of everything. If you never open your
> mouth you may trot along in the same old harness for
> years."[1]

Trying to support his family on an annual teaching salary of $450 forced Graham, like many teachers, to seek a second income. Publishers frequently sought teachers for summer work as book agents and uncle George Graham had contacts in this field. In the spring before daughter Rettie's birth, A.B. met a representative of Ginn & Co., Chicago text-book publishers, at the Kline Hotel in St. Paris and discussed the possibilities for work during the summer either on salary or commission. Graham chose to work for 25% commission and pay his own expenses. It was a courageous choice, some might say gamble, at a time when elementary readers sold for 30 to 50 cents, and high school texts such as Latin or geometry for only $1.25.

Graham was delighted to clear $100 over his expenses and the company was so pleased they offered him a job at $600 annually, more than he had ever earned teaching. But Graham was a committed teacher, and although he continued to work for Ginn & Co. parts of the next several summers at $75 per month, his work as a book agent was simply supplementary income. Some writers have criticized such associations as an attempt by publishers to control educational texts, but book fairs and classroom discounts currently create a similar influence. The misuse or benefit from such relationships still depends upon the educator. Graham used the contact with one of the largest text-book publishers of the time, as an opportunity to become well acquainted with available school books, and it seems to have stimulated his interest in school libraries. Graham's association with Ginn coincided with their attempt to strengthen sales to rural schools. One advertisement invited, "The township schools are adopting many of our books. We are especially interested in corresponding with any district teachers who are earnest in their desire to better their schools by the introduction of up-to-date text books."[2]

Before his second summer as a book agent, Graham was offered and accepted new duties as teacher-principal of Terre Haute High School and part-time superintendent for the southern half of Mad River Township. His $70 per month salary for an eight month term remained the same for four years, 1896-1900, and summer work as a book agent continued to be a critical second income for the Grahams.

The first year the Grahams rented a home at Thackery for $5 per month. This village west of Terre Haute had developed with the railroad and its attraction was the accessibility it provided to relatives in Conover and Piqua and to Maud's sister Minnie who had married George Stephenson, a high school teacher at St. Paris. The Graham and Stephenson families had much in common and visited each other often.

The responsibilites at Terre Haute were quite similar to those Graham had held at Lena-Conover during the 1890-91 school term. The difference was a principal who was not an idealistic twenty-one-year- old trying to impress his hometown neighbors, but an experienced rural teacher who had developed a philosophy of education, confidence in his teaching abilities, and a missionary zeal about the gaps between needs and opportunities in rural schools.

Terre Haute had become a two room school about 1890 when district directors erected a new room at a right angle to the old one and connected them with a steepled entry. Each room accommodated up to forty-five pupils and had its own heating stove and slate blackboards around three sides of the room.[3] Anne Peiffer began teaching the primary room at the same time Graham began in the high school. Both became popular teachers in the community, with the local reporter describing the closing exercises in 1899 in detail and noting, "Both (Graham and Peiffer) have given entire satisfaction and the patrons are in hopes they will be employed for another term."[4] Graham's students presented him with the gift of a chair, an unusual occurrence which was noted in the paper.

Another innovative young educator began teaching in the one-room school between Terre Haute and Thackery the same year that Graham became part-time superintendent for that half of the township. A.C. Neff was excited by the new manual training courses being introduced into urban schools such as New York, Boston and Philadelphia. He and Graham persuaded the local school directors to allow him to move his own small foot-powered lathe and assorted carpenter's tools into a corner of the one-room school and after regular hours teach some basic manual training. Both boys and girls participated in this early rural experiment in manual training. Girls made comb cases, decorative boxes and calendar easels, while boys usually make small furniture items or repaired furniture brought from home.[5]

During his four years at Terre Haute, Graham gradually introduced a number of teaching innovations for such a rural district. High school students participated in debates on a variety of topics to sharpen their research, reasoning and communication skills. Civics study was heightened by excursions to Urbana to visit county government offices. The entire trip, from the purchase of railroad tickets to a meal in the hotel dining room, became learning experiences for subjects as diverse as mathematics and etiquette. The high school reading table regularly included the *Pathfinder, Youth's Companion,* and *Cosmopolitan* and the local reporter complimented, "Mr. Graham's efforts to place before the children the best weekly newspapers and literary magazines is highly appreciated."[6]

One of Supt. Graham's most significant practices went largely unnoticed outside of the community. School programs for holidays such as Washington's Birthday and exercises for the last day of school had for some time been occasions to invite parents in this part of the midwest. Regular teachers' meetings to discuss professional concerns were becoming common even in rural areas. At Terre Haute Graham combined the two, inviting parents and teachers to meet together to discuss topics such as school discipline, compulsory attendance laws, and the selection of books to encourage student reading. The Terre Haute reporter commented on the lively discussion by sixteen parents and four teachers at one such meeting and promised another meeting would be held before the close of the school term.[7] Although the

National Congress of Mothers Clubs was organized about this time in Washington, D.C. and the Ohio Congress of Mothers clubs five years later, it would be at least two decades before Parent and Teacher Associations began appearing in local schools. Graham's meetings were well ahead of such formal organization, but the idea was so successful he would transplant it and expand it when he moved to Springfield.

Graham's most visible step toward educational professionalism, however, occurred September 9, 1897 when he was elected editor of the Champaign County unit of the Ohio Teachers' Reading Circle at its business meeting in conjunction with the county teachers' institute. The report noted that, "County papers have granted us space for the presentation of school matters and for the purpose of creating educational sentiment and keeping alive educational interests."[8] The O.T.R.C. was a statewide organization for teachers interested in professional improvement and Champaign County had 140 members that autumn among the county's 226 teachers. In many ways, 1897 was a turning point for Champaign County educators and it reflected what was going on across the country.

In 1890, A.C. Deuel, long-time superintendent of Urbana city schools had retired and been replaced by William McKendree Vance. But it was the summer of 1897, shortly before Deuel's death that Vance replaced him as Clerk of the School Examiners. Between 1896 and 1897 the Champaign County Teachers' Institute changed dramatically. The schedule was cut from two weeks to one and local speakers were replaced by state or nationally known educational experts. Teachers registered for a variety of lectures and professional workshops each day and for the first time the public was also invited to attend evening lectures. The location was changed from Urbana High School to the recently built Market Square Theatre, and the evening lectures were intended to be both entertaining and educational.

As Urbana superintendent, Clerk of the School Examiners, and executive committee member of the Champaign County O.T.R.C., William McKendree Vance, was easily the most important educator in the county. He became an important mentor for A.B. Graham, introducing him to the Western Ohio Superintendents' Roundtable and to the National Education Association. A decade later it would be his recommendation which earned Graham one of his most valued assignments, membership on the N.E.A. committee of five which recommended a plan for junior high schools.

But in 1897, Graham was speaking for the first time as educational spokesman for concerned teachers. Champaign County newspapers had never had a regular educational column and the O.T.R.C. had not had an editor before 1897. One strongly suspects that Graham sold both the association and local papers on the idea and volunteered for the position of editor. In any event, educational columns soon began appearing regularly in the two Urbana papers, the *Champaign Democrat* and the *Urbana Citizen and Gazette,* as well as the *St. Paris Era Dispatch,* and Graham was re-elected editor as long as he stayed in Champaign County. It is worth noting that at the same time his brother-in-law, George Stephenson, was elected president of the group which planned the annual teachers' insitute and the bi-monthly county teachers' meetings. For the first time, Graham had an influential position and influential professional friends and he lost no time in speaking out on educational issues.

One might expect that the educational columns would be devoted primarily to announcements of teachers' meetings and reports of their activities, but such items were limited to a few paragraphs, and from the beginning these columns were primarily editorials on educational issues. Three of the first columns dealt with attendance; the recently enacted state law regarding compulsory attendance, the philosophy behind compulsory attendance, and enforcement provisions. Graham showed an ususual capability for relating concepts to the practical experience of his audience. A major portion of one column dealt with the question, "What is time in school worth?" By setting up a hypothetical situation for readers proposing that eight years of common schooling was worth at least $5000 to an individual throughout a lifetime, he broke this down into days and hours and concluded that a parent who kept a boy home to cut corn was costing him 80 cents per hour or more than $4 per day; far more, of course, than any farmer was then paying to hire corn cutters.[9] This is one of the earliest examples of Graham's ability, as a writer or speaker, to utilize interesting homilies to provoke thought.

Through three years of these columns, Graham developed positions on educational concerns which would occupy his attention for the next several years. The importance of improving school libraries and providing funding for them, the need to plant trees and shrubs to beautify school playgrounds, and means for providing a healthy and attractive interior school environment were recurring themes. One early column pointed out that churches hired sextons so ministers need not clean their churches, and that county officials were not expected to sweep and dust their own offices, so why were so many country school teachers still expected to be the school janitor?

Later columns often dealt with a single issue in depth and frequently appeared on page one. A record cold spell in February 1899 registered 32 degrees below zero at Terre Haute. The following week a front page, two column article described "Centralization of Schools and Transportation of Pupils — Modern Conveniences in Country Life."[10] Accompanying photographs of transportation wagons being used at Westville and Terre Haute were most unusual for small newspapers of the day. In 1897 Westville, in northern Mad River Township became the first school district in western Ohio to consolidate by transporting pupils. Parents decided to pay a driver rather than build a new school. Early in 1898, the Ohio Legislature passed legislation allowing districts throughout the state to use school tax funds for pupil transportation. That same fall Neff's School (Mad River Township District #4) under Graham's jurisdiction, began paying a driver $17 per month to transport pupils to Terre Haute. Graham's February news article showed Champaign County readers these transportation wagons, presented a summary comparing costs, and shared some of the reactions of parents.

Other educational columns show Graham's extremely current awareness of educational issues being researched by N.E.A. committees and commissions. One dealt with the problem of teachers receiving work and pay for only seven to nine months per year and appealed for teachers to be paid for compulsory attendance at the county institute. Graham evidently worked with his directors to see that they practiced what he preached for the Terre Haute reporter noted, "Our school board made a move in the right direction at its last meeting by making the attendance upon teachers' meetings sort of compulsory. They give each teacher the last Friday afternoon of each month for attendance with pay, but no attendance, no pay."[11]

One issue Graham emphasized that fall was the need for Ohio to support a public normal school. A column pointed out that the state universities educated engineers, geologists, lawyers, physicians, horticulturists and other professionals but not a single teacher. Among the forty-five states Ohio was one of six which did not support a public normal school. Graham pointed out to his readers that this was a particular disadvantage to country districts because many of the larger cities supported their own schools for teacher training.

Another column in the fall of 1899 cited statistics on the rising influence of agricultural colleges and pointed out how rapidly agriculture was being accepted as an applied science. It was accompanied by a photograph of an irrigation system, another interesting early example of Graham's ability to catch the attention of his audience with an application of the theoretical concept he was explaining.

The education columns in the Champaign County papers carry no "by line," but no one who reviews Graham's articles and speeches over the next twenty years can doubt the author when the same themes, sometimes even the same phrases and examples, recur again and again. The fact that Graham was re-elected editor by his peers each fall suggests support for the numerous controversial positions he was taking. It seems amazing, however, that the issues being discussed in meetings of national educators were being featured almost concurrently on the front pages of weekly newspapers in a rural county of southwestern Ohio. One clue to the interest and support lies in the names of featured speakers at teachers' institutes. For example, in August 1899 Dr. A.E. Winship of Boston, editor of the prestigious *New England Journal of Education* gave a report of the N.E.A. meeting at Los Angeles a month earlier. This also undoubtedly explains how Graham later came to publish some articles and photographs on country schools in the *Journal*. What could be more natural than for the local educational editor to interview and exchange ideas with institute speakers?

During his four years at Terre Haute Graham was a progressive teacher and local administrator, a participant in professional meetings exchanging views with experienced local and national colleagues, and spokesman for the county teachers' association on educational issues. He also made the commitment to an educational career by earning his life certificate as an Ohio teacher. During three days of examinations June 20-22, 1899 in Columbus, applicants dealt not only with dozens of subject matter questions in all areas, but also with many aspects of educational history, science, theory and practice. "Name the leading educational reforms in America in the last fifty years." "Distinguish between work and play. Show their relation to each other, and their true place in any system of education." "How can self government be developed in the child?" "Shall pupils be promoted before the end of the year?" "Enumerate the chief contributions of Rousseau to the history of pedagogy."[12]

One wonders whether Graham was amused or insulted to read in the *Champaign Democrat* a week later that, "Prof. Graham was one of the lucky boys to get a life certificate at the examination at Columbus last week."[13] Seven of the thirty-two successful candidates were women not "boys," and A.B. Graham would certainly have assured anyone that there was much more work than luck in earning that certification. A measure of the value which Graham placed on the accomplishment is the fact that he treated himself to having his silhouette cut by Lonzo Cox at the Southern Hotel before returning home. By the late 1890s Graham clearly perceived himself a professional educator and acted in accord with his definition of that role.

Chapter 5
Innovative Superintendent, Springfield Township, Clark County, Ohio

> "Will you not help to have the children see some of the most interesting things around them: The Historical Society's Room in the Bushnell Building, the electric light plant on Washington St., the type setting machines in either the *Democrat* or *Gazette* office or at the Crowell Publishing Co., "pouring off" at a foundry, and many other interesting and instructive places .... All of learning is not of books. Won't you please give the children your everyday problems arising from the selling of produce and purchasing of groceries?"[1]

It was barely ten miles from Terre Haute to Springfield, close enough surely for the Springfield Township school directors to be aware that they were hiring an enthusiastic educational advocate and for A.B. Graham to realize that he was accepting an uncharted educational challenge. Springfield Township had a number of experienced teachers with a tenure of ten or eleven years, far more than the state average of between two and three years.[2] The twelve autonomous sub-districts had never had a full-time superintendent and some of these teachers naturally worried that the added cost of a special district superintendent would be at the expense of their own salaries. Graham literally had to prove his worth.

By the turn of the century superintendents were common in Ohio's urban school districts, but Commissioner Bonebrake reported only 68 of the 1,335 township districts had superintendents devoting half or more of their time to supervision.[3] Only five could claim a full-time rural superintendent and one of these was Harmony Township just east of Springfield. These pioneers increased community members' awareness of school activities, their expectations of educational quality, and their willingness to provide financial support. It would be another decade before Ohio established a system of county superintendents with the intent of standardizing educational supervision in rural areas.

Springfield Township had been surveyed as a rectangle but by 1900 the city had encroached until it resembled a short handled skillet cradling the city on its eastern, southern, and western borders. That year the census recorded 3,608 persons in the township and 38,253 in the city it encircled.[4] The city was the most central location in the township and the new superintendent rented a home at 89 Rice Street accessible to the electric street-cars. At that time there were thirty cars and more than 12,000 passengers daily paid the five cent fare to ride.[5] Graham used them to reach the county building and also used connecting inter-urban lines to Dayton, Urbana, Xenia, and London to travel within walking distance of his twelve schools. When necessary, he hired a horse and buggy for a half or full day, carefully noting it in his journal.

Graham's $675 salary for the 1900-01 school year was the largest he had ever earned. While low compared to many profes-sions of the day, this was considerably more than the state aver-age of $30 to $35 per month for rural school teachers, and about average for part-time township and village superintendents, which in Clark County ranged from $520 to $1000.[6]

When the new Springfield Township superintendent arrived, 832 youth from six to twenty-one years of age had been enumer-ated and 530 were enrolled for the fall school term. In October 1900 Graham reported an average daily attendance of 447.[7] This enrollment of 64% of the enumerated youth reflects the fact that many older youth had already left school to become homemakers or full-time workers, and others were needed on the farm during fall harvest.

Like most rural townships, each Springfield sub-district had its own school building. These included eight one-room schools with the smallest, Pleasant Ridge, Sinking Creek and Mill Creek usually having about 20 students in attendance. The largest building in the township, three-room Rockway, regularly enrolled more than 100 students per term. In between were the enrollments of the three two-room buildings.[8] During Graham's tenure the township school board had twelve members, one from each sub-district, and in Graham's words, " . . . a few of these represented the long ago, the rest stood for progress."[9]

In modern terms Graham's role as a township superintendent is best described by comparing it to the principal of a seventeen-room school, with over 500 students enrolled in classrooms separated by more than ten miles. Reading his schedule, current principals might be surprised and amused by the similarities of their jobs. He often recorded visiting the parents of a truant child and frequently carried a measure to check distances and assure parents which building was within the prescribed two miles of their home. He often authorized the purchase of shoes from a special fund so that a child might attend school, substituted for a sick teacher until a replacement could be obtained, and arranged for the repair (or in an emergency did it himself) of a leaky roof, broken window or smoking stove.

His first month on the job the new superintendent recorded thirty-three school visits, observing all of his teachers at least twice. His journal reveals his particular concern for student reading abilities. He was distressed by teachers who did not use the phonetic system or allowed pupils to recite in a monotone. Graham observed and counseled teachers or taught a class himself to demonstrate teaching methods and judge pupil skills. He noted in his journal, "At each place made offer to take any class at any time when making a visit except when in some class the teacher had partially developed some subject and should continue by himself or herself without interruption."[10] One has to imagine eight grade levels and the diversity of mathematics, geography, grammar, history, spelling, reading and science to place such an offer in perspective. Perhaps the new superintendent was seeking acceptance of his teaching abilities among his staff as well as assessing pupil performance, but he continued to average at least two unannounced visits per month in each classroom throughout his tenure. Pupils were given monthly evaluations of their work and formal examinations twice yearly.

Some of the Springfield Township buildings had been constructed prior to the Civil War, but the newest, Locust Grove, was only four years old. The fact that this newest school was a single room structure while three-room Rockway consisted of an 1858 building with additions, reflected population growth and a continuing philosophy that school buildings should be within walking distance of student homes. It is an example with a touch of irony considering the heated discussions among professional educators during the 1890s regarding school size in relation to efficiency and quality. The construction of Locust Grove School two years after Ohio enacted legislation to permit transportation of pupils at public expense reflects prevailing community attitudes regarding the importance of neighborhood schools under local control; a challenging issue which is still hotly debated.

Learning environment was a priority for Supt. Graham and he immediately began emphasizing improvements to school building interiors and exterior grounds. Photographs of the renovated interior of one-room Reid School, built in 1858, dramatically illustrate that schools did not need to be new or large to provide an excellent learning environment. The ideal included healthy and attractive classrooms, well equipped libraries, a graded curriculum, and landscaped playgrounds with sanitary restrooms.

Graham had no doubt that "The growth of moral character is more rapid and substantial where the surroundings arouse an emotion of pleasure."[11] He encouraged attractively painted or papered walls and insisted on window shades which could be used to control light within the room. To introduce students to an appreciation of art, he persuaded Springfield's Crowell Publishing Company to present each of his twelve schools with a set of six pictures which school directors had framed and hung. Graham saw to it that each building obtained a flag for patriotic exercises and jacketed its stove for more even heat distribution. In December 1903 the township board, undoubtedly with Graham's encouragement, hired a music teacher for all schools on a rotating basis, and during Graham's tenure five of the twelve were able to purchase an organ to accompany musical instruction.[12]

Graham's ideas were not revolutionary. Children attending city schools were already experiencing many of these advantages, but in rural Ohio supervision by professional educators was so rare that most schools were as good or poor as each teacher made them, and teachers rarely taught in the same school enough consecutive terms to make dramatic improvements.

Although Graham spent much time improving the school environment, he was even more concerned with the quality of the learning experiences students were receiving. In 1901 he noted in his journal that no reading lesson should be conducted without time for interpretation, but noted on the other hand that a need for extensive explanation from the teacher was evidence that selected materials were too difficult or that a pupil was in the wrong grade. He placed an emphasis on competence which modern educators accustomed to a more formally graded structure might find surprising.

Graham had been on the job a month when he persuaded school directors to spend $10 for each of the twelve schools to purchase supplementary books, a practice he convinced them to repeat each fall. No decision was more important to Graham than the selection of these books. October 28, 1902 he noted, "Made final selection of books. Much more difficut to spend $10 than $100." During Graham's tenure directors spent more than $1000 to create well stocked bookcases of about 200 volumes in each of the district schools and standardize the resources available to students throughout the township.[13]

Graham's missionary zeal was most apparent in his high regard for library books. Springfield Township schools benefited handsomely from the traveling libraries inaugurated in 1896 by the state library in Columbus. By 1900, boxes containing twenty to fifty books could be requested for a loan of three months or longer. Graham saw to it that each of his schools received a box liberally stocked with books pertaining to agriculture and books suitable for parents as well as students. In February 1902, when the legislature was considering extensive library legislation, he spent a day in Columbus contacting legislators and state librarians requesting their support for a law allowing school boards to use contingent funds to purchase books for township school libraries.[14] It was an important step in the days when public libraries were usually confined to a few cities beyond the reach of most rural residents. A survey by Commissioner Corson in 1897 revealed that 60% of Ohio's rural schools had no library facilities. But Ohio was not a backward state, in 1900 it ranked first in the nation in the number of libraries in public high schools and third in the number of total volumes. Some students had access but many did not.

Springfield Township students also received *The Pathfinder* and *The Youth's Companion,* newspaper magazines popular among youth of the day. About 250 students annually, almost half of the enrollment and probably most of those old enough, participated in the Ohio Pupils' Reading Circle which awarded certificates as an incentive for assigned reading in literature, history and science. By the time Graham left the township, students were being accepted as transfers into Springfield city schools grade for grade.

The beautification of school grounds was another area which received much of Graham's attention. He believed they should be as beautiful as home yards, and should, in fact, present an example of beauty to the community. He applauded the school grounds which had retained some of their magnificent old trees and always used Arbor Day as an occasion to plant new ones so children might have shady grounds on which to play. During his tenure hundreds of shrubs such as lilacs, hydrangeas, japonicas, and rambling roses were set out on school grounds and thousands of bulbs were planted for spring bloom. At Reid School several hundred tulip bulbs were combined with whitewashed stones to form a dial on which an elm tree's shadow marked the hours. In 1904 beautification efforts were extended to homes with pupils obtaining thousands of ferns, geraniums, pansies, and chrysanthemums in the spring and thousands of tulip, daffodil, hyacinth, and narcissus bulbs in the fall at reduced prices from Good and Reese Nursery and Fair View Floral. Springfield was headquarters for nine greenhouses with the largest nursery selling 2,500,000 rose plants annually,[15] so it was natural that the superintendent's efforts would be encouraged.

As an administrator, Graham's commitments to professional associations increased markedly. He regularly attended township and county teachers' meetings and participated in the Western Ohio Superintendents' Association. November 3, 1900 he attended the Central Ohio Teachers' Association and, "To my surprise was elected first vice president of the Association. Did not know name had been presented to the nominating committee." December 26, 1900 he was elected president of the State Township Superintendents' Association at their meeting in Columbus[16] and the following day attended the County Examiners' Association since he had been appointed to a vacancy on the Clark County Board. These responsibilities increasingly made him an educational spokesman, such as his testimony to the State School Board regarding minimum salary levels for teachers.[17] Continuing disparity between rural and urban teaching salaries caused Graham to consider his own options and as early as 1902 he had sought and received his principal's certificate from the Springfield City Board of Examiners.[18]

What Graham lacked in professional credentials, he sought to compensate by utilizing professional meetings as personal learning opportunities. During the last week of February 1901 he participated in the N.E.A. department of superintendents' meeting in Chicago and found time to visit first, sixth, and eighth grade classes at John Quincy Adams School, where he observed the use of Speer methods. He also noted visiting the Chicago Institute and Col. Parker's School.[19]

Graham's love of teaching and learning was not confined to a classroom. With the superintendent, every trip was a learning experience. A walk to school was a chance to discover new weeds, flowers, insects, birds, or rocks. A trip into town offered opportunities to explore stores, the telephone exchange, a creamery, or the post office. Parents were regularly admonished regarding such opportunities and Springfield Township teachers took students on field trips to the courthouse, the historical society, and local businesses with their superintendent's blessing. Three notable excursions during Graham's tenure involved older students from the entire township under his personal supervision.

The first and best known of these was a visit to the Ohio State University on June 5, 1903. More than one hundred students and parents took the electric cars of the Columbus, London and Springfield line to the capital city. On campus they visited the domestic science laboratories in Hayes Hall, saw an illustrated lecture on "Color Photography" by Prof. Thomas of the physics department, enjoyed a picnic lunch near the famous Neil spring, visited the museum in Orton Hall, and spent much of the afternoon in the soils and dairy laboratories of Townshend Hall, where they were greeted by President Thompson and Dean Hunt of the College of Agriculture.[20] Supt. Graham concluded that "Every taxpayer who spent that day at the University left it feeling that the $550 that Springfield Township contributes annually toward its support is money well spent."[21] Several students who took that trip decided that a university education might be a possibility, even for them.

A very brief stop at the Capitol near the end of that June excursion led to a specifically planned visit the following year. April 6, 1904, more than fifty Springfield Township seventh and eighth grade students visited the General Assembly, the Governor, and several state officials. Judging from a poem written by Fern Haley of Possum School, the highlights for the students were hearing the Senate debate an automobile law, seeing bags of gold and silver stored in the vault of the state treasurer's office, and viewing Relic Room treasures such as Ohio's Civil War battle flags, and the desk of Governor Tiffin, Ohio's first governor.[22]

A different type of tour November 11, 1904 took 76 students to the National Cash Register Company in Dayton. This was a career exploration visit in every sense, observing not only the manufacturing process, but the social and educational activities provided for employee welfare, and a variety of employee responsibilities from manufacturing to maintaining the landscaped grounds.[23] Graham had clearly gotten the idea the previous spring after the company had hosted the Western Ohio Superintendents' Round Table in Dayton and Graham described the experience in his journal as "an educational feast."[24] This is an excellent example of a teacher's ability to distill ideas from varied life experiences and find suitable methods for sharing them with students.

One of Graham's first actions to unite his district schools and create community support at the township level was to prepare and reproduce more than 300 copies of a monthly report to parents. His second year he inaugurated monthly parent-teacher meetings in the evening similar to those he had begun at Terre Haute. Sessions were rotated among district schools and featured topics such as "Rural Life vs. City Life," "Consolidation of Schools," "School and Home Ground Improvement," and "The Library and the Home."[25] Graham's journal hints at the popular acceptance of these meetings. On January 17, 1902, "House well filled with adults, 17 parents from Reid, 12 came up from #1 in the transportation wagon besides others who came in their own conveyances." October 30, 1903, "About 75 present for school meeting at Reids. Songs by school. Subject, 'Art for Rural Communities'." October 28, 1904, "Night meeting at Locust Grove. About 50 present. H.H. Eberhart gave, 'How to Determine a Child's Vocation'."

At their August 1904 meeting the Springfield Township Board of Education appropriated money from the contingent fund to provide one evening lecture in each school the following year. The topics selected were: "The Church in U.S. History," "History of the Ohio School System," "Milk and Its Care," "First Aid to the Injured," "The Soil," and "Other Worlds" (astronomy).[26] Graham spent October 5th in Columbus securing lecturers from the university and the Commissioner of Education's office, but his own resignation prevented the fulfillment of these plans. It was an extraordinarily broad adult education effort for the times and the commitment of public funds by a township board was most unusual. One can only speculate how it might have developed had Graham continued to give it leadership.

Springfield Township schools had become a source of community pride with activities frequently being described in the city's daily and weekly newspapers and being copied a year or two later by nearby townships. Joint closing exercises for all twelve township schools became so popular that the commencement program in 1904 was held at the county fairgrounds and attracted nearly 500 people for recitations and musical selections lasting most of the day. The number of students going from the township into the city for a high school education increased from five Graham's first year to twenty-seven his last year.[27] From an historical perspective, however, all of these innovations and achievements were eclipsed by an experimental agricultural program which began in January 1902.

After laying the groundwork among teachers and parents, Supt. Graham invited students from all schools in the township who were interested in doing some experimental work in agriculture to meet at the county building on Saturday while their parents were shopping in town. Neither Graham's journal nor the Springfield papers recorded the date or activities of the first meeting, an omission he later stated was a deliberate attempt to avoid having the idea "shot down" before it had a chance to develop. His journal entry for Wednesday, January 15, 1902 reads, "At Rockway during the whole afternoon. Completed B & G list for Expmt Club."[28] This date on which Graham recorded completing the roster for his "Boys' and Girls' Agricultural Experiment Club" is now widely proclaimed as the birth of the 4-H Club movement which evolved, although it is quite possible that the group first met on the preceding Saturday.[29]

Some thirty students attended the first meeting and were given litmus paper obtained from Garwood's Drug Store and shown how to test their home soil for acid or alkaline qualities. Plans were made for those interested to grow experimental plots of corn and later another group formed to grow flowers from seeds obtained by Congressman Cox. Some of the club members had disasters and became discouraged during the growing season, but many were successful and participated for several years. Surviving lists from some of the early meetings show a typical session might attract forty or fifty youth with parents sometimes helping teachers demonstrate how to test seed germination or splice a rope. By planting season eighty-three youth were involved.

By 1903 Graham was seeking help. He corresponded with Professor Liberty Hyde Bailey at Cornell who indicated that New York had nature study leaflets which they were using with youth, but nothing to offer in terms of agricultural experiments or club organization.[30] Supt. Graham wrote to Dean Thomas F. Hunt of the College of Agriculture at Ohio State University who referred him to L.H. Goddard of Washington Court House, Ohio who was directing agricultural experiments for the Ohio State University Agricultural Student Union. This group affiliated with the Agricultural Experiment Station was organized in 1895 with a nucleus of alumni from the O.S.U. College of Agriculture and gradually expanded to include any progressive farmer who was willing to conduct scientific crop experiments. They agreed that Springfield Township students under Graham's supervision could obtain several varieties of seeds from the Agricultural Experiment Station and use the planting instructions and report forms of the Agricultural Student Union for their work. Supt. Graham rented a horse and spring wagon to deliver the seed corn to students at various township schools.

Graham's efforts to improve school grounds and his work with agricultural experiment clubs led the State Commissioner of Schools to appoint him as the Ohio representative in the School Garden Department of the American Park and Outdoor Association.[31] Members of the Agricultural Student Union in other counties began to tell their school people about the experimental work of the agricultural club in Clark County and soon the College of Agriculture was receiving requests for more information. Dean Hunt published a bulletin *Rural School Agriculture* describing Supt. Graham's program so that interested teachers or superintendents might begin their own. Graham devoted much of the 1903 summer to the program, personally visiting each club member's project, but he attributed much of the group's success to the teachers who assisted with Saturday meetings and the parents who took an interest in the home projects.

During the Clark County Fair the main building provided space for a dining hall on the first floor and an eighty foot "Educational Hall" for school exhibits on the second floor. Each township which made an exhibit received $10 worth of books for its schools, and Springfield Township, quite naturally, featured the accomplishments of the agricultural club members.[32] In the winter club members exhibited their results at the Farmers' Institute meeting in Springfield, and Theodore Spears, one of the Negro boys in the club, became the proud winner of a handsaw donated by a local hardware store for the best exhibit of corn.[33] Supt. Graham had found that youth could demonstrate results to farmers, many of whom were still reluctant to accept advice from educational "experts."

Like all evolving organizations the membership of the experiment club was fluid. Members joined or dropped out as they became old enough or graduated from the township school, became interested or discouraged, enjoyed or lacked the encouragement of parents and friends. There is no evidence that the Springfield Township club ever stopped and then reorganized between January 1902 and Graham's resignation in November 1904, but there is considerable evidence that it was a continuous organization with fluctuating participation depending on the season.[34]

It is important to note that both the groups commonly referred to as the "boys' agricultural club" and the "girls' flower club" were actually co-educational throughout this period. Members were free to select what they wanted to do, and while soil testing and corn projects were more frequently chosen by boys, Graham recalled that some of the best results were achieved by girls, citing particularly the work of Margaret Strong who lived northwest of Springfield.[35] Two of the most successful members of the group were Negro boys, Theodore and Clarence Spears. The city of Springfield had a significant Negro population and had discontinued separate schools for white and black youth in 1887. When Graham came to Springfield Township about 11% of its households were Negro but few of these were farmers.[36]

The innovative work of the agricultural club and Graham's increasing skill as a public speaker began to bring him invitations from a variety of groups. In October 1903 he described the club's work to the executive committee of the Ohio State Grange, whose Master, Frank A. Derthick, was soon to become a member of the Ohio State University Board of Trustees.[37] That same fall Graham's mentor, William McKendree Vance, now superintendent at Miamisburg, invited Graham to speak to the Western Ohio

Superintendents' Round Table on the attitude of the schools toward country life, and to include a description of his work with the boys' and girls' experiment club. In congratulating Graham he noted "Of course you know that No. 22 of the University Bulletin was reproduced almost entirely in the *New York Journal of Education. The Youth's Companion* had a paragraph the other week based on an utterance of yours. It was quoted in an impersonal way, — no name mentioned, — but I recognized the signet of A.B. Graham."[38] Graham's work was obviously getting national attention although it was frequently anonymous.

In January 1904 Graham spoke to the state-wide meeting of the Agricultural Student Union, the group with which he had been cooperating, and noted in his journal they "Voted to ask legislature for $3000 for agricultural extension work."[39] A few weeks later he spoke to the Farmers' Insitute at Troy and noted, "My dear mother present. Somewhat embarassing to me but of great pride to her."[40]

It was soon apparent that Agricultural Experiment Clubs were a grassroots movement too appealing to be confined to Springfield Township. In the autumn of 1904 Homer C. Price, who had succeeded Hunt as Dean of Agriculture at O.S.U., was reporting to the United States Department of Agriculture that Ohio had "sixteen regularly organized clubs with a membership of six hundred and sixty-four, distributed in ten counties of the state . . . A great many children carried on experiments in the schools who were not organized into clubs."[41] The college furnished seeds for a total of 2838 experiments with vegetables, corn, and flowers. Like many who succeed anonymously for years and then appear to be an overnight success, Supt. Graham found that the agricultural experiment club made him an authority whose writings and speeches were sought. It was a glorious opportunity to proclaim some of his long nurtured ideas about educational improvements for rural communities.

9 Carmony School, Johnson Twp., Champaign County, Ohio, where Graham began teaching in 1885

10
First teaching certificate earned by sixteen-year-old Graham before completing his last year at Lena-Conover School

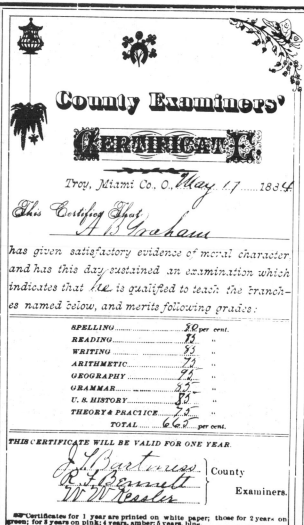

County Examiners' Certificate

Troy, Miami Co., O., May 17 1884

This Certifies That

A B Graham

has given satisfactory evidence of moral character and has this day sustained an examination which indicates that he is qualified to teach the branches named below, and merits following grades:

SPELLING	80 per cent.
READING	75 "
WRITING	85 "
ARITHMETIC	75 "
GEOGRAPHY	95 "
GRAMMAR	65 "
U. S. HISTORY	85 "
THEORY & PRACTICE	75 "
TOTAL	665 per cent.

THIS CERTIFICATE WILL BE VALID FOR ONE YEAR.

J. L. Bartmess
R. F. Bennett } County
W. W. Kessler } Examiners.

Certificates for 1 year are printed on white paper; those for 2 years on green; for 8 years on pink; 4 years, amber; 5 years, blue.

11 Lena-Conover School, Miami Co., Ohio: A. B. Graham, Principal, April 1890

12 Auditorium at National Normal University, Lebanon, Ohio; seating capacity 1400

13 Two-room Terre Haute School, Mad River Twp., Champaign Co., Ohio, A. B. Graham, Principal, 1896-99

14 Principal Graham with students at Terre Haute School, 1898

15 Landscaped exterior of one-room Sinking Creek School built in 1862, Springfield Twp., Clark Co., Ohio, 1904

16 Wallpapered interior of Sinking Creek School with artwork provided by Crowell Publishing Company

17

Boxes of books on loan from State Library of Ohio to a Springfield Twp. school, 1904

18 Student using one-room school library, Springfield Twp, Clark Co., Ohio, 1904

19 Children at play on landscaped school grounds, 1905. Playhouse stimulates imagination

20 Softball encourages group cooperation

21 Springfield Twp. teachers, 1903-04. First row, l to r, Etna Griffith, A. L. Frantz, Supt. Graham, Jesse Fross, Pat L. Maughan, Anna Kissell; 2nd row, W. S. Maxwell, Charles C. Stoker, Maggie Hinkle, W. H. Lewis, J. E. Barnhart, J. Q. Grisso, George T. Crawford; 3rd row, H. H. Eberhart, J. M. Collins, Ella Kissell, J. Albert Kirby, Glenna Snavely, J. Warren Arthur, O. P. Hause

22   Horse drawn school transportation wagon, Lima Twp., Licking Co.,
Ohio, 1906

23   Principal Graham teaching at the racially integrated Frey School,
Springfield, Ohio 1905

PART III
Extension Educator

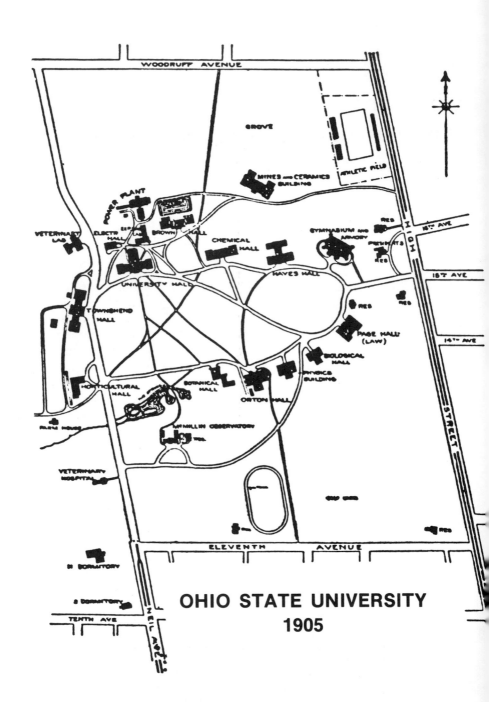

OHIO STATE UNIVERSITY
1905

Chapter 6
Agricultural Clubs, Seeds for Learning by Doing

> "Not only must provision be made for the three R's,
> but for the three H's as well; the *head* for a wealth of
> information and knowledge, the *heart* for moral and
> spiritual strength, and the *hand* for manual dexterity
> and skill."[1]

Graham could recall teachers speaking of the 3 H's along with the 3 R's from the time he began teaching at seventeen[2] and President Beardshear of Iowa State College had used these symbols in his address to the National Education Association in 1902,[3] but applying this concept and encouraging his teachers to do so brought rewards beyond Graham's expectations.

During the summer of 1903 he spent many hours visiting his pupils' corn, flower, and vegetable plots. He constantly urged them to report and evaluate their results and they came to believe that he sincerely wanted to know about their successes and failures. Many attached notes to their report forms, and some included a touch of humor which was completely unintentional.

"Dear Superintendent,
I write you a few lions in regard to my garden . . ."

Soon the trickle of personal reports became a flood: "Dear Sir," "Dear Mr. Graham," "Dear Friend." The boys and girls of the agricultural experiment club were taking their efforts quite seriously. Their frank descriptions of successes and failures provide a candid picture both of crop results and teacher-learner relationships.

Dear Sir,   Nov. 12, 1903
The seeds that I planted are beets, radishes, lettuce, spinach and I forgot the watermelons. The things I planted were fine and I raised them myself. They were bigger than we ever raised before. I was going to sell the lettuce but our folks ate it all up before I had time to sell it.
Sincerely,
Clara Valentine[4]

Dean Hunt's bulletin on *Rural School Agriculture* ignited rural Ohio like a spark in dry grass. Many rural teachers had long sought materials to relate school work to the homes and farms of their students. They were perfectly aware that the majority of their students would not go beyond their district school and the education they received there must open doors to their lifetime work.

Soon after he succeeded Dean Hunt at Ohio State University's College of Agriculture, Homer C. Price wrote to Supt. Graham, whom he had not yet met, telling him how the bulletin on *Rural School Agriculture* had been distributed. High school superintendents had received 781 copies, agricultural newspapers 100, county newspapers 138, former students of the College of Agriculture who were living in Ohio 350, Ohio legislators 143, secretaries of county Boards of Agriculture 69, members of the State Board of Agriculture 10, Ohio State University trustees 7, general distribution 187, and 215 were still on hand in September 1903.[5]

The request for help with agricultural materials had originated in Clark County, but the Ohio State University College of Agriculture quickly saw the advantages of enlisting students in agricultural experiment work, and responded with assistance to assure that such opportunities were available throughout the state. Supt. Graham's use of the Agricultural Student Union materials soon revealed a need to adapt the planting directions and reporting forms for use by elementary students. This was done early in 1904 with Graham contributing many suggestions. The "Ohio Federation of Rural School Agricultural Clubs," was formed in cooperation with the Agricultural Student Union. Pupils could still choose from the four experiments offered the previous year: testing soil or growing corn, flowers, or vegetables. The agricultural college provided seeds, directions for planting, and forms on which to report progress.

The forms for reporting soil tests gave directions for determining soil acidity with litmus paper and provided enough blanks to report results from six different soil samples. Students who chose to raise flowers had directions for planting and caring for calendulas, petunias, nasturtiums, phlox, candytuft, portulaca, and sweet alyssum. They were to report when the seeds were planted, when they first came up, when they first bloomed, and how many weeks they bloomed. A similar form for vegetables included radishes, lettuce, beans, beets, carrots and tomatoes. Students were to record the date on which the seeds were planted, the date the first plants appeared, the date seedlings were thinned, the date the first vegetables were ready to use, the amount marketed, and the total yield.

In the corn experiment students were expected to grow a shock of at least two varieties, one of which might be from their father's own seed corn. They were to mark off an area 42 feet square for each shock and to follow careful instructions regarding the planting and cultivation of this area. They were to record the variety planted, how the ground was prepared, the date the corn was planted, when the seeds sprouted, when the corn was cultivated, when the first tassels appeared, the number of stalks with two ears, the number of stalks with no ears, the soil litmus test, the yield per shock, and the computed yield per acre.

In March 1904 Dean Price issued an updated bulletin *Agricultural Clubs in Rural Schools,* a large section of which had been written by A.B. Graham. It included a proposed constitution for agricultural clubs and the college requested that it be notified of the name of the club, the date of its organization, the names of its president, vice president and secretary, and a list of its members. The college would recognize and provide forms and seeds for one club per township providing the club had ten or more members and did not include pupils less than eight years of age. Graham suggested distributing the bulletin at teachers' institutes with the astute observation, "Sometimes I have found that a wide awake teacher can stir a slow and ultra-conservative superintendent."[6] In 1904 the Agricultural Student Union reported agricultural clubs in twenty-two townships of fourteen counties with approximately 1400 students participating. One hundred and one of these were in the Springfield Township Club of Clark County with Elliott Goodfellow, president and Abbie LeFevre, secretary.[7]

Three new categories were added to the corn, vegetable, and flower experiments of the previous year: *Observations* of wild flowers and the making of dried herbariums; *Identifications* of trees, birds, or insects; and *Collections* of weeds and seeds. An interesting feature of the new bulletin was the inclusion, at Graham's suggestion, of a photograph of Townshend Hall on the final page. The caption beneath it read, "The Goal Toward Which Clubs Lead." It had already occurred to Dean Price in the spring of 1904 that the agricultural experiment clubs throughout the state could be an excellent device for recruiting students for the College of Agriculture.

Graham's leadership of the new movement was recognized on many fronts. Ginn and Co. publishers sought his endorsement for their new text, *Agriculture for Beginners,* about which Graham stated, "Every farner's son who reads this book will have a far better opinion of his father's business. He sees farming as an art intimately related to the sciences which aid him in understanding agricultural conditions. The book creates a desire to question and test the traditional priorities of the father."[8] Graham's previous employment as a sales agent for the same firm presented a conflict of interest which probably made such an endorsement unwise regardless of his judgment regarding the quality of the text.

That fall the Ohio State University *Agricultural Student* published a series of articles written by Graham, "Rural School Agriculture," "An Experiment With Corn," and "Naming and Testing — Weeds, Birds, Insects, Flowers, and Rocks."[9] In January 1905 he spoke on the "Value of Elementary Agriculture in Rural Schools," to between 400 and 500 members of the Agricultural Student Union attending their annual meeting in Columbus.[10] President Thompson of Ohio State participated in this meeting and agricultural leaders pushed the university even harder than they had the year before to establish an extension department in the agricultural college. Graham had developed quite a following who saw him as the man to head such a venture.

For several months Price and Graham had been discussing such a possibility and Dean Price had offered a part-time position with a simultaneous opportunity for Graham to earn a degree in agriculture.[11] None of their correspondence contains Graham's reply but he evidently rejected this in person; perhaps because it was financially inadequate for a family man, perhaps because he considered his educational experience compensation for the lack of an agricultural degree. At the same time Graham had been considering several other employment opportunities, any of which offered a considerably higher salary than his Springfield Township position. He had received overtures from the science departments of Otterbein College and Miami University and he was still considering an administrative position with the Springfield city school system. The result was his resignation from

Springfield Township to serve as teaching principal of the three-room, racially integrated Frey School on Springfield's south side beginning November 28, 1904.[12] It is not clear whether this was a move to pressure Ohio State or simply an opportunity to move into the better paying urban system. Graham actually took a pay cut from $100 per month for a nine month year in Springfield Township to $80 per month for a ten month year at Frey School, but the city promised him a $1200 position the following year, and the township had no possibilities for advancement.[13] President Thompson actively entered the Ohio State negotiation after the January 1905 meeting of the Agricultural Student Union and at their April meeting the University trustees appointed Graham to a newly created position as "Superintendent of Agricultural Extension" at an annual salary of $1500.[14]

In his final report to Springfield Township students, teachers, and parents November 25, 1904, Supt. Graham thanked them for the accomplishments he felt had been made during his tenure. He particularly highlighted the agricultural work. "During the past two years, in a very simple and unpretentious way the initial step leading toward *some very simple* work in elementary agriculture and nature work in rural schools has been taken not only for Springfield Township but for our state. It is now a recognized branch in the new school law and has been adopted by many elementary graded schools and township high schools. If your township is to be remembered for nothing more, it has passed into the school history of our state for this very necessary work. Should not this work lead to establishing a County Agricultural School at no distant day? Wisconsin has two such schools now."

Supt. Graham envisioned the agricultural club work in Springfield Township having a place in history, but he clearly saw it within the context of the public school system. One strongly suspects that he dreamed of being the administrator of a county agricultural school right there in Clark County. Few places in the state or the nation at that time could have provided better support for such a dream. The county population of 58,939 at the turn of the century was dominated by eleven agricultural implement companies employing more than 4000 persons. Springfield's strong publishing enclave was led by Crowell's *Farm and Fireside,* the largest farm paper in the country.[15] Its early editor, Charles E. Thorne, was a powerful voice influencing federal legislation. When the Hatch Act established experiment stations throughout the nation for agricultural research, he became director of the Ohio Agricultural Experiment Station, the same institution the Agricultural Student Union and Graham's agricultural experiment club were working with so closely. Graham's proximity to the agricultural power base was impeccable, but Ohio was a decade away from requiring county school districts, and more than a half century removed from the establishment of joint vocational school districts.

Local support for boys' and girls' agricultural club work, however, was growing too rapidly to be denied. By 1904, Graham was beginning to receive reports and letters not just from Clark County youth, but from across the state. He encouraged this as a means of keeping in touch with the relevance of the program. He labeled one folder "successes" and another "failures" and kept a collection of notes describing each:[16]

> "I tried so hard to keep the weeds out of the flowers and I succeded after all."
>
> Clovas Stalts

> "On account of the rain the ageratum seed roted."
>
> Lillian Cross

> "The ground I used was not good for flowers. Your beans were just elegant. We have used nearly all."
>
> Lida M. Davis

> "On account of so much wet weather the Leaming (variety of corn) did not mature and filled on one side cause it blowed down when it began to fill out. I am not satisfied with results but will try it again. Please send me seed for next year."
>
> R.O. Botkin

> "I have enjoyed my flowers very much. I took some to the sick and took some to school with me."
>
> Alice Dial

> (re: poppies) "There was only one came up and it died."
>
> Edna Thorn

> "My largest carrot weighed one pound and three ounces."
>
> Helen Davis

Had Supt. Graham been a fifth grader, one suspects that his own report might have described his work in detail much like the following from District #3, Bath Township, Greene County:

> Dear Sir:
>
> Mr. Barnes gave us our corn, flower and vegetable seeds from the Agriculture Department the last day of school. I took corn and flower seeds. I sowed my flower seeds May 9, 1905. The Helichrysum Bracteatum came up May 17, 1905. The Gaillardia came up May 27, 1905. The Pansies came up May 25, 1905 I had Scabiosa and Helichrysum Bracteatum of many colors. The Asters bloomed during the month of Sept. The Scabiosa and Helichrysum Bracteatum bloomed from the first of Sept. to the last of Oct.
>
> I planted three hundred and eighty-three hills of corn. Water washed some out before it came up. We plowed it three times. I rode the horse each time we plowed it. I hoed it twice. The wind blew it down when the ears were about half grown which injured it. It yielded twelve bushels.
>
> Jacob W. Barr, 5th grade

Such reports from students begin to reveal why the concepts of the Springfield Township agricultural club became so basic to an educational program which grew beyond school boundaries and was copied around the world to an extent Graham could not have imagined when he left it in 1904. Similar concepts were developing almost simultaneously in several locations. Educators nationwide were anxious to adapt John Dewey's philosophy of "learning by doing" to the rural environment. Cornell University employed John W. Spencer, a farmer who had become interested in scientific agriculture, to conduct nature study through the schools using leaflets prepared by university faculty. By the turn of the century, Will Otwell, a nurseryman from Macopin County, Illinois, was conducting corn growing contests for boys as a means of creating interest in the local farmers' institute. This became so popular that University of Illinois specialists met with a group of boys assembled by O.J. Kern, Winebago County Superintendent, late in February 1902 to explain procedures for conducting scientific experiments in relation to corn growing. In Iowa, Keokuk County Superintendent Cap. E. Miller's students exhibited their agricultural and homemaking projects at township fairs as early as 1904 and similar groups under the supervision of Wright County School Superintendent O.H. Benson and

Page County School Superintendent Jessie Field began using the 3-H symbol for recognition pins in 1907. But nowhere were these pioneers employing more of the enduring concepts of the 4-H Club movement at an earlier date than A. B. Graham.

From the beginning in January 1902, the Springfield Township agricultural experiment club had:

> — met outside of school hours and across school district boundaries for the purpose of learning
>
> — committed each member to undertake an agriculturally related project.
>
> — learned through scientific experiments and demonstrations.
>
> — relied on land-grant university specialists as the source of knowldege
>
> — kept records of work done and results achieved
>
> — organized clubs and elected youth to fulfill leadership roles
>
> — based membership on subject matter interest without regard to race, sex, or economic status
>
> — encouraged parents and other community adults to assist in teaching youth
>
> — exhibited results to the community with the expectation that adults would learn from the youth's results
>
> — recognized achievements of the group through educational trips and merchandise awards provided by local businesses
>
> — demonstrated a philosophical commitment to the development of the 3 H's as well as the 3 R's

Some of these concepts so widely accepted today were considered radical by the standards of some educators in 1902 to 1904. Co-educational groups, racially integrated groups, clubs using school property outside of school hours or under the direction of parent volunteers were ideas carefully omitted from most official reports.

But colleagues with similar goals began to learn of each others' work and offer support. Graham provided a number of the photographs Kern used in his book, *Among Country Schools.* Graham's evangelical style was very similar to Perry G. Holden who several years later wrote, "Your work with boys and girls was the first to attract my attention in the United States and at one time I had set my heart on having you with me in the Extension Department at Ames, Iowa."[17] Graham did travel to Iowa at Cap Miller's invitation to describe his club work to teachers, but his pioneering efforts in developing an extension program for adults as well as youth were to be in his home state.

Chapter 7
Rural Educator in the College of Agriculture

> "A twenty dollar cow and a fifty dollar cow may pass
> by the same name, but the blue milk and thin cream of
> one and the rich milk and thick cream of the other make
> a great difference in the cows. So it is with the centralized
> or consolidated schools: the product is the gauge of
> efficiency."[1]

As an advocate of educational change, A.B. Graham never
skipped a beat when he accepted a position which expected that
he would illustrate his educational philosophy with agricultural
examples. Graham was an educational practitioner advocating
the approved practices of current experts. He lived long enough to
see research raise questions about both centralized schools and
thick cream, but he welcomed change without feeling threatened.

The substantive discussions which created a position to
direct agricultural extension education were conducted face to
face between President Thompson, Dean Price, and Superintendent Graham, so one can only obtain clues from remnants of
correspondence regarding their intentions for this new venture.
It is quite clear that there was no legislative mandate for this
function, but that these men were working cooperatively to
achieve mutually supportive goals. A.B. Graham was turning to
the university for assistance in improving the teaching environment and curriculum of country schools, Dean Price was searching for ways to reach farmers throughout the state and to
encourage more students to attend the agricultural college, President Thompson was placing high priority on developing a broad
leadership role for the university in relation to teacher education
state-wide. The willingness of all three to search for areas of
compatibiity among these goals led to some innovative arrangements for organizing and financing Ohio's first agricultural
extension efforts.

The formal tone of President Thompson's initial letter suggests the two men had barely met, but it also indicates that the agricultural faculty had already agreed to Graham's selection.

> Dear Sir:
>
> We are anxious to undertake some agricultural extension in the rural schools. It is the opinion of our Agricultural Faculty that you would be a desirable and suitable man for that work. We have discussed the matter at considerable length and if there is any disposition on your part to engage in that work we should like to have an interview with you at some convenient time to yourself. I wish you would do us the favor to give the matter consideration and let us talk it over with you. I cannot write the details of our plans in a letter but an hours chat would bring us to a pretty full understanding of the situation.
>
> With appreciation,
> Yours very cordially,
> (W.O. Thompson)
> President[2]

Graham obviously responded promptly, for a week later Dean Price referred to Graham's meeting on Saturday (Jan. 28th) with President Thompson and addressed two concerns which Graham had evidently raised regarding his acceptance by the agricultural faculty and the permanence of the projected work. "We believe your training has been deficient in some regards but we believe that you have other qualifications that compensate for this fact . . . from a professional standpoint I do not see that you can in any way endanger your future. I have no fear but what this work will be permanent."[3] Graham responded the following day, (Feb. 2nd) agreeing to meet both Price and Thompson on Saturday (Feb. 4th). At that time they evidently reached an understanding regarding Graham's salary and the agricultural extension structure and budget which the trustees formalized in April.[4]

A noteworthy sidelight for modern readers is the evident speed of the U.S. Postal Service in the days when trains crisscrossed the country linking cities such as Columbus and Springfield several times daily. It also points out the informality with which decisions were made prior to regulations requiring equal employment opportunities.

Another aspect of the time period appears in Graham's unofficial assignments before he began work. E.A. Jones, Commissioner of Common Schools requested that Graham be on the program of the State Association of School Board Members on March 17th to discuss elementary agriculture, and Graham wrote

Price, "I hope you can be there. It seems to me that there should be as little crossfiring as possible in furthering a work of this kind."[5] June 27th he fulfilled a similar request for the State Teachers' Association meeting at Put-in-Bay, and wrote the lead article for the July issue of their journal. His description of agricultural work in Springfield reveals the wide range of topics being studied through the experimental club: soil formation, drainage, fertilizers, tillage, testing and selecting seed corn, prevention of oat and wheat smut, potato scab, butter making, insecticides and spraying, grafting and budding fruit trees, and rope splicing.[6] Events were moving so rapidly it must have been difficult at times to distinguish leaders from followers, and perhaps the roles alternated as the new organization evolved. Similar events in other states emphasize the many instances in which agricultural extension originated as universities responded to grassroots demand, not as a program conceived and promoted by department faculties. This was a distinction with significant implications for the future.

The Ohio State University to which Superintendent Graham reported July 1, 1905, was growing rapidly in physical facilities, students, and faculty. Now past its thirtieth anniversary, enrollment was approaching 2000 students and more than one hundred faculty were distributed among six colleges.[7] The university was about to outgrow its east-west boundaries between High Street and the Olentangy River, and north-south between Woodruff and Eleventh Avenues. President William Oxley Thompson, a graduate of Muskingum College and an ordained Presbyterian minister, had come to Ohio State six years earlier from the presidency of Miami University at Oxford, Ohio. During the first quarter of the 20th century he guided the university's development at a rapid pace which would not be approached again until after World War II.

In 1904, fifteen buildings for instruction were grouped near the famous Neil spring. University Hall had been joined by elaborately designed buildings such as Orton Hall, Hayes Hall, and the Armory. Brown Hall had just been opened for the College of Engineering. Eight campus residences accommodated the university president, several faculty members, and the farm manager. Two dormitories near the end of the electric car line at Neil and Eleventh Avenues had rooms for up to 84 students at rates of

$3.25 per week or less depending upon the number of meals desired.[8]

Townshend Hall, where an office was established for the new Superintendent of Agricultural Extension, was a 260 foot long building completed in 1898 for a little over $100,000.[9] It was the largest agricultural building on a university campus throughout the country and accommodated most of the needs of the agricultural college. This included the college offices; classrooms, and laboratories for courses in soils and crops; dairy classrooms with adjacent refrigeration facilities for pasteurizing, butter and cheesemaking; a basement livestock judging arena; agricultural chemistry laboratories; and a 200 seat classroom also used by the Townshend Society for agricultural students. Horticultural Hall was just to the south, and toward the river behind both buildings stretched the 200 acre farm with necessary barns and equipment. The space allotted to agricultural extension was initially just space; Graham began operations with his own rolltop desk brought from Springfield.

In the academic year ending June 30, 1904, the College of Agriculture enrolled 255 students. This compared with 744 in the College of Engineering, 521 in Arts, Philosophy and Science, 171 in Law, 91 in Veterinary Medicine, and 47 in Pharmacy.[10] The college granted degrees in agriculture, domestic science, horticulture, and forestry, and offered short courses in these areas as well as dairying. Dean Homer C. Price, a native of Licking County, had graduated from the college in 1897, earned his M.S.A. from Cornell University, and served two years as professor of horticulture and forestry at Iowa State College, before returning to Ohio State as professor of rural economics in 1903. Like the university, the college was poised for growth.

The university farm fulfilled its primary missions providing laboratory experiences for agricultural students and facilities for experimental work by faculty and students, but receipts from sales of farm products provided the college with some very useful funds from an unappropriated source. It was from this "produce fund" that agricultural extension was financed prior to its first legislative appropriation in 1909. Receipts of slightly more than $12,000 for the year July 1 to June 30, 1905 were relatively insignificant within a university budget of approximately $600,000, but it was enough to launch an innovative idea.[11]

A major expense for agricultural extension that first year was Graham's $1500 salary plus expenses for traveling more than 10,000 miles speaking to farmers and teachers. At the time, President Thompson was receiving $5000 and Dean Price $2750, the maximum salaries permitted Ohio State faculty under existing state law. With the assistance of a part-time clerk, teaching and writing contributions from willing faculty members, and a modest budget for printing expenses, agricultural extension began operations with a $5000 budget.[12]

Graham's first task was to commit to writing the general plan for agricultural extension, the organizations and agencies through which it would be implemented, and the teaching methods which would be utilized. July 1st fell on a Saturday, but the new superintendent must have been anxious to begin. Years later he recalled the quiet Sunday afternoon, July 2nd, on which he developed an outline plan and addressed it to President W.O. Thompson, with copies to Dean Homer C. Price and Secretary Wm. R. Lazenby, College of Agriculture and Domestic Science. It included the following purposes:

> To elevate the standard of living in rural communities.
>
> To acquaint boys and girls with their environment and to interest them in making their own investigations.
>
> To give to the boys who shall become interested in farm work an elementary knowledge of agriculture and farm practices; and to girls the simplest facts of domestic science.
>
> To cultivate a taste for the beautiful in nature.
>
> To emphasize the importance of hard work and habits of industry which are essential in the building of strong character.
>
> To inspire young men and women to further their education in the science of agriculture and domestic economy.
>
> To educate the adult in the elementary science of agriculture and the most up-to-date farm practices.[13]

Several aspects of the initial organization are worthy of further note. While Supt. Graham was appointed in the department of rural economics and paid from the agricultural produce fund, he directed this plan to President Thompson with a copy to Dean Price; a chain of command which evidently evolved when the trustees had assumed responsibility for "produce fund" accounts. It is quite clear that all three men envisioned an agricultural extension program which reached out to adult farmers and homemakers as well as youth. For the first time, domestic science was specifically included for women and girls. Graham was to continue the work begun in Clark County with boys' and girls' agricultural clubs, but the organizations cited for reaching youth focused primarily on teacher training through institutes, normal schools, and teacher associations and through local officials serving as township boards of education and county teacher examiners. It was clearly assumed that agricultural clubs would be associated with public schools, organized and supervised by local teachers. It was recognized that adult farmers would be reached through farmers' institutes, livestock breed organizations, and a variety of publications from the college's own bulletins to local newspapers. From an historical perspective the surprising breadth of the new organization is surpassed only by the speed with which it was implemented and accepted.

An enduring and influential extension method was launched within three months of Supt. Graham's appointment. Volume 1, Number 1 of *The Agricultural College Extension Bulletin*, was mailed in October 1905. Initially it was a monthly news bulletin issued September through June primarily for rural teachers, but welcoming advanced students and farmers as readers. It was mailed without charge to everyone who annually requested that they be on the mailing list. In 1905 this averaged 5000 copies, but by 1914 it was 29,000 copies monthly.[14] Issues typically ran from 16 to 32 pages and included several illustrations. Early issues usually contained a poem and a song appropriate for rural classroom use. James Whitcomb Riley was a favorite, but Wordsworth, Whittier, and a variety of lesser known poets were featured.

The bulletin was also a vehicle for announcing teacher education opportunities. The first issue offered the services of eleven Ohio State University faculty members for Saturday lectures at county teachers' meetings or summer teachers' institutes which would pay their travel expenses. Surprisingly, the list of topics was broad and Supt. Graham was the only representative from the College of Agriculture. A choice of seventeen possible lectures included "The Mineral Resources of Ohio," by Edward Orton, Jr.; "Educational Psychology," by D. R. Major; "The School as a Social Institution," by J.E. Hagerty; "The Teaching of English Literature," by J.R. Taylor; "United States History and Civics," by A.H. Tuttle; "Educational Value of Manual Training," by T.K. Lewis; or "Nature Study as a Basis for Elementary Agriculture," by A.B. Graham. President Thompson's goal that the university become a center for teacher education was clearly receiving early emphasis.

During his nine years at Ohio State, Supt. Graham served on the faculty for thirty summer teachers' institutes in twenty-four different counties representing all sections of the state.[15] In the critical years from 1905 to 1909 preceding and following Ohio State's establishment of a College of Education, no O.S.U. faculty member represented the insitution more visibly among local teachers than Supt. Graham. His teacher institute presentations were double the combined appearances of Prof. W.W. Boyd and Prof. D.R. Major, the university's experts in educational administration and psychology.[16] In his presentations Graham had already developed the straightforward speaking style which became his trademark. Reporting on the Logan County Teachers' Institute, the *Bellefontaine Examiner* stated, "The teachers enjoyed a treat in hearing Prof. Graham who is connected with the O.S.U." As usual, Graham used his platform on nature study to urge teachers to take the lead in influencing community attitudes about the quality of education. "We ought to have our meetings in the evenings in the school house when the farmer can get in and discuss centralization and libraries. Talk school until the patrons dream of libraries and pictures. Don't worry if there is a patron who doesn't agree, for he will, after a while. We must prove to our patrons that we can lead."[17] His concerns included, but were not limited to, agriculture and his words were chosen to stimulate action just as they had been in Terre Haute and Springfield.

From the beginning, each monthly extension bulletin contained at least one article on agricultural applications of natural science written by one of the college professors. These included topics on insects, trees, birds, soils, crops, livestock, and plants. Early issues were actually teacher workbooks giving several experiments to be conducted by individuals or groups of students. "Some warm day this fall, place in the sun three tin pans. In one put some dry sand, in one some wet sand, and in the third water. Let them remain for an hour or more. Which one has become the warmest? Which will become the warmest, well-drained land or land not drained?"[18] Supt. Graham expressed his belief in the value of experimental experience succinctly, "Who cares for a correspondence course in swimming?"[19]

Rural teachers were encouraged to incorporate elementary agriculture into almost every subject, and almost every issue of the extension bulletin posed questions for observation, discussion, or problem solving. "Why do kettles boil dry? What becomes of the water?"[20] "Which will a brook carry farther, fine sand or pebbles?"[21] "Select ten ears of corn from the field and weigh them. Some time during the first week in January weigh them again. Do the same about the first of March and the first of April. Calculate the percent of loss at each weighing. If corn can be marketed in the fall at 35 cents a bushel, would it pay to keep it until the first of March and sell it at 40 cents a bushel?"[22] It soon became obvious how closely Graham's concept of nature study was integrated into studies of mathematics and science.

Early issues of the extension bulletin informed readers of services which they might request. Teachers and students were encouraged to send unknown items from nature study field trips to the agricultural college for identification. All forms of insects, rocks, and plants began to arrive, and subsequent topics suggest that professors found this a useful device for determining future bulletin topics and appropriate levels of knowledge and interest.

Graham also began describing scientific experiments in a regular column, "Agriculture for Elementary Schools," in the *Ohio Educational Monthly* using some of the same information.[23] He introduced nature study by quoting a familiar maxim, "Things seen oftenest are seen least," and gave some specific suggestions for making nature study field trips educational excursions, not just outings.[24]

The first issue of the extension bulletin contained an article by Graham, "Planting on Rural School Grounds," a theme he would emphasize again and again as he sought to improve rural school environments. Agricultural extension offered to draw a planting plan, listing suggested varieties of trees, shrubs, and bulbs for any teachers who sent diagrams of their school grounds. Lists of appropriate plantings were printed periodically and price lists were given in planting season for bulb orders from the Livingston Seed Company in Columbus for those who could not purchase them locally. For several years the bulletins featured before and after photographs, many taken by Graham in his travels and talks, emphasizing the esthetic value of attractive interior and exterior rural school environments.

Graham's interest in rural school libraries naturally suggested that the bulletin would recommend appropriate texts and supplementary reading for nature study and agriculture. May 12, 1906 the Board of Control of the Ohio Teacher's Reading Circle adopted the *Agricultural College Extension Bulletin* as a reference for its members and directed the secretary to send its membership list to Ohio State University for future mailings. Within its first year, the bulletin had become firmly established among rural teachers as a primary resource for nature study.

Ohio State's campaign for a College of Education culminated in 1906. At every opportunity President Thompson had been stressing the inadequacy of normal schools to prepare secondary teachers and school administrators. He was greatly concerned that of 1,331 townships in the state, only 189 then had high schools, and only six of these were able to prepare students adequately for direct entry to Ohio State.[25] In April 1906 the Ohio General Assembly passed legislation permitting Ohio State to establish a Teachers' College, and the same month the university issued its first summer term bulletin aimed primarily at teachers. For an instructional fee of $6 (and approximately $3 to $4 weekly for room and board in a nearby home) teachers were offered a variety of subjects and several courses in educational psychology and methodology.[26] Agriculture offered a course in soils and one in plant and animal culture while domestic science offered two in theory and practice of domestic science. This summer session coincided with President Thompson's report to the Governor June 30, 1906, in which he pleaded for a legislative appropriation, not just permission, to create a Teachers' College at Ohio State University which would emphasize the preparation of secondary teachers.[27]

The Ohio State University Trustees supported a faculty committee committed to moving ahead, and by the following spring the university bulletin was announcing the opening of a College of Education for autumn term, 1907. ". . . opportunity is offered for preparation for the work of teaching in high schools and normal schools, of superintending schools, of supervising special branches, and of acquiring a knowledge of, and right attitude toward, education."[28] So many persons and events influenced this outcome, it would be impossible to appraise the proportionate contribution of each. But the complete omission of Graham's name in the definitive history of the college[29] is a curious error which speaks dramatically of the isolation among university departments and colleges which had occurred by the time the college celebrated its fiftieth anniversary in 1957. This history does not mention Graham's influential role among teachers throughout the state, with the state department of education, or with key legislators at the time the college was evolving. Rural education was not only disadvantaged, but its grassroots spokesmen were frequently ignored by the professionals in teacher education.

There was much less separation between departments when the entire university faculty was small enough to know each other personally. At the time agricultural education was mandated in the Ohio public school curriculum in 1911, university departments were sometimes cooperative and sometimes competitive. A university spokeman described its teacher education program, perhaps ·with some idealism, as an elective system in which, "students in the college of agriculture may prepare for teaching by electing work in the college of education and students in the college of education may prepare for teaching agriculture by electing courses in the college of agriculture."[30] The College of Education offered four courses in agricultural education: elements of general agriculture, teaching agriculture in the high school, teaching elementary agriculture, and rural life and institutions, as well as special summer sessions for teachers. Competition for student enrollment and the funding based upon it was incompatible with an elective system. After federal funding was provided for vocational education in 1917, a new Department of Agricultural Education was established combining both subject matter content and methodology within the College of Agriculture.[31]

At the turn of the twentieth century, quality of life in rural areas was a key issue. The 1900 census showed 11% of the men of voting age were illiterate, a figure undoubtedly higher in rural areas and among women. The average school term was 144.6 days and the average attendance per pupil 99.1 days, figures which were no doubt lower in rural areas.[32] One writer has described the period from the turn of the century to World War I as "the Indian summer of rural America."[33] Scientific agriculture was yielding bountiful production but rural population was declining and urban areas were growing. Both those who lamented the social-cultural deprivations of farm life and those who prized the independent farm life style focused on rural schools as the key to retaining young people in rural areas.

The National Education Association had thrown a spotlight on rural schools with extensive study and recommendations by a

"Committee of Twelve" in the 1890s. Their recommendations regarding school consolidation for supervision and funding, obtaining qualified teachers and superintendents, and standardizing the curriculum became the basis of extensive discussion among educators and the impetus for much of the educational legislation during the next two decades. This committee cited Ohio as "an excess of democracy" for its 1875 situation, with 15,087 teachers employed in common schools and more than 35,000 school directors and board members charged with their administration.[34] This was the climate which led Graham and other professional educators to advocate consolidated schools so urgently.

Feelings were strong throughout the midwest about the degree to which rural schools were to be controlled by local farmers or professional educators. In the 1890s Ohio legislative action to abolish sub-district directors met such opposition it was repealed and the state entered the 20th century with a dual system of township and district boards making decisions on buildings, teachers, texts, and curriculum. By 1900 Ohio was the only midwestern state without a system of county superintendents. By the time he came to Ohio State University, A.B. Graham had been employed for seventeen years by district and township schools and he understood clearly the need for involving local people and seeking their support for making needed changes in the schools.

In northeastern Ohio in 1892 Ohio became the first state outside of New England to consolidate a rural school. The directors of the Kingsville District in Ashtabula County sought legislative approval to transport pupils rather than build a new building. This was granted with great care to limit permission to this district, not to open the gates for widespread transportation of pupils at public expense. But nearby districts were soon desiring to transport pupils, and by 1898 the General Assembly passed a law permitting boards throughout the state to transport pupils with public funds. In 1904 legislation further encouraged consolidation by permitting boards to consolidate any school of less than twelve students.[35]

In the fall of 1900, O.J. Kern, the innovative superintendent of Winnebago County, Illinois, toured several northeastern Ohio centralized schools and talked with teachers, students, and parents.[36] His enthusiastic reports were given wide circulation by the U.S. Commissioner of Education and midwestern educators began to emphasize consolidation as the answer to the problem of small rural schools with a tax base too poor to provide quality education. Ironically, it was neither Ohio nor Illinois, but Indiana, which already had a township structure of school organization, which moved most rapidly to centralize township schools.

A.B. Graham strongly supported centralization as a means for improving rural schools beginning with his experience as superintendent in southern Mad River Township. In 1898, the year state law first permitted public transportation, students were transported under his supervision from Neff's School to Terre Haute. By the time the *Ohio Teacher* published a series of articles on the topic, opening in October 1902 with an article by Graham, centralization was becoming an important issue among Ohio educators.[37] It was quite logical that Supt. Graham would give this issue priority attention and use his new state-wide position to influence its progress.

In the fall of 1905, Supt, Graham sent a questionnaire to several hundred parents in townships already having centralized schools. Some of the questions dealt with community attitudes. "What effect has centralized or consolidated schools had on the social and educational interests of the township?" "What is the general sentiment of those not having children to send to school?" Other questions dealt with specific operations. "How does the driver announce his coming?" "Is it necessary to clothe your child as heavily for winter trips as under the old plan?" "Does your child attend school more regularly than under the old plan?"[38]

These survey responses were combined with Graham's photographs and published as *Agricultural Extension Bulletin,* Number 5, "Centralized Schools in Ohio." This became so popular that it was twice updated and reprinted and was distributed to over 100,000 school directors, teachers, and parents. Ohio's Commissioner of Common Schools, who had no funds to do the job himself, approved enthusiastically, but local critics were plentiful. One Clinton County township clerk complained that it was illegal to use public funds for such a publication, an issue that was essentially avoided since extension publications were then being funded from the agricultural college "produce fund."

An Ohio map in the original 1906 bulletin identified 32 completely centralized township schools with another 60 sub-district schools consolidated by transporting pupils to an adjacent school.[39] Some educators tried to sell the idea as less costly, but not Graham. During his first six months on the job he visited twenty townships and was many times asked, "Is it cheaper?" and many times answered, "It is not how cheap, but how efficient." He cited the example of Madison Township, Lake County, where per capita expense on the basis of enrollment decreased from $16 to $10.50 and on the basis of average daily attendance, from $26.66 to $16.07. While the total expense was about the same under the new plan as the old, more children were able to attend school and to attend regularly.[40]

Graham had summarized the advantages of centralization in terms of ability to secure and retain better teachers in larger schools; to provide a graded curriculum; improve the children's health by reducing wet feet and clothing; reduce the immoralities of fighting and vandalism which sometimes occurred on the road to school; provide opportunities for nature study and agriculture, and domestic art and science; and increase land values by providing better educational opportunities in the neighborhood. A comparison of this list with others written by educators across the country in this time period reveals one striking difference. Almost no one else emphasized land values, yet it was common for parents to move into town to assure children better schooling. It is an item which demonstrates Graham's ability to seek out and utilize reasons which would counteract rural people's prejudices against change. It was essential that teachers be concerned with community issues beyond their classrooms. Some of the most severe limitations to an improved learning environment were the transportation difficulties posed by bad roads.

Consolidation progress was slow but steady. In 1907, Kern estimated that in many states 85% of the students attending one-room schools did not go beyond the boundaries of the home district and he pleaded for consolidated schools offering some agricultural education.[41] Some local school boards feared loss of prestige and some rural teachers feared consolidation would mean loss of jobs. Sometimes sentimental voters resisted abandoning the community landmark of spelling bees, box suppers, and voting days. The latter was probably the main reason the Country Life Commission appointed by President Theodore Roosevelt held much discussion but did not take a stand regarding consolidated schools. Chairman Liberty Hyde Bailey of Cornell University was reluctant to support consolidation until provisions were made for community halls in rural areas.

Graham envisioned new centralized schools as community centers where parents could be involved in a wide range of activities. He advocated "patrons' meetings" on a variety of topics and exercises for special days such as Thanksgiving, Christmas, Washington's Birthday, Arbor Day, and Closing Day. He wanted centralized schools to provide an enlarged and enriched community for adults as well as youth. He had already demonstrated to his own satisfaction that this could be done, and his leadership of such meetings at Terre Haute and Springfield had won wide community support.

Educators continued to cite examples of deficient one-room schools such as one in Delaware County, Ohio where reportedly *no* pupils attended all winter, but the teacher faithfully rang the bell and then spent the day reading by the stove.[42] By 1912 one source showed 192 of Ohio's 1370 rural schools had been consolidated.[43] Another credited Ohio with 350 consolidated schools and ranked it second to Indiana among midwestern states in adopting the concept.[44] The difference in numbers probably lies in the distinction between township centralized schools and abandoned sub-district schools where pupils were transported to a nearby school. Most states had consolidation of both types. Graham left Ohio long before the one-room school disappeared, but he never quit preaching the concept of schools large enough to provide optimum learning with efficiency. His last year as Superintendent of Agricultural Extension he recorded eleven talks on school centralization.[45]

The editor of the *Journal of Education* was particularly impressed with Graham's photographs. "Among the men who are doing great things in a noble way for rural schools, Professor A.B. Graham of the extension work of the department of agriculture of the Ohio State University takes high rank. He has visited a thousand rural schoolhouses in Ohio, and has photographs of most of them. With all my study of school conditions, and after reading all that Fowler, Stetson, and Kern have printed upon the subject, I never had the faintest conception of the degradation until I saw the photographs of Professor A.B. Graham. Ohio has some of the best rural school properties in the country, and he shows these in contrast. Mr. Graham is showing the farmers of Ohio that they can have the best as well as the poorest if they want the best for their children. His work is already bearing fruit, and is certain to revolutionize conditions."[46]

The extension bulletin on centralized schools was not only reprinted and widely distributed, but was condensed in the *Ohio Teacher,* a monthly magazine edited by the Marietta, Ohio superintendent and widely read, particularly by eastern Ohio teachers.[47] Graham continued to write or update a special bulletin on rural school conditions each year. "Township High Schools of Ohio" in 1908,[48] and "The Country Schools of Ohio" in 1910,[49] both contained his survey results which were widely quoted, and photographs which were widely reproduced. Educational historians cite 1905 as a turning point marking rapid growth toward rural high schools. As usual, Graham was on the cutting edge of change, speaking out on an educational issue. Frank Miller, Commissioner of Common Schools, considered Graham's series of bulletins the most concise statement of rural school conditions in Ohio. He credited them with creating an awareness which helped to contribute to significant revisions in the Ohio School Code in 1914, which created rural school districts and county superintendents.

Graham maintained good relationships through several personnel changes in the Office of Commissioner of Common Schools. Appointed as a member of the committee to plan an educational exhibit respresenting Ohio at the 1907 Exposition in Jamestown, Virginia, Graham saw to it that Boys' and Girls' Club Work was represented by club record forms, corn samples, litmus tests for acidity, and a variety of the 1905-06 Ohio State University *Agricultural Extension Bulletins* for school nature study.[50] It was an early and extensive exhibit of the work accomplished through a partnership formed by a land-grant university, the public school system, and local volunteer leaders.

About the same time Graham authored a symposium on rural school problems for the *Ohio Educational Monthly.* It featured the viewpoints of ten experienced rural teachers discussing current issues such as rural supervision, teacher training, centralization, and examinations for high school admission.[51] The method was even more remarkable than the content, for by using spokesmen from all parts of the state, Graham was localizing his appeal at the same time he was gaining endorsements for his position. It was a technique he was to use many times in the future.

As Superintendent Graham's writings and speeches regarding rural schools began receiving national attention, the National Education Association appointed a committee of five to study a growing problem in regard to the division between primary and secondary courses in public schools. Chaired by Gilbert B. Morrison, Principal of McKinley High School, St. Louis, Missouri, this group included Wilson Farrand, Principal of Newark Academy, Newark, New Jersey; Edward Rynearson, Director of High Schools, Pittsburgh, Pennsylvania; Albert B. Graham, Superintendent of Agricultural Extension, Ohio State University, Columbus, Ohio; and J.H. Francis, Principal of Polytechnic High School, Los Angeles, California. The committee's report and recommendations July 26, 1907, at the association's national meeting in Los Angeles, outlined a new concept for a junior high school and sparked a lively discussion among educators for years.[52]

The issue was the division of the twelve years of public school course work and a proposed change from an eight-four curriculum to a six-six or six-three-three division. The N.E.A. committee considered both the pedagogic and economic aspects of the question and strongly recommended that secondary education be extended downward two years.

The pedagogic reasons for the committee's recommendation may be summarized in four categories: FIRST, 1) Pupils would have the advantage of being taught by teachers specially trained for the different branches. As the committee said, "It takes a musician to teach time and harmony so that it will be appreciated. Although there is not a consesus of opinion on this point, the belief is growing that it should not be different with the teaching of arithmetic, of geography, of history, or of grammar." SECOND, Students in the seventh and eighth grades would have the advantage of daily contact with several personalities. "The consensus of scientific opinion is that the dawn of adolescence calls for a change in the child's environment, that the period of love of change, adventure, and individual initiative has arrived and should be indulged by giving him more freedom and elbow room than are usually accorded in the seventh and eighth-grade rooms of an elementary school." THIRD, It would mitigate the abruptness of the transition from the elementary schools and remove what is now regarded by parents as a natural stopping place. ". . . this erroneous notion of finality and completeness at any point in the system might in some measure be avoided and pupils and parents be spared the fallacy that there is any logical stopping place in a process of education." FOURTH, It would permit a variety of options in laboratory sciences, manual training, modern languages, and college preparation which were not possible in the crowded four-year secondary curriculum.

The committee recognized that the economic aspects of the question were not favorable because it would require a greater proportion of school buildings and classrooms to have equipment and teachers for secondary style instruction, and these were more expensive than primary schools. Free textbooks and calisthenics were cited as examples to indicate that taxpayers had in the past responded with support for changes they perceived as positive. The committee concluded that their suggestions would first be perceived necessary in larger cities. Of particular interest is the statement, "The necessities of a change in the smaller towns are not so great as in the large cities which are deprived of many of the natural and stimulating conditions afforded by the country. The extensive laboratories, workshops and museums in our large city schools may indeed be considered in part as an attempt to restore to the pupils those forces, exercises, and experiences which are the inheritance of youth in the country." How one would like to know whether that statement expressed the sentiments of the innovative rural superintendent whose students studied nature but also took field trips to businesses, colleges, and government offices, or the philosophy of a city administrator who remembered with nostalgia the practical examples of a rural school environment.

As this committee predicted, change came slowly and gradually. But Columbus, Ohio was soon interested and one of the first schools in the country built specifically for junior high instruction was Indianola Junior High School near the Ohio State University campus.[53] When it opened in 1909, twelve-year-old Walter Graham was one of its first students. N.E.A. committee member J.H. Francis later became Columbus Superintendent of Schools.

In 1909 N.E.A. created a rural and agricultural professional interest section, and in July 1910 at the Boston annual meeting, Supt. Graham reported to the department of secondary education as chairman of a committee "Encouraging College Entrance Credit in High School Agriculture."[54] This group had conducted a survey which found numerous colleges willing to give credit for courses taught by trained teachers (not those who remembered growing up on a farm) conducting appropriate laboratory experiments with soils, plants, insects, and farm animals.

Of the 93 colleges responding to the committee's survey nationally, 36 were giving credit for agricultural courses including Ohio's Wesleyan, Miami, Ashland, and Defiance. Eight were preparing to give credit, including Wittenberg, Rio Grande, Antioch, and Wilmington. Twenty-seven indicated they would give credit if asked and if work had been properly done. These included Ohio Northern, Mt. Union, Marietta, Buchtel, and the University of Cincinnati. The 23 colleges not giving credit included Wooster, Denison, and Kenyon, but the latter two indicated willingness to consider it. Efforts to establish agriculture as a scientific study worthy of college entrance credit were evidently widespread, but one suspects they had been particularly intense in Ohio where the committee chairman had been performing an advocate's role. This trend would later be reversed as agriculture assumed the vocational role of an applied science at the secondary level.

Encouraging the progression from nature study in the elementary grades to agricultural education in high schools and colleges remained a Graham priority, but the agricultural experiments with clubs of boys and girls which had drawn the university's attention to Supt. Graham, now had to compete with other issues for his time. Graham may have had more opportunity to motivate teachers to conduct club work as a school superintendent than he had in his position at the College of Agriculture.

When the agricultural college created the "Ohio Federation of Rural School Agricultural Clubs" in connection with the Agricultural Student Union, the federation distributed instructions for experiments and report blanks to be completed by students. Early issues of the extension bulletin encouraged teachers to send for directions for organizing agricultural clubs for 1906, and reminded teachers that names of students had to be submitted by March 1st to receive seeds and report forms from the College of Agriculture.[55] It also suggested to teachers that they plan exhibits for county fairs, and included photographs of such exhibits which showed that domestic arts and sciences were already being included for girls.

The Agricultural Student Union considered its mission accomplished with the establishment of an agricultural extension division in the college and voted to disband their organization. There continued to be enthusiastic teachers who encouraged agricultural clubs and their activities, but much of the work was conducted at student homes, and crops and garden experiments needed attention during the growing season when the teacher might be employed elsewhere or attending school. Work begun in the spring might be ignored by a new teacher in the fall. Few local school board members knew enough about the work to reward teachers for the extra effort, so clubs usually relied on an individual teacher's motivation and knowledge.

The most visible results of the boys' and girls' clubs were the exhibits made at county fairs or farmers' institutes. It was easy to arouse interest in the best products and to encourage local businesses to award prizes for such efforts. It soon became popular to hold judging contests where youth competed for the ability to rank several ears of corn, or judge a class of livestock, much as they competed in spelling bees. Breed associations began to encourage these contests as a means of arousing attention for the qualities of their livestock. When agricultural extension received state funding, exhibits and contests became an increasingly important focus of the extension youth program.

It was agricultural extension's successful bid for state funding which reinforced faculty perceptions in the College of Agriculture that Supt. Graham was an educator, at the same time that faculty perceptions in the College of Education branded him an agriculturist. Only time would reveal the true scope of the difficulties for those who attempted to walk the middle ground.

Chapter 8
Ohio State University: A Land-Grant University Reaching State-Wide

> "One who is desirous of being a really helpful agent dare not be a destructive critic, a cynic, or a gossip; he must be one who is able to take into consideration the conditions under which people live, their interests and financial resources which, in great measure, form the foundation upon which better things are to be constructed."[1]

Graham was an articulate spokesman for this new style of educational programing. After more than three years of ad hoc financing through the college produce fund, political groundwork had been laid to seek a legislative appropriation for agricultural extension. February 15, 1909, Democratic Senator Walter A. Alsdorf, a grain dealer from Johnstown, Ohio introduced S.B. 50, "To provide for agricultural extension work by the College of Agriculture and Domestic Science of Ohio State University, and making an appropriation therefor."[2] Specific provisions by the finance committee and floor amendments were included before the bill passed unanimously February 25th, with an appropriation of $20,000 for the fiscal year beginning July 1, 1909. The House of Representatives concurred unanimously on March 5th. The unanimous vote reflected the political support which had been generated throughout the state for agricultural extension by various farm organizations, but the sponsorship by the senator from Licking County, where Dean Price owned a farm, should not be overlooked.

The bill specifically authorized the college to arrange for the extension of its teaching throughout the state, by holding schools of not more than one week with not more than one per year in each county. Such schools were to include soil fertility, stock raising, crop production, dairying, horticulture, domestic science, and "kindred subjects." The college was also instructed to give demonstrations at agricultural fairs, institutes, granges, clubs, and organizations, and to provide instruction by mail or through the publication of bulletins. The law prohibited this appropriation from being used for the payment of rent, heat, light, janitor service, or other local expenses. Communities requesting local schools were to be responsible for local arrangements and expenses, an important concept which would be reinforced in future funding legislation.

Meeting April 9th, the O.S.U. Board of Trustees appointed two of their members, F.A. Derthick of Mantua and O.E. Bradfute of Cedarville to assist President Thompson in directing this work. A.B. Graham was appointed Superintendent of Agricultural Extension at a salary of $1800 to work "under the direction of this special committee."[3] No reference was made to the role of the Dean of the College of Agriculture.

Late in 1908, Charles H. Allen, a bank president in Paulding, Ohio, had written to agricultural extension asking if it might be possible for farmers in that county to receive a week of local instruction from the university. After consulting with faculty departments, Supt. Graham offered a five day short course. This was held December 29, 1908 through January 2, 1909, without a New Year's holiday, at Paulding with Professors Shoesmith, Williams, and McCall teaching crops and Professors Marshall and Shields teaching animal husbandry.[4] Other counties immediately began to request such schools, creating a demand which coincided nicely with agricultural extension's request for state funding.

After the passage of the Alsdorf Act, procedures were soon established for working with local organizations requesting extension schools and the first was taught September 6-10, 1909 in Athens County at Amesville. Organized and supervised by A.B. Graham personally a pattern was established for future schools which fortunately was captured by W.J. Warrener, secretary of the Athens County Grange, writing extensive reports of all lectures for the daily paper.[5] Concurrent sessions for farmers and farm wives featured the latest scientific information through demonstrations as well as lectures. Mrs. E.W. Foulk lectured to the homemakers on topics as diverse as vegetables, home furnishings, and household economy, illustrating her points with numerous demonstrations. Instructors attempted to adapt their teaching methods to adult learners and she may have had the most humorous and successful critique by students. While teaching food chemistry, she asked six homemakers each to bring a loaf of bread for the class to evaluate quality of texture and flavor. When she rated the top score a tie between two loaves, class members were amused and delighted, for they had tested the university teacher by submitting two loaves from the same batch of dough!

Throughout the week six teachers from the agricultural college alternated in presenting four sessions each day. Prof. Alfred Vivian, for example, lectured on soil tillage and commercial and natural fertilizers. Prof. V.H. Davis followed his lecture on controlling insects and diseases with demonstrations in a nearby orchard to show spraying, budding, and grafting techniques. This school established a pattern which was well accepted by the public. By November President Thompson was able to report that provisions had been made for thirty-six schools under the Alsdorf Act and that a demonstration at the state fair and some county fairs showed potential for very useful instruction in that area.[6]

Initial results were overwhelmingly successful with participants so enthusiastic the university was able to increase its state appropriation for agricultural extension to $50,000. During that 1910-11 budget year seventy-nine extension schools were taught with about 17,000 persons in attendance.[7] The popularity of these five-day schools taught by college faculty threatened the established two-day farmers' insitutes which were locally organized under the auspices of the State Board of Agriculture. In 1890 they had been authorized to share a county tax of three mills per resident,[8] and some local organizers brought political pressure to bear to assure their retention. In 1911-12 the agricultural extension budget was reduced to $40,000 and a pattern was established to hold extension schools in about one-half of Ohio's counties each year. Clark S. Wheeler was appointed to coordinate these schools and a schedule evolved for conducting sessions in three counties each week during a period of approximately fifteen weeks from mid-November through mid-March.

In his 1914 report Supt. Graham commented favorably on the success of extension schools as a teaching method, indicating that the leading farmers of each community had been involved in organizing and attending these schools. During that year 5,304 persons attended 43 schools, for an average of 123 persons per school.[9]

The popularity of local extension schools led to the birth on campus of an enlarged program for a much more diversified audience. As Supt. Graham stated, "Instruction taken to the home or community of the learner will never push back the intellectual or spiritual horizon so far as will instruction received in the parent or central institution, because the conservatism or inertia of a community asserts itself over the individual."[10] The man who had implemented the agricultural extension philosophy in Ohio was admitting that the quality of education which can be extended locally will differ from the interactive atmosphere of the campus classroom. State-wide response to the new offering was dramatic evidence of the extent to which the Ohio State University's College of Agriculture had bridged the educational gap to farmers by demonstrating its ability to teach relevant material.

The first "Farmers' Week" on the O.S.U. campus in 1913 attracted 140 persons, and was in a sense a revival of a program held in 1881 and dropped for lack of staff support. The new attempt was a resounding success with the second session in February 1914 enrolling 770 persons from 77 of the state's 88 counties, and establishing a pattern which enabled the program to double its attendance each of the next three years (reaching over 4000 by 1917).[11] Lectures featured the college's most highly regarded faculty using the latest laboratory equipment for demonstrations. Courses were arranged morning, afternoon, and evening throughout the five days so participants could attend a five session shortcourse on a topic such as dairying, soils, or horticulture, or day students could attend and benefit from a single session. Agricultural organizations began to hold annual meetings concurrently with this progam and the sheer volume of the event for many years emphasized a mutually beneficial relationship between farmers and the campus. Like local extension schools, "Farmers' Week" included courses in home economics for farm wives, and contests and agricultural career information for older youth.

Because extension schools and "Farmers' Week" so successfully attracted those interested in farming and homemaking topics, both Supt. Graham and Pres. Thompson, a minister by training, were interested in sponsoring a "Country Life Week" in the summer which would emphasize the socializing aspects of country life. Concern for the declining rural population and the inferior educational opportunities for country children had been widespread for more than a decade, but the country life movement had been given national focus by the Country Life Commission appointed by President Roosevelt in 1908. The leadership of this movement came largely from educators and church groups and was never completely successful in arousing the rural residents they were most interested in helping. A Country Church Conference was called by Graham July 25-27, 1911 "for the purpose of discussing the real causes underlying the decline of the country church and to start a state-wide, non-denominational movement which will ultimately result in a return of strength and influence to the country church and make it the center of rural activities"[12] A name change to "Country Life Week" in 1913 failed to broaden the audience beyond ministers or to increase the program's impact.

One of the most exotic teaching methods used by agricultural extension under Supt. Graham originated when the railroads offered free trains to agriculture and domestic science for educational exhibits and programs. The idea originated in Iowa in 1904 and similar programs developed in several midwestern and southern states. The motive of the railroads was, of course, to promote a positive image among farmers and to increase the agricultural tonnage which they hauled. In the years from 1907 to 1913 the principal railroads operating in Ohio offered one or more trains for several days each year, and C.R. Titlow was employed as an extension assistant to handle arrangements.

It was an attention getting educational idea which drew crowds and made farmers aware that the agricultural college could help them. During the peak year from July 1, 1911 to July 1, 1912, fourteen trains were operated, making 360 stops in 68 counties, involving a total audience of 42,198 persons.[13] Graham believed, "No one should leave the train without something in his hands to carry home. The train is an exponent, an advertiser, if you please, of the agricultural college. Many students come to college saying that they heard this man or that on the agricultural train, were attracted by him and so decided to enter college."[14]

Agricultural trains were usually scheduled in early spring before the planting season or after fall harvest. A typical train had a baggage car for equipment and livestock, a dining car for the traveling faculty, and at least two lecture cars. "Our news man and his portable typewriter occupied an important place in the baggage car; he had a local story for every stop having a newspaper."[15] Stops were usually an hour and a half or two hours, sometimes offering varied lectures on livestock, crops and fertilizers, other times offering programs for special audiences such as dairymen, orchardists, or poultry farmers. At least two of the trains offered special lectures for homemakers.

When space was limited, demonstrations were performed on the platform of the baggage car or railroad station with the audience gathered below. A photograph from the Erie Railroad's Dairy Special clearly shows that on a rainy day the cow had the dry position and the spectators held the unbrellas!

These trains were quite popular, but time consuming for faculty resources. One of the chief disadvantages was that extension at that time could only provide bulletins for follow-up and many farmers needed more personal instruction. Later trains focused on exhibits of agricultural products instead of lectures. The largest of these was the "Ohio Booster" mounted in cooperation with the Agricultural Experiment Station and the State Board of Agriculture. It ran over the New York Central Lines for 100 days beginning in January 1912. In Ohio, the era ended the following year with the "Better Farming" train of the Norfolk and Western, March 19-27, 1913.[16]

But none of the early extension methods outshone the overwhelming popularity of the *Agricultural Extension Bulletin.* When the Alsdorf Act encouraged instruction by mail and bulletins it opened avenues for expanding the monthly bulletin begun in 1905. Extension created a full-time editorial position in 1910. The monthly bulletin quickly evolved a new look, concentrating most of each issue on a topic of some depth written by a faculty member of the college. Originally the primary audience had been rural teachers with farmers a secondary audience, but now these roles were visibly and intentionally reversed. During the 1910-11 year, monthly press runs increased from 25,000 to 35,000 copies and the university editor's annual report showed that agricultural extension's printing expenses at $3,627 nearly equalled the entire printing costs of all other units of the university combined at $3,843.[17]

A significant portion of this cost was the addition of seventeen supplemental bulletins, from 4 to 24 pages in length, printed in quantities of 5,000 to 25,000 copies, labeled as "Farmers' Reading Course" and "Homemakers' Reading Course." These titles probably reflect Supt. Graham's experience with the Ohio Teachers' Reading Circle. "Reading Course" conveys the impression of a correspondence course, but that was not the primary purpose. Although extension did offer to respond to readers' questions, the supplements were not written in a questioning format, and they were not designed to provide college credit by correspondence as some states were doing by that time. These publications were simply single topic brochures designed to be kept for reference, much like modern extension publications. Early titles in the farmers' course included, "Soil Formation," "Drainage of Farm Land," "Orcharding," "Spraying Fruit Trees," Weather Forecasts," and "Home Butter Making." The homemakers' course offered the first bulletins written by members of the domestic science faculty, "The Canning of Fruits and Vegetables," "Jellies, Jams, Preserves and Pickles," "Bread and Bread Baking," and "Sanitation."[18]

The format of single topic supplemental bulletins permitted printing flexibility based on demand and became quite popular because they could easily be revised and reprinted. In time the bulletins did lead to requests for true correspondence courses, and in 1914 J.E. McClintock was appointed to supervise an operation of 25 courses prepared on a variety of topics by members of the college faculty.[19]

From the beginning, Dean Price and Supt. Graham had been aware of the benefits to be received from cooperative efforts with rural newspapers. It will be recalled that Graham had experience writing an educational column for the Champaign County papers as a township superintendent in the 1890s. He had developed skills which were very useful as he began writing regularly for the *Ohio Farmer,* a bi-weekly magazine widely circulated throughout rural Ohio. In his final report as Superintendent of Agricultural Extension, Graham clearly stated extension's goal, "It has been the aim of the department to furnish information concerning both the approved agricultural practices and the social life in the country, and news concerning the University and the Agricultural College in particular."[20]

After extension employed an editor, press coverage expanded dramatically. In the year ending June 30, 1914 a feature article with photographs was prepared every three weeks for both the American Press Association and the Western Newspaper Union. A multigraphed newsletter was mailed bi-weekly to 750 newspapers throughout the state. Some of these papers printed the entire letter, some used parts of the material for editorials, and some clipped and used items of particular interest to their subscribers.[21]

When the Ohio legislative appropriation as the sole source of funds for agricultural extension peaked in 1910-11, the work was organized under eight areas: 1) *Extension Schools* for farmers and homemakers on a week-long, county-wide basis, 2) *Demonstrations* on specialized topics such as fruit tree pruning, 3) *Agricultural Trains,* 4) *Fair Exhibits,* 5) *Bulletins,* 6) *Identifications* of items (such as insects) sent to the university, 7) *Agriculture in the Schools* through educational programs for teachers, and 8) *Personal Visits* to agriculturists.[22] President Thompson was reporting enthusiastically, "The University has now had sufficient experience in the work of agricultural extension to offer a deliberate judgment as to its value. The beginning of this work was speculative and altogether experimental. Experience has, however, demonstrated the educational values of this work and the interest shown by the communities has been so well sustained as to thoroughly justify the expenditure of the money."[23] His opinion was particularly significant because as spokesman for the executive committee of the Association of American Agricultural Colleges and Experiment Stations, he was currently testifying before Congressional committees considering federal funding for extension work.[24]

But, increasing scope and visibility was generating competition. From its inception, the *Agricultural Extension Bulletin* had annually devoted its February issue to the results of Graham's surveys and his comments on rural school issues. In 1911 the topic was "Practical Agriculture in Rural Schools." By this time agricultural education in the schools had become a topic which "warmed up the proceedings," when superintendents got together.[25] Ohio legislation permitting agricultural education was enacted in 1905 and the efforts of the agricultural college significantly affected the fact that 225 schools were teaching agriculture and/or home economics six years later when the

Cahill Law was enacted to *require* that agriculture be taught in all township, village, and special district schools.[26]

Graham was an influential spokesman advocating the scientific bases of agricultural study, but along with zoology, chemistry, and genetics he made an interesting plea, "A high school offering an agricultural course should not look entirely to its sciences for manual exercise and gross experiments through which to perform its functions. Enough remains of its literature, history, and art in rich contributions, that tell of the pleasure of the farm as sung by American and English poets; that tell of the results of the great plant and animal breeders and the inventors of farm machinery whose labors in the peaceful arts have redounded quite as much to their glory as have the labors of the statesman or warrior; on the painter's canvas, domestic animals, the farmyard, and beautiful fruit have found a place where they may be admired no less than historic or sacred subjects."[27] The expression of such sentiments in favor of liberal arts set Graham apart from many colleagues in both agriculture and education, earning admiration from some but isolation from others.

When the Ohio legislature passed Senate Bill 18 in February 1911, it not only required agricultural education state-wide but established four agricultural supervisory districts responsible to the Commissioner of Common Schools. Each supervisor was to be paid a $2000 salary and had a $1000 travel allowance. They were appointed for a two-year term with no more than two from the same political party. A broad range of responsibilities directed them to attend teachers' institutes in each of their counties to conduct instruction in the teaching of agriculture, and to cooperate with county agricultural societies in exhibiting agricultural work by students.[28]

Schoolmaster Graham expressed satisfaction that the nature study work and agricultural experiments begun by the boys' and girls' clubs were now officially imbedded in the school curriculum, but he and Dean Price were distressed that responsibility for teacher education in agricultural subject matter had been delegated to politically appointed supervisors reporting to the Commissioner of Common Schools rather than to the College of Agriculture. An adversary relationship developed based on the university's feeling that they had generated public support, and then watched the State Commissioner reap luxurious financial benefits.[29] The following year, the college established a four-year curriculum in cooperation with the College of Education to prepare graduates to teach agriculture in secondary schools, and the Department of Agricultural Education was established five years later after federal funds were appropriated for vocational education.[30]

Across rural Ohio, agricultural extension had very quickly become one of the most visible areas of the land-grant university, and with rural areas proportionately over represented in the state legislature, its political strength was significant. A complete description of the growing interactions and conflicts between the agricultural college, state agricultural agencies, the agricultural press, and university administration is impossible within the confines of this biography. Enough background must be given, however, to explain the context of Supt. Graham's resignation when extension became caught in the power struggle, and the subsequent evolution of extension education. The events which led to the battle for control of Smith-Lever funds in 1914 were remarkably similar to the battle for a narrow or broad interpretation of a land-grant university at the time Ohio State was established.

The years from 1909 to 1914, between the passage of the Alsdorf Act providing state funding for agricultural extension and the Smith-Lever Act providing federal funding on a cooperative basis, were a period of rapid growth for the College of Agriculture. Student enrollment of 475 in 1909-10 had grown to 1234 by 1913-14, an increase of 260%. During the same period the total enrollment of the university had grown from 2765 to 3609, an increase of only 85 students beyond agriculture's growth. The college budget for instruction in 1909-10 was $60,000 compared to $82,000 in 1913-14, an increase of 37%. The university appropriations for instruction in all seven colleges during the same period had grown from $325,000 to $575,000, a 77% increase. Dean Price was quite vocal in expressing his belief that the College of Agriculture was not being treated fairly.[31]

While there was some substance to his argument, these figures did not include the state appropriation for agricultural extension, or some of the college's other sources of funds such as short course fees and farm produce sales. The purchase of land west of the river for farm expansion and the construction of several new livestock buildings were visible evidence to faculty in other colleges that agriculture had growing influence with a constituent base throughout the state. It revived a heated debate regarding a broad or narrow intrepretation of land-grant college purpose which dated to the university's birth. Into this power struggle between the university and its most rapidly growing college stepped the Ohio legislature.

In the 80th General Assembly in the spring of 1913, Democratic Senator John Cunningham, a farmer from Knox County who chaired the agricultural committee introduced S.B. 178 to establish a State Agricultural Commission of four members, three appointed by the Governor, and the fourth to be the Dean of Agriculture designated by the Trustees of the Ohio State University. Each was to be paid $5000 annually and effective August 6, 1913 the commission was to assume the powers of the State Board of Agriculture, the Veterinary Commission, the Livestock Commission, the Experiment Station, the Dairy and Food Commission, the Fish and Game Commission, and part of the responsibilities of the Pharmacy Board.[32] University trustees were concerned that in many matters the College of Agriculture was being made accountable to the Governor rather than to the president of the university. They reluctantly complied with the law and elected Dean Price to represent the university.[33] Effective August 6th, Dean Price was paid by the State Agricultural Commission rather than the Ohio State University.

The Agricultural Commission began to exert control over agricultural extension preferring that it emphasize exhibits and contests rather than lectures and demonstrations. This was noticeable in extension schools and on the agricultural trains, but it became especially true in boys' and girls' agricultural clubs which had been dropped as a component of agricultural extension when agricultural education was mandated in the public schools. Extension programs for youth were concentrated on corn growing and livestock judging contests. There were difficult philosophical moments for Supt. Graham, who had consistently emphasized learning in the context of group experiments rather than individual achievements. He had emphasized to teachers that "The field seeds that are sent to boys and girls are not just to satisfy a fancy. They are not worth planting if the desire is only to raise something larger than has been raised. The best ear of corn is not always the largest. The size and shape of the grains, the arrangement of the rows, the relation of the distance around to the length of the ear are also points to be considered. . . . a large head of cabbage may be a bunch of loose leaves, and a large potato may be a black hearted one. Size alone doesn't mean much."[34] Judgments based on quantity rather than quality provoked discussions which extension, like many organizations, would debate again and again.

By 1911 when the Association of American Agricultural Colleges and Experiment Stations held its 25th annual meeting in Columbus, it had created a Section on Extension Work, of which Graham had been elected secretary. In a discussion of boys' and girls' club work during the sectional meeting Graham raised some thought provoking questions. "How long can this prize-giving system be kept up as an educational feature? I have directed agricultural club work for nearly ten years, and am of the opinion that it can be carried on without the prize incentive. Yet generally the custom obtains; but who will offer these prizes from year to year? There are men, railroads, manufacturers interested in it; but where is it going to stop? It has to stop some place; and is it a means to be justified by the end to be attained? There is altogether too much prize-giving to children. This sort of work can be managed without giving prizes."[35] These were questions few of Graham's colleagues in the room, and few who followed in later decades, really wished to discuss. Graham obviously held a minority opinion regarding competition and rewards.

A related issue discussed at this meeting was the size of "clubs." Some southern states were reporting as high as 400 to 500 members. Graham considered these to be lists rather than interactive groups and questioned, "Can one man take care of more than sixty or seventy? We hear so much of big things in these days. We are giving too much time to these big things; and I think the work will be accomplished better through smaller clubs."[36] By current standards of social interaction it seems a surprising argument, but such differing viewpoints provided the basis in southern states for a youth program largely taught in classrooms by county agents, while clubs led by volunteer leaders outside of school classrooms prevailed throughout much of the rest of the nation.

The Ohio Agricultural Commission favored big events which drew significant press attention and one of their most visible efforts was the "Ohio Corn Boys Train" which December 1-6, 1913 took several hundred youth to Washington, D.C. Most of the participants were prize winners whose expenses were paid by local public officials, bankers or businessmen. They visited the White House and the Capitol where they were greeted by the entire Ohio congressional delegation, and enroute they had sight-seeing excursions in Philadelphia, Harrisburg, and Pittsburgh.[37] Such contests and trips, modeled on Otwell's work in Illinois, were becoming popular in many states. Like most sponsors, the Ohio Board of Agriculture did not operate an educational club program for participating youth.[38]

It was in this climate of newly legislated agricultural education for public schools and contests organized by the Agricultural Commission, that Graham remarked during a round table discussion among state and national extension leaders, "I formerly thought that it (the extension department) could do much in organizing boys' and girls' clubs, but I am not of this opinion now, even though I know that almost every extension worker in the country is against me. . . I cannot see that we are making headway in raising such work to the level we desire; and I do not care to assume a class of work which properly belongs to the district school. If we can train the teacher to do the work in the district school, well and good. . ."[39] Graham consistently emphasized the university's role as the teacher of teachers, and he visualized boys' and girls' club work as a supplement to the public school curriculum not as a separate educational organization.

Ohio did not have county agents in agricultural extension at this time and Graham's concern with the university's inability to deliver a quality product directly to local groups was realistic. Graham's statement is consistent with his definition of extension's role in his original statement of purposes, July 2, 1905. As a former teacher, Graham probably had far more faith in the public school system than some of his agricultural colleagues. He appears to be expressing more concern for the quality of the product than regard for which agency delivered it; a logical position educationally but a potentially disastrous one politically. Graham's independent expression of convictions again seems to have earned him both cautious admiration and distrust among agricultural extension peers. In later years, Graham's own opinion changed dramatically when vocational legislation defined specific limits for agricultural education in public schools and extension began to develop a network of county agents to organize and supervise local work.

Coincidentally, 1914 was a year of significant transition for agricultural extension nationally. Graham's appointment as Superintendent of Agricultural Extension in 1905 made Ohio one of the pioneers of a national movement. Fred H. Rankin had been appointed with a similar title at Illinois in June 1902, primarily to coordinate farmers' institutes, and Iowa secured state funding to appoint Perry G. Holden to develop an entension program in April 1906, but developments were occurring in many locations with most of the early staff employed on a part-time basis.[40] In 1907 the United States Department of Agriculture Office of Experiment Stations began reporting annually on extension activities throughout the country.

The U.S.D.A. Office of Experiment Stations had contributed to the birth of extension education when it began issuing educational bulletins on the results of its experiments in 1887. These were creating a desire among some farmers for more scientific agricultural information. This was paralleled by the farmers' institutes established in 26 states during the 1880s. Ohio's first institute in October 1880 led to 40 during the winter of 1881. These were sponsored by the State Board of Agriculture with local committees making the arrangements.[41] When the American Association of Farmers' Institutes held its second national meeting in Columbus in October 1897, one of the topics discussed was a proposal for the federal government to provide aid to land-grant colleges to support agricultural extension work.[42] It was an idea still nearly two decades away from fruition.

Many people in different states contributed to the diversity of the movement. During the 1890s Pennsylvania State University began offering agricultural correspondence courses and Professor Liberty Hyde Bailey at Cornell secured a state appropriation to conduct horticultural demonstrations throughout New York state. In Texas, soon after the turn of the century, Seaman A. Knapp began farm demonstration work using local agents as teachers. With special federal and private funding to combat the cotton boll weevil, local demonstration agents were soon hired throughout the south. By 1905 the American Association of Agricultural Colleges and Experiment Stations established a standing committee on agricultural extension with Kenyon L. Butterfield as chairman.[43]

In 1907 this committee reported thirty-nine states were doing some type of extension work, primarily farmers' institutes, but only nine states had a superintendent or director at the agricultural college. Ohio, of course, was among those leading nine, and its organizational structure and programs were a typical example of the diversity the national program would assume a few years later. By 1913, thirty-eight states appropriated more than $1,000,000 to employ 182 full-time and 217 part-time persons in agricultural extension work.[44] It was in this climate that requests for federal funding finally succeeded and May 8, 1914 President Wilson signed the Smith-Lever Act providing federal funding for agricultural extension work on a cooperative basis between the United States Department of Agriculture and state land-grant colleges.[45]

In Ohio, as in many other states, numerous people had plans about what should be done with this new federal money. Two months earlier Dean Price had introduced a resolution to the Agricultural Commission which stated in part,

"Whereas, The Agricultural Commission is charged with the supervision and direction of all agricultural extension work supported by the State, and

Whereas, One of the principal reasons for creating the State Agricultural Commission was to unify and correlate the agricultural extension activities of the State, . . ." and concluded with a request that Ohio State University Trustees appoint a committee to implement plans and policies regarding funding.[46]

Supt. Graham envisioned a broader approach and within a week of the federal legislation he outlined a list of recommendations to Pres. Thompson concluding, "It is my opinion that with future development in sight, this department could be more or less individualized if it were located in some building where it would not be surrounded by departments purely agricultural."[47] Dean Price, without consulting Supt. Graham, recommended that he himself be appointed Director of Extension, and that the Agricultural Commission coordinate the work of a newly appointed corps of county agricultural agents.[48] The stakes were high since the 1915-16 appropriation of $61,114 (including the required state matching funds) increased to $103,710 the following year and implied similar increases to come.[49] Ohio's disputes were in some respects a microcosm of the national debate regarding a broad or narrow subject matter interpretation of this funding for agricultural and home economics education. Dean Price envisioned an applied agricultural extension program administered by the

Agricultural Commission. Supt. Graham envisioned extension education for rural familes which drew from *all* departments of the land-grant university.

The prospect of nearly doubling the existing state funding was a mixed blessing succinctly described by President Thompson: "(The) Federal Act makes possible a very generous provision for Extension Work. There is some doubt whether the state will be sufficiently well organized to expend economically and efficiently the maximum appropriation. . . The fact the legislature in its wisdom at the last Session divided the Extension funds between the College and the Agricultural Commission will make it necessary to reconstruct the legislation for the future or to continue an uneconomic and inefficient piece of administration."[50]

The personal toll extracted by the organizational structure under the Agricultural Commission was expressed by Graham in a confidential letter May 24, 1914 to a friend and colleague in the United States Department of Agriculture. "I have about concluded that I should give up my work in Ohio. Of the nine years, the last two have brought about more serious changes as to organization than all the remainder. The worry and strain under which I have been placed, that the work may appear to be going on smoothly to our constituents, have come nearly being more than I have physical strength to bear. . . A man must be happy in his work or no measure of success can be attained. . . Do you know of any place where I may be considered?"[51]

The issue was quickly resolved, perhaps too quickly. In his letter of resignation to President Thompson and the Board of Trustees June 24, 1914 Graham stated, "I find it impossible to serve faithfully and agreeably two masters, one the best interests of the Ohio State University and the other the demands of the Agricultural Commission. . . The Dean demanded of me that I show my loyalty first to the Agricutural Commission or step down and out. The former I cannot do and maintain the proper degree of loyalty to the University and the College of Agriculture. . . . The Board of Trustees of the New York School of Agriculture on Long Island have elected me as head of their Extension Department and it is my desire to accept this position."[52] The O.S.U. trustees requested that Supt. Graham withdraw his resignation or take a year's leave of absence, but he declined.[53] The provisions of the Smith-Lever Act were accepted for Ohio by

Governor Cox, and Homer C. Price was appointed Director of Agricultural Extension while simultaneously retaining his roles as Dean of the College of Agriculture and member of the Agricultural Commission.

At the same time, Dean Price was reporting, "through the Agricultural Commission the work of the College of Agriculture has been brought into closer relation with all other agricultural agencies of the state."[54] Price was obviously pleased that the administrative design through the Agricultural Commission emphasized coordination with state agricultural agencies rather than other departments of the university. Graham's decision to resign rather than disagree publicly with his dean may have been hasty, for powerful forces were aligning themselves to argue both sides of the question. The issue was so political that it became a factor in the 1914 election and when Democratic Governor Cox was defeated by Republican Congressman Willis, it became clear that legislative changes would be forthcoming. In the next session Senator Mallow, a farmer and banker from Ross county, introduced S.B. 250 to replace the Agricultural Commission effective July 20, 1915 by a ten member State Board of Agriculture appointed by the Governor to serve without compensation.[55] They would, in turn, be authorized to appoint boards for regulation and licensing, and for operating the state fair. The Dean of the College of Agriculture was returned to the university payroll, and extension administration reverted completely to the university.

On March 30, 1915 the Ohio State University Board of Trustees adopted a resolution "That it is the sense of this Board that Professor H.C. Price can serve the University best as Professor of Rural Economics on and after June 30, 1915."[56] Dean Price declined to accept this change of status and his bitter resignation to the president and trustees was submitted simultaneously to the alumni association and to the press. The resulting furor in local newspapers and farm press did not subside until President Thompson met with several hundred representatives of agricultural organizations and alumni during June commencement events.[57] It was a power struggle in which both the university and the college lost face through their bitter fight in the public press, but the result reaffirmed the principle that teaching units of the university were responsible to the university administration.

Late that fall Prof. Alfred Vivian, a respected faculty member in the College of Agriculture, was selected as Dean and the wounds began to heal. November 8, 1915 Clark S. Wheeler was appointed Director of Extension within the College of Agriculture. A new structure divided extension activities into eight bureaus: 1) farm bureaus, 2) boys'and girls' club work, 3) publications, 4) public meetings including farmers' institutes and extension schools, 5) farm management demonstrations, 6) cow-testing associations, 7) demonstrations by specialists, and 8) home economics.[58]

Ohio was among the pioneering states during the era in which innovative ideas, persuasive outreach to new audiences, and experimentation with varied teaching methods gave birth to a new educational organization of national scope. It was too soon to realize how widely this agricultural extension model would be sought around the world.

The Cahill Law which mandated agricultural education in 1911 was later modified to eliminate requirements at the elementary level, but the four agricultural supervisory districts it established were utilized when federal legislation funded vocational education. The 1912 convention to revise the Ohio constitution created a State Superintendent for Public Instruction appointed by the Governor, a change which brought added responsibility and authority. An extensive survey of Ohio schools by external consultants led to major changes in the Ohio School Code in 1914.[59] Perhaps the most significant aspect of this legislation was the creation of county school districts with specifications for county boards of education and county superintendents. Agricultural extension work had been very helpful in creating awareness of rural school conditions, but now the State Department of Public Instruction and the university College of Education were structured to provide solutions.

When agricultural extension was formally developed within the College of Agriculture after passage of the federal legislation to provide cooperative state and federal funding in 1914, Ohio decided to organize into departments. Dean Price envisioned that "These departments will be in charge of men of collegiate training and academic rank, who will be members of the University faculty."[60] This was a key decision which affected both the university and agricultural extension far into the future. As specialization increased within agricultural extension, generalists like Supt. Graham who had been able to walk with one foot in the world of education and the other in the world of agriculture found the road becoming increasingly complex. It was, indeed, time for him to seek new challenges.

In 1915, Pres. Thompson projected, "The far reaching importance of this work in Agricultural Extension is only dimly comprehended by the most intelligent of men. There is reason to believe that a generation of important service lies ahead of the Agricultural Colleges of the country."[61] This prophecy was fulfilled and the wounds inflicted with the dramatic changes of 1914 were significantly healed by the time Agricultural Extension celebrated its 25th anniversary in 1939. Both Homer C. Price and A.B. Graham were among the honored guests who spoke of its pioneering efforts.[62]

Chapter 9
U.S.D.A. — Teacher of Extension Teachers

> "It would appear that our teaching work would be a
> little more acceptable to educational men and particu-
> larly to our extension forces in the States, if there could
> be a larger injection of the philosophy of education and
> the principles of teaching . . . We really need more work
> on how to deal with people. We may call it personality,
> we may call it human engineering, or what we will, today
> the outstanding cry everywhere is 'How can we deal with
> human beings that they may be stimulated to act from
> within rather than from repression or from forcing
> them?' "[1]

At heart, A. B. Graham was a motivator and teacher, not a
regulator. Through twenty-two years of work in the United States
Department of Agriculture bureaucracy he retained his strong
educational roots and his philosophical commitment to the
unique partnership between a federal agency and the national
network of land-grant universities. His Ohio experience was
excellent preparation for the role he assumed as an educational
conscience within the organization responsible for agricultural
policy and funding, but his arrival there was almost accidental
and his role evolved gradually.

Between 1909 and 1912, Supt. Graham had been invited to
consider and had declined several positions which offered a
higher salary than he was receiving at Ohio State. These positions ranged from the Dean of Agriculture at Morgantown, West
Virginia to Superintendent of Farmers' Institutes at Manhattan,
Kansas; Southern District Supervisor of Rural Schools in the
U.S. Bureau of Education; and Assistant Superintendent for the
public schools of New Jersey.[2] The diversity of these positions
reflects the breadth and respect which Graham's work in Ohio
had achieved. His loyalty to Ohio ran deep, however, and his
emotions probably affected his decisions about staying as much
as they affected his quick acceptance of the offer from the New

York State School of Agriculture on Long Island in 1914, when he felt his position in Ohio had become untenable.

The school on Long Island was a new institution and Graham had barely arrived before its serious problems became evident. Some of the promised faculty failed to arrive and Graham was there three months before he received his first salary check. Nevertheless, he declined an offer from South Dakota and one from Connecticut to become their Director of Extension, feeling that he owed the New York school at least a year of service.[3] The situation failed to improve and the director of the school spent much time away from the institution soliciting funds. Graham carried a heavy load teaching students, representing the director on programs during his absence, and managing the school farm. After a year, in September 1915, he wrote a friend that he had not been paid since July and "I am very tired. I think I shall make some effort to shake loose."[4]

Graham maintained an active correspondence with several Ohio State faculty members and had enjoyed a visit from Professor French of the College of Engineering during the summer of 1915. He was well versed regarding the reorganization of the College of Agriculture and the resignation of Dean Price, and he was clearly encouraging some of his supporters who were urging his return to Ohio as Director of Extension. Although President Thompson and Graham remained friendly correspondents for several years, Thompson quickly rejected any consideration of Graham's return to the College of Agriculture, fearing such a move would inflame supporters of the recently abolished Agricultural Commission.

Several Graham supporters then encouraged him to seek the Extension Director's position in Pullman, Washington, and one of them recommended him there as a fluent speaker who had developed Ohio's extension budget from nothing to $50,000, describing him as a "big, generous-hearted man with a real vision of the ideal country life."[5] But other forces were at work. On the same day that Ohio State University trustees selected Alfred Vivian as Dean of the College of Agriculture and Clark Wheeler as Director of Agricultural Extension, President Thompson sent C.B. Smith, Chief, North and West, States Relations Service, U.S.D.A., a handwritten note regarding this action.[6] This may have provided Smith the incentive he needed. Two weeks later he offered Graham a temporary position to study the efficiency of "movable schools" conducted under the Smith-Lever Act, and to assist in preparing the States Relations Service first report to Congress.[7] Graham accepted immediately and reported to the U.S.D.A. December 16, 1915.[8] He evidently managed to leave the unhappy New York situation on congenial terms, for three months after his departure Director Johnson's letter enclosing his last salary check included the friendly invitation to "drop in and see us any time."[9]

Graham plunged almost immediately into the bureaucracy of administering the new federal money. Smith-Lever appropriations for extension programs were confronted with an existing patchwork of activities across the country which had developed under a variety of state, local, and private funding. Within the Department of Agriculture the States Relations Service had been created with former Office of Experiment Stations Director Alfred C. True becoming the new director of the enlarged unit combining both experiment station and extension functions. Fifteen southern states, which had been developing a system of county demonstration agents in conjunction with the Bureau of Plant Industry, were placed under the jurisdiction of the Office of Extension Work South and the remaining thirty-three states from New England to the west coast reported to the Office of Extension Work North and West headed by C.B. Smith, also formerly from the Experiment Station Office. For eight years these two parallel extension services operated with distinct differences.[10]

Graham's first assignment was to collect data on "movable schools," a catchall term for the off-campus teaching being conducted by extension staff in various states. Graham's survey collected innovative examples throughout the country; the demonstration railroad car equipped by the Household Science Department of the University of Illinois with household equipment and home furnishings "to show the machines, the kitchen utensils, and the color schemes, not just to talk about them;"[11] a three-day "soil fertility school in the county agent's room over Moore's Drug Store in Ellsworth, Maine;"[12] a conference on community planning conducted jointly by the Massachusetts Agricultural College Extension Service and the Massachusetts Federation for Rural Progress at Smith's Agricultural School in Northhampton, Massachusetts."[13] Graham's report included a recommendation to adopt the term "Extension Schools" rather than the phrase "movable schools."[14]

Much of the information he compiled was used in the States Relations Service report of extension programs during its first year of operation, July 1, 1915 to June 30, 1916. C.B. Smith's instructions were, "Make it optimistic, make it encouraging, put in no controversial material."[15] Graham followed instructions but he remained skeptical of official reports throughout his U.S.D.A. career, believing that reports for political consumption were inherently biased.

Extension budgets and staff soon increased dramatically to meet the demand created by war mobilization, for increased productivity from agricultural resources. Graham's temporary appointment soon became permanent and he became one of several administrative specialists conducting state audits of Smith-Lever programs and accounts. This work typically involved trips of one or two months duration to spend a week per state conferring with program specialists regarding plans of work and reviewing the records of fiscal officers on an item by item basis. One 1920 travel schedule shows both the typical pattern of operation and the way in which Graham managed to keep in touch with his sister in Piqua and son in Columbus, Ohio during these years:[16]

August 23-29 — Lafayette, Indiana
August 30-September 1 — Piqua, Ohio (on leave)
September 2-4 — Columbus, Ohio
September 6-11 — East Lansing, Michigan
September 13-18 — Madison, Wisconsin
September 20-25 — St. Paul, Minnesota
September 27-October 2 — Urbana, Illinois

Graham's administrative experience in Ohio was a distinct advantage in understanding the problems state directors faced in interpreting which programs were eligible or ineligible for Smith-Lever funding, and how state or local money might be utilized concurrently. But Graham's real strength was his educational background, and amid growing numbers of subject matter specialists he quickly became the expert on educational methods. By the end of the war the regulations of the new organization had stabilized and while Graham continued to perform some state fiscal and program audits throughout his twenty-two year career, he increasingly became the teacher of teachers within the U.S.D.A. extension service.

One of Graham's strengths was his ability to convey the same philosophical principle to different audiences by carefully altering his language and examples as he spoke or wrote. For instance, in a printed U.S.D.A. circular dealing with adult motivation, he wrote, "The fact is that possessing knowledge does not necessarily throw people into action. So, our information and knowledge which we endeavor to transmit to him, or to develop a desire in him for acquiring, comes to naught, if we do not appeal to his inherent characteristics — pride, curiosity, ingenuity, creativeness, desire to help others — in our efforts to build up an interest within him to acquire, to want, to hunger for the information and knowledge which we have."[17] In speaking, he gave a personal example and expressed the concept more pungently, "The commercial world has long ago learned that in order to sell its products it must create within the individual a desire for them. A mere display of notions on the counter will not sell them."[18]

A.B. Graham can be given much of the credit for defining the relationship between U.S.D.A. extension specialists and their counterparts in land-grant universities across the country. In a 1921 speech he outlined the qualities of an extension specialist in a masterful blend of idealism and reality.

> "An extension specialist should know his subject thoroughly, understand the research work upon which conclusions are based, and be familiar with farm practices of the most successful farmers. He should have not only the ability to adapt his work to varied conditions, but also willingness to coordinate it with that of other specialists whose work might be directly related to his own. He should be able to form sympathetic contact with all rural people. He should understand the psychology of both the youth and the adult, and should determine his methods of teaching through his knowledge of this fundamental feature. He should divest his subject of those phases too difficult to be accepted and adopted by community leaders in agriculture and home economics, and should present it in such a way as to establish confidence and to inspire the desire to rise above present conditions or practices. Since all of these desirable features may not be found in one individual, his teaching power, next to his knowledge of the subject, should be the distinguishing characteristic of the extension specialist. . . .
>
> The extension specialist, in his relation to the institution, either from the standpoint of investigation or teaching, should, if possible, be so located on the campus that he will come in contact with the greatest resident teachers of his subject and those who bear in mind the application of results to ordinary farm conditions, to labor, to capital, markets, climate, soil, etc. . . .

> The extension specialist should be equal, if not greater, even, in his power to teach, than resident instructors, for his function is largely that of teaching those who have already become fixed in their thought and their manual habits. . . .
>
> The real function of an extension specialist, therefore, is not to do again and again the thing that he wants the people to do; it is to inspire the desire within them, and then, under his leadership and participation, teach them the operation in order that they may attain a certain degree of self-mastery and self-confidence, and may in turn, teach others, thereby extending the influence and thought of the one specialist far beyond what could be otherwise attained. . . ."[19]

This entire speech contains some of the earliest, most eloquent, and most enduring concepts of the Cooperative Extension Service teacher ever written.

Since Director True and Chief Smith entered extension work through their experience in the U.S.D.A. Office of Experiment Stations, they relied heavily upon Graham's teaching experience and administrative experience within a land-grant university agricultural and home economics faculty to define an appropriate role for extension subject matter specialists. This informal role became official in 1922 with the establishment of a Division of Extension Methods with A.B. Graham in charge.[20] This coincided with the consolidation of the northern and southern extension offices into one federal Cooperative Extension Service, and a growing national need for local extension staff trained both in subject matter and in teaching methods.

While it is impossible today to separate tentative inquiries from firm offers, it is clear that Graham could have chosen among several administrative options during the U.S.D.A. changes of the 1920s. Some Ohio friends were urging President Harding to appoint him Assistant Secretary of Agriculture, but as Graham later wrote a co-worker, "Those who came to see me were somewhat disappointed when I told them I wouldn't trade a certainty for an uncertainty." This strongly suggests that Graham had reached a point in his career where he treasured security in the civil service over political appointment, but he indicated other factors as well. "It had always been a job of picking up chips for the Secretary . . . who at that time I did not admire."[21] When Dr. True retired, friction between Secretary Wallace and Dr. Smith prevented the latter's selection as Director of the new combined Extension Service. According to Graham's recollection years later, Extension Directors from four states refused the appointment,[22] and in 1923 Clyde W. Warburton of the Bureau of Plant

Industry became director. All internal memoranda and correspondence with state directors portray Graham as a team player throughout these administrative changes, but years later he did reveal some of his private feelings. "There are many in the states who have and others who will refuse a federal position for a variety of reasons. Lack of freedom in thinking and acting, having to compose letters and talks for others to sign or deliver as if their own, long distances from home and families and long duration of field trips throwing too heavy responsibilities on the other members of the family."[23]

Most of Graham's work during these years, in fact, did appear anonymously or was credited to others. Close study of interoffice memoranda reveals some, but probably only a portion, of his contributions. An excellent example is Graham's list of extension accomplishments during the first decade of Smith-Lever funding, which he submitted to his superiors with the notation, "I trust that these few thoughts may be helpful as well as provocative of others much more important."[24]

1) "The people have been made aware that there is an educational organization for teaching the best practices in agriculture and home economics. This is comparable with the fact that before 1840 the people were not aware of such a thing as a public system of secondary education. . . (only) privately endowed academies. . .

2) (State) Legislatures as well as many counties are taking it now as a matter of fact that they are to appropriate for extension work just as they would for public schools or roads. The offset feature of the Smith-Lever Act stopped a great deal of vacillation in State legislatures as to the amounts of money they should appropriate for extension service. . . . (and) contributed much to stabilize both the lines of work and the amounts of money that could be budgeted from year to year. . .

3) The system has made possible immediate contacts through county agents with the State agricultural colleges, and is the only organization directly tied up with a central subject-matter State educational institution. . .

4) The experiment stations are being brought a little closer to the farm problems needing investigational work. . .

5) Practices of merit by laymen are being brought before more people. . .

6) College teaching is being affected and improved because of practical results secured on the farms and because of a gradual bringing into the classroom of more actual farm conditions. . .

7) It raised the plane of farm-paper contributions and editorials. . .

8) The present system of extension work is standardizing the means and agencies through which extension teaching is being done.

9) It has made possible a more extensive and more uniform cooperation of educational work with business agencies such as breeders' organizations, commercial fertilizer firms, farm implement manufacturers, fruit, vegetable, and grain dealers. . .

10) The present system has provided a uniform plan of work for young people out of school. The agricultural extension organization is one of the outstanding agencies through which to appeal to those who have become disconnected with the schools. . .

11) Hundreds, if not thousands, of community organizations have sprung up in the name of the extension service. These have not only provided a local and voluntary educational organization, but it has furnished an opportunity for social intercourse, thereby bringing about more of a community of interest and cooperation in action."

Many of these concepts were developed in more detail as U.S.D.A. adminstrators reported extension's accomplishments during its first decade.[25] They were certainly many of the concepts which made extension education a model sought by developing countries around the world. Many persons wrote and spoke of extension's early accomplishments, but Graham's unpublished list remains one which captured the philosophy of the organization in a succinct but eloquent manner.

Some of Graham's field reports and memos to superiors provide delightful clues to his style of consultation with state extension workers regarding their programs of work. By modern standards these early field reports are models of simplicity: "Date and Place, Purpose, Names and Titles of Persons Met in Conference, What I Did, Comments and Recommendations." Graham was noted for a frankness which many long-time colleagues appreciated, but it no doubt intimidated some new acquaintances. A report following one New England trip shows his typical style of specific criticism or praise, "Specialists are in most of the States rendering entirely too much personal service or are making their appeals to a circle of susceptibles — a group of people with whom they like to work because they more quickly accept their reasoning. The great fear that many of the specialists have is that they must do the work to have it done right. They seem to be unable or unwilling in many of the States to develop their work through leaders. This is particularly true of the agricultural subjects, but it is not true of the home economics subjects. The women seem to have little or no difficulty in teaching through the local leadership plan."[26]

One of Graham's assignments in the reorganized extension unit was to review and comment on annual plans of work from each state. Whether positive or negative his comments usually went straight to the heart of the matter. "The Agronomy plan is very good on subject matter but nothing is given at all as to methods of carrying out the work." (Oklahoma) "The clothing plan contains nothing more than a calendar." (New Jersey) "It may not be amiss to call your attention to a particularly strong plan. I think the nutrition plan in Massachusetts is exceedingly good."[27] Graham never mastered the art of using words to obscure rather than convey meaning, and he had little patience with any plan of work which did so. Commenting on a proposed project in rural sociology and community organization he said, "There is so much of this social work that is of a general nature or is so very light that it does not get anywhere... It is a good deal like some of these indefinite projects in child care and training; that is large enough to include everything under the heavens from educational methods to corrective surgery."[28] Statistics presented in a manner to enhance the facts were likely to draw equally harsh criticism. Graham noted that increases in 4-H enrollment reported in percentages and averages needed close scrutiny and pointed out that, "A D.A.R. (Daughters of the American Revolution) group could increase its membership by 100% by growing from one to two members."[29]

Graham's combination of directness tempered by a sense of humor served him well in his primary assignment in charge of U.S.D.A. extension specialists. During the sixteen years Graham held this assignment the group usually contained from twenty to thirty subject matter specialists affiliated with units such as plant industry, animal industry, or the forest service. Their extension assignment made them responsible to Graham for their program of work, travel schedule, and budget. This was a challenge in earned leadership for which Graham was uniquely qualified. He had already spent nearly forty years in education and his image as a father figure to many of the group was enhanced by the familial style of the extension organization. Graham's primary contribution to the unification of this diverse group from nutritionists to agronomists to animal scientists, was a series of provocative meetings on Wednesdays at 11 a.m. For sixteen years these sessions, which participants christened "Bright Hope School," had a challenging array of discussions and speakers which often attracted bureau chiefs from throughout the department.

Normally these sessions featured a presentation followed by group questions and discussion, with a secretary making a transcription for those absent on a travel schedule. As the group began its seventh year Graham emphasized to newcomers that one of the primary purposes was to get acquainted and thereby "avoid or destroy unwarranted prejudices against our fellow workers... and create a spirit of good fellowship which is absolutely essential to real cooperation."[30] In its formative stages when the group was small and field experience provided bonds of common concern there were notable successes, but even before Graham's retirement the divisions and competition of specialized concerns became as real among federal extension specialists as they were among university departments.

Various members of the specialist group shared responsibilities for presentations relating to teaching methods, frequently using examples from their field work. Sometimes Graham joined with a staff member in presenting a topic such as the discussion Feb. 11, 1925 on "Undeveloped Opportunities in Extension Work," He called attention to the needs of part-time farmers living on 20 or 30 acres in the country but able, thanks to Henry Ford's cars, to work elsewhere as well. Grace Frysinger, of Home Economics, suggested reaching new audiences by working with merchants through window displays and demonstrations in stores.[31] Most of Graham's presentations at these meetings quite naturally dealt with some aspect of educational methodology: "Some Limitations in Extension Teaching,"[32] "Suggestion and Reason as Applied to Extension Teaching Methods,"[33] "Leadership and Personality,"[34] "Grooming Our Extension Teaching Materials."[35] Graham excelled in the role of devil's advocate and encouraged spirited discussions.

The annual planning committee for these sessions frequently took advantage of resource persons within the U.S.D.A. or other government agencies, or visitors who were studying U.S. government operations: "The Status of Rural Education," Catherine M. Cook, U.S. Bureau of Education,[36] "Goitre in Humans," Dr. Taliferro Clark, Public Health Service,[37] "Reaching the Public With the Printed Word," Nelson A. Crawford, U.S.D.A. Information Specialist,[38] "Women's Institute Work in England and Wales," Edith Nightingale, National Federation of Women's Institutes,[39] "Chinese Rural Life and the Stimulus of the Chinese Youth to Secure an education," Wm. P. H. Hwang, Ph.D. student from

China,[40] "Rural and Urban Migration and Its Consequences," Dr. O.E. Baker.[41]

When guest speakers with educational expertise were featured, invitations were often extended well beyond the extension staff. A number of outsiders responded to hear Prof. A.M. Field from the University of Minnesota, College of Education discuss "The Extension Specialist as a Teacher."[42] One of the liveliest question and answer sessions followed Prof. B.H. Bode of the Ohio State University, College of Education, who contended in his presentation on "Teaching the Habit Fixed Mind" that docile minds are inferior minds.[43] A presentation by Prof. O.G. Brim of the Ohio State University, College of Education on "Conflicting Philosophies of Rural Education"[44] was included together with the ensuing discussion in the yearbook of the National Society of Rural Education. A special two-day professional improvement conference in 1936 featured two of the best-known educators of the day, Dr. Edmund deS. Brunner and Dr. Irving Lorge of Columbia University.[45]

But meetings were not the only tool utilized by Graham to see that extension staff members were currently informed on educational methods. One three-page memorandum to his supervisor reporting the status of extension teaching methods contains several revealing comments. "I am anxious to see, and I hope you will see, Dr. Thorndike's new book that is supposed to be out in a few weeks on *Adult Education.* Such men can speak with some authority. We are quite willing to bow at the feet of such men who are recognized the world over as investigators in educational fields, but I am not inclined to believe that there is going to be very much of a new birth in extension methods of teaching born in the Department of Agriculture. I am somewhat doubtful about the degree of acceptance of present studies in our own office. We are in need of an awakening on the perfecting of methods based on human behavior as the investigators have been able to determine."[46] It is obvious that Graham read current research on the psychology of adult learning and that over a period of years he continually advocated more application of this theory within the Department of Agriculture. It was a needle which may not have been appreciated by personnel in the division of extension studies and evaluation.

In state extension conferences Graham became a popular speaker on educational methodology whose "no nonsense" style and consistent emphasis of basic principles appealed to field staff. "A leader should bear in mind that repetition of an idea or of a practice is essential, that results of but once seeing the demonstration are not lasting. The leader should therefore repeatedly call attention to the practice, using many ways and forms to do so. People may read of the demonstration or may hear it spoken of once or twice, but the great, intelligent mass is not thus successfully appealed to. The idea may be 'dressed in different clothes,' one day in a bulletin; next in a county newspaper; a month or so afterwards, during an automobile tour, when someone may casually mention it; and later, the same idea may be brought out in an exhibit at the community fair, and still later at the county or State Fair. Again, the same ideas may be hurled forth from a lantern slide projector, and the people may remember previously seeing the picture in a bulletin. A chart tacked to the barn may include the table last seen in a bulletin or in some publicity article. Whatever the method adopted, there must be continuity of thought and suggestion through repetition."[47]

A circular he wrote for department publication on "Some Fundamentals of Extension Teaching" was first published in 1926 and reissued in 1935. Its opening sentence is classic Graham style, "At the outset it is desirable to call attention to something as old as the hills, and that is the fundamental teaching principles, which lead from the known to the related unknown, from the concrete to the abstract."[48] Once Graham accepted an educational principle he irritated a few but charmed many with his missionary zeal.

A wide variety of educational methods were subjected to Graham scrutiny and comment during these years: radio talks, circular letters, exhibits, bulletins. His eye for detail and perfection is illustrated by two memos relating to teaching charts. In 1933 he compiled and sent to federal extension specialists a listing of the dimensions of the rooms in which each state held extension conferences so that they might prepare better charts for use in their presentations.[49] The issue was obviously still on his mind a year later when he attached a pointed postscript to his two page evaluation of an U.S.D.A. Economic Outlook Conference, "Charts that can't be read and speakers that can't be heard are poor economics for a $10,000 conference."[50]

Graham's responsibility for extension specialists included those in home economics, and it was perhaps only natural as a former one-room school teacher that he should assume special interest in the area of child development. One radio talk he prepared for womens' clubs in Maryland resulted in so many requests for the script that he printed, "Let's Pretend," a fascinating little treatise on imaginative play.[51] Charmingly illustrated with Graham's own photographs of his two youngest children, this little brochure is surprisingly modern in the specific contributions it advocates for parents to aid the development of a child's imagination.

During the Great Depression extension was deeply involved in attempting to alleviate its catastrophic effects, working closely with a variety of federal agencies, and often touching needs which they had inadequate resources to resolve. In 1934 the extension editorial division advised Graham to delay plans for sending a new bulletin, "Farm House Plans," to county agents nationwide because, "Director Eisenhower[52] informed us that since the first order for 50,000 copies, a second order for 100,000 copies and a third for an additional 50,000 copies have been placed. He stated that relief agencies are advertising this publication extensively and that members of Congress are asking for large quantities, some for as many as 10,000 copies, for distribution to their districts. Large numbers of requests are also being received from builders, carpenters and others interested."[53] As it became increasingly common for Extension to provide subject matter expertise and to cooperate with a variety of agencies in the dissemination of information, it became more and more difficult for the public to credit who was responsible for their assistance or lack thereof. This was a significant problem for administrators dependent upon public funding and one not always appreciated by extension educators concerned with people and their problems.

Graham was one of several extension staff members who had to wrestle with problems of program versus policy throughout his U.S.D.A. career. The Land-Grant College Association had appointed a Committee on Extension Organization and Policy and Graham's interoffice memos often suggested that matters be referred to them when related organizations seemed to be crossing the line between subject matter and policy. When the American Home Economics Association involved extension specialists on a committee to assess the needs and interests of "The Older Girl," Graham stated, "It appears to me that the relationship of the American Home Economics Association to the problems of farm young people is no different from that of a National Poultry Association, Dairy Association, or some other group interested in a particular phase of extension work. . . "[54] Graham contended that no group of people belonged to any agency but that specific populations could be appropriately assisted by a variety of organizations, preferably working cooperatively.

Relationships among agencies had always been a concern, and at least as early as 1932 U.S.D.A. extension personnel were assigned liaison with specific organizations and associations. Subject matter speicalists were assigned to related professional organizations and Graham was assigned the U.S. Office of Education, then located in the Department of the Interior; the American Association of Adult Education; the American Sociological Association; the American Psychological Association; and the National Recreation Association.[55]

There were many times when Graham walked the tightrope between program and policy and he expressed his reason for protecting subject matter specialists rather forcefully to Dr. Smith. "My opinion is that whenever a subject matter man is put in the position of pulling chestnuts out of the fire, he is in that degree, creating an unfavorable atmosphere in which to do educational work."[56]

Graham's role as an auditor of Smith-Lever programs and accounts revealed frequent need for interpretation of policy relating to boys' and girls' club work. The passage of the Smith-Hughes Act funding vocational education included subject matter in agriculture and home economics. Responsibility for administration rested with the U.S. Bureau of Education which did not have subject matter experts in these areas. As state departments of education frequently sought subject matter assistance from extension units in land-grant universities, problems sometimes developed. As Graham explained to one state director, "The entire arrangement of funds makes it very easy to slip from what may be questionable under a Smith-Lever project to that which is not at all questionable under a state project. It would seem to me that the frequent reference to cooperation with the public school forces should be eliminated or we should be clearly informed as to the plan of cooperation of the State College of Agriculture with the State Education Department in reference to vocational education."[57]

Although the Land-Grant College Association and the Federal Board for Vocational Education developed a memorandum of understanding as early as 1918, modifications and interpretations continue to define this relationship to the present day. In 1922, Graham requested a conference with his superiors prior to the Land-Grant Association meeting to discuss his specific concerns that a modified memorandum in 1921 was permitting vocational education to define extension's role both in pre-vocational agriculture and home economics education and in adult education for farmers and homemakers. In describing his concern Graham defined his own concept of the fundamental principle of boys' and girls' club work. "Boys' and girls' club work is the agency in cooperative extension work whereby boys and girls are enlisted through a community program of work, to conduct demonstrations in agriculture and homemaking... Every boy and girl of the community is considered a potential demonstrator. . . a social motive and a natural environment are provided. These two elements are recognized by educational leaders as very desirable but often difficult to provide in the school room."[58] Graham clearly saw the extension youth program open to all youth as an extracurricular educational program operating in support of, but outside the jurisdiction of, the public school system. That was not a viewpoint shared by all states in 1922 when the northern and southern extension services were merging.

Graham's concern about infringement from another direction was directed to G.E. Farrell who was giving leadership to boys' and girls' club programs. Calling attention to the newsletter of the "National Committee on Boys' and Girls' Club Work" which had been organized in 1921 with Guy L. Noble as Secretary, Graham stated, ". . . it is my opinion that, either intentionally or otherwise, Mr. Noble is using a heading on the sheet which would lead one to believe that the U.S. Department of Agriculture maintains a Chicago office and that he is connected therewith."[59] Farrell's response two months later suggests extensive internal discussion of the question and provides background for what is at times still a controversial issue. ". . . It is true that Mr. Noble uses the four leaf clover insignia used by the Boys' and Girls' Club Work in cooperative extension work. I do not believe, however, that it is possible to discuss this matter with Mr. Noble, because he feels that this insignia is common public property. The letterhead used by Mr. Noble does set forth rather clearly the relation of

Mr. Noble to the committee of which Mr. E.T. Meredith, ex-Secretary of Agriculture is chairman. . . In the program prepared by Mr. Noble he wishes to secure a special appropriation from Congress to support County Club Agents in each of the agricultural counties of the forty-eight States. . . This committee is similar to the committee that was organized for the promotion of vocational education previous to the passage of the Smith-Hughes Act. . . The plan seems to meet with the approval of a great number of club leaders. . . I should hesitate to take this matter up with Mr. Noble."[60] Graham had obviously prodded a hornet's nest. To this day, the extension youth program attempts to accommodate both educational projects whose primary rewards are intrinsic, and educational contests which feature rewards from a variety of special interest organizations.

Although Graham never had administrative responsibility for boys' and girls' club work, Dr. Smith frequently sought his counsel because of his early association with the movement. Commenting on proposed "Objectives of Club Work" in 1927 Graham emphasized his view that the program needed to be project centered with a subject matter base. He felt strongly that social-cultural activities should grow from this content base.[61] Later, responding to a request from Smith for an opinion on a congressman's proposal to award certificates to club members, Graham was moved to ask, "Did you ever stop to think about the disappointments, embarrassments, feelings of envy, etc. that come to many others as against a very selected few who from the point of biological advantages, accident or early environment, and perhaps some other things, have a better chance? The prejudices of judges, as is well illustrated sometimes at fairs when those officially in charge request the judge to distribute the winnings geographically, or on some other basis, rather than on the basis of merit, produce an unpleasant condition. . . I realize that I belong to the minority that does not believe in the offering of prizes. . ."[62] When the stakes became higher, Graham's criticism became sharper. In 1934, he recognized the "lure of educational scholarships," but lamented the various prizes offered by the National 4-H Committee as commercial "exploitation of boys and girls" which lowered the educational value of their work.[63]

The larger the rewards became, the more Graham sounded like a purist for instrinsic motivation. Yet as a teacher and superintendent, from spelling bees to vegetable gardening, he had consistently rewarded accomplishments with some type of recognition. One suspects his increasingly strong rhetoric was intended as an antedote for a pendulum he felt was swinging too far in one direction. He consistently favored group recognition over individual recognition. His opinions were, however, increasingly minority opinions among those giving leadership to the 4-H Club program; especially those working extensively with private sources of funding support. It is a measure both of Graham's stature and those who disagreed with him that they continued to work for the growth of the program while discussing their philosophical differences.

One of the personal goals which Graham tried to implement by private persuasion was his dream of a 4-H Club march written by John Philip Sousa. The maestro died before this became a reality, but Graham persisted and "The Pride of the Land" National 4-H Club March, written by Edwin Franko Goldman, Bandmaster of the National Broadcasting System, was introduced at the National 4-H Camp in June 1933. It was a goal achieved through Graham's personal dedication but he was on a travel schedule and did not hear it until a month later when his family tried it out with his daughter playing the piano, and he wrote Goldman, ". . . we all enjoyed it immensely."[64] It was soon recorded and both record and sheet music were made available nationally.

No one doubted Graham's emotional commitment to youth and no one was more eagerly sought as a speaker for state and national 4-H conferences. One of his finest presentations was prepared for the National 4-H Club encampment in Washington, D.C. in June of 1935 on "The Importance of Vision." Beginning with the Latin word "videre" from which vision derives, Graham emphasized the concept of future planning which reaches beyond seeing. He challenged delegates with an array of role models; inventor Thomas Edison, publisher Horace Greeley, President Abraham Lincoln, W.C.T.U. founder Frances E. Willard, and Antarctic explorer Richard E. Byrd among others. The diversity of their visions reveals much about Graham and the idols from whom he personally drew inspiration. One brief excerpt perhaps reveals Graham's power and popularity as a motivational speaker. "Benjamin West, the great artist, was once asked with what he mixed his paints, and his answer was 'With brains.' And so it is with many of our visions. We mix them with our own personality, our own character traits, and our own intelligence."[65]

In the mid 1930s A.B. Graham was approaching his seventieth birthday and the completion of five decades as a professional educator. One would expect that he might be slowing down, but all available evidence suggests otherwise. In a rare written commendation in 1935 Smith noted, "I have been reading over the things you have been doing in the field lately. I am impressed with the versatility you possess in meeting all Extension situations as they come up, also the wealth of background you have as a result of your study, your years of experience, and your native ability. We are happy that, through Extension, the nation is getting the benefit of your ripe judgment and counsel."[66]

In 1935-36 travel allotments were reduced to $700, less than half of the $1500 U.S.D.A. extension specialists had been receiving at the beginning of the depression, but this still went some distance at the government maximum of $5 per diem. Civil service positions provided greater security than comparable responsibilities on state university faculties or among county extension agents. In 1924 Graham had received a P5 classification, the same as his superiors Dr. Warburton and Dr. Smith, and from 1928 until his retirement his annual salary was $5600, very good indeed by depression standards.[67] By comparison, Extension Director Ramsower at Ohio State was receiving $5550 and most department chairmen in the College of Agriculture ranged somewhat below that figure.[68]

During July 1936 Graham was in New England auditing extension programs and accounts in Bangor, Maine; Durham, New Hampshire; and Burlington, Vermont. By the end of August he was in New Mexico, Arizona, and on to Berkeley, California by the first of September. An invitation about this time from the Michigan Director offers a unique bribe. "Our State Leaders and myself feel the need for a voice in our conference which will express those higher human values which are the final objectives of the whole service and which are often vaguely felt through the material phases of projects and programs. . . I understand Mr. Graham is near retirement age and this may be our last opportunity to have him in Michigan. . . Mr. E.L. Austin, our Professor of Education in whom Mr. Graham has been interested, will also be on the program."[69] As he approached retirement Graham was still actively seeking out people from whom he could learn a thing or two!

As that year ended, Graham made news across the country by proposing that a 4-H type of educational program be extended to city youth. The *Columbus Dispatch* headlined "Farm Life with City Convenience is Aim of U.S. Agricultural Club Founder."[70] Similar versions of an apparent U.S.D.A. news release appeared in the *Washington Star*[71] and the *Boston Globe*,[72] while a *Philadelphia Bulletin* editorial urged support for Graham's proposal.[73] It was an idea ahead of its time in terms of funding, but one which achieved significant progress within Graham's lifetime. Several state 4-H leaders began working towards this goal with state or local funding, and one suspects that the U.S.D.A. used Graham, known affectionately within the department as the "Daddy of the 4-H Club program,"[74] as the spokesman to draw media attention.

Graham's leadership style with the U.S.D.A. extension specialists reveals a collegial unit resembling a university department rather than an autocratic bureaucracy. He was a firm taskmaster whose rule was "no reports, no travel," but he was just as firm in defending the rights of his colleagues to make their own program decisions. In one instance he strongly defended a home economist's choice of words in a circular letter which the extension editor wished to change, assuring the editor that she knew her clientele better than either of them.[75] In a modern context Graham's writing style often appears sexist but his delegation of committee responsibilities, his equal division of travel budgets, and his recommendations regarding civil service classifications show that professionally male and female extension specialists were treated equally. One exception, in the name of chivalry, did occur when the unit was assigned a couple of choice parking spaces. Graham informed one of the recipients, who was on a travel schedule when the allotment was made, that the decision was women first, "as per custom of the sea."[76]

The strongest evidence of the specialists' regard for Graham is a memorandum in Director Warburton's correspondence file dated Oct. 5, 1937, signed by twenty-one extension specialists pleading for an exception to the U.S. Civil Service policy of mandatory retirement at age seventy. "Representing as we do a wide field of agricultural and home economics endeavor, and having had the opportunity to appraise Mr. Graham's value to extension work from close personal association and as reflected to us by State workers, we have no hesitancy in stating that the services which he is rendering in the Department are peculiarly and specifically due to his broad experience in educational work, and to his outstanding personality and his unusual ability to understand and inspire people. His pioneering in junior work while a rural school teacher, his early association with State extension work and his insatiable determination to keep abreast of modern thought in all fields affecting extension, all have served to set him apart from other extension leaders. His full knowledge of extension problems, his inspiring personality and broad wisdom are too valuable to be lost by the Department if it can be avoided."[77] They indicated they were writing without Graham's knowledge and that their suggestion was subject to his willingness, but an attached professional vita suggests at least some level of awareness by Graham's devoted head clerk, Bertha M. Bennett.

But federal retirement rules were not made for bending. Director Warburton, Dr. Smith and most of the specialists who had worked with Graham were present to have lunch and participate in the final exercises of "Bright Hope School" on March 12, 1938. Graham began his remarks on the occasion, "The hired man is moving to town."[78]

One aspect of Graham's retirement, the family's return to Ohio, was taken for granted by family and colleagues. No one was surprised either that A.B. should be asked and that he would accept speaking engagements from a variety of educational groups in several states. But a groundswell of support was growing in his home state to recognize his contribution as a 4-H pioneer, and this culminated in 1952 with a golden jubilee celebration which eclipsed all else.

24
A.B. Graham silhouette made June 1899
at the time he earned a life
teaching certificate

25
Corn plot report
form, agricultural
club, 1904

REPORT BLANK (FILL OUT AND RETURN)

	VARIETY NO. 1	VARIETY NO 2
Name of variety..........	Boone bo White	Warner's White
Date on which the land was plowed...........	May 23, 904	May 23, 204
What was done in preparing the land for planting	The ground was harrowed	
Date of planting...........	May 23, 904	May 24, 1904
How many days was it before the first stalks appeared	Seven	eight days
Dates on which the corn was cultivated or hoed	Plowed & hoed June 3, 13, & 27.	
When did the first tassels appear........	July 25, 1904	July 25, 1904
How many stalks had two ears........	very few.	
How many stalks had no ears	Many	very few.
Did the litmus paper test show the soil to be acid or neutral...........	Tests will be made soon.	
How much corn did each shock yield? How much would this be per acre 27–36	1½ bushels	2 bushels.

NAME... Carl F. King.
CLUB... Bath Township Agricultural B.
ADDRESS... Harshman Ohio. R.R.#1.
COUNTY... Green co TOWNSHIP... Bath Township

	RADISHES	LETTUCE	BEANS	BEETS	CARROTS	TOMATOES
Date planted	May 14	May 14 1904	May 14...	... 14 1904	May 14 1904	May 14, 1904.
Date at which first plants appeared	May 22	May 21	May 24	May 26	May 29	May 22.
Date of thinning	Did not thin any. We planted them for a pa
Date when ready for use	June 10	June 10	July 10	July 4.	July 25	August 20
Amount marketed	give lots away did not sell any.
Total yield	one half	good bit	three	one bu	three bu	good many

REMARKS The vegetables did fine and they got
a very large size. They produced lots of seed.
NAME Grace Willis. CLUB Agricultural Clubs.
ADDRESS Fletcher R.F.D. COUNTY Miami. TOWNSHIP Brown.

REPORT BLANK (Fill out and return to the College of Agriculture, Ohio State University)

	AGERATUM POTOX.	PETUNIA Chinese Pink	NASTURTIUM Scabrosa	POPPY Helichrysum	ZINNIA Gaillardia
1. Date planted	May 1, 1905	May 1, 1905	May 1, 1905.	May 1, 1905.	May 1, 1905.
2. Date at which first plants appeared	May 17, 1905.	May 17, 1905.	May 18, 1905	May 18, 1905	May 18, 1905
3. Date when first bloom appeared	July 1, 1905		July 14, 1905	July 22, 1905	Aug 1, 1905
4. Number of days or weeks the plants were in bloom	4 wks. 1 da.		2 wks 1 da.	3 wks. 1 da.	2 wks 1 da.
5. Which produced seeds	Potox.		Scabrosa	Helichrysum	Gaillardia

REMARKS The Chinese Pinks did not come up.

NAME Icie M. Claar. CLUB Rural School Agricultural.
ADDRESS R.F.D. #6. COUNTY Clark TOWNSHIP Springfield

26/27 Federation of Agricultural Clubs report forms for vegetables and
flowers, 1904

28　Springfield Twp. School exhibit at Clark Co. Fair, 1905

29　Agricultural Club exhibit, Springfield Farmers' Institute, 1903

30 Springfield Township Agricultural Club members on excursion to Ohio State University, June 1903. Top left, Supt. Graham, Dean Hunt, Prof. Decker

31 Farmers' Week, Ohio State University, 1913. Supt. Graham lower left

32 Agricultural Extension Corn Judging School, c. 1910

33 Agricultural Extension School, foods class for homemakers uses school gymnasium, c. 1910

34 Clerks Tom Wheeler and G. H. Bricker in the Agricultural Extension
mailing room from which 750 bi-weekly news releases and 20,000
monthly bulletins were distibuted, c. 1910

35 Agricultural Extension clerks Ruth Jones and Alice McMillan, c. 1910

36/37/38   Agricultural Extension Trains: Dairy Special, Crops Car, Better
Farming Special

39 U.S.D.A. States Relations Service, North and West, 1920. C. B. Smith at desk; l to r, Florence E. Ward, A. B. Graham, Gertrude Warren, Miss Harris, William A. Lloyd, Hans W. Hochbaum, Oscar S. Fisher, Mrs. Salisbury, Henry J. Wilder, Grace E. Frysinger, Milton Dantziger, Mark Thayer, T. Weed Harvey

40
U.S.D.A. Supervisor Graham checking extension programs at Ohio State, 1930

41   Graham at U.S.D.A. desk, 1937

42   Graham family and colleagues at U.S.D.A. retirement, March 1938;
      seated, l to r, Helen G. Baker, Maud L. Graham, E. Blair Graham,
      Joseph R. Graham; standing, Bertha M. Bennett, Kenneth Warner,
      Mrs. C. B. Smith, Harlan L. Shrader, H. W. Brokaw, A. B. Graham,
      Harry Brown, C. W. Warburton, Gertrude Warren, C. B. Smith

PART IV

Recognition for an Educational Pioneer

Chapter 10
4-H Club Jubilee —
50th Anniversary

> "This recognition, as I see it, is much more for a cause resulting in what is now known as 4-H Club work than for any one individual connected with its initiation."[1]

When Russell Agle opened his wholesale "first-day" window at the Springfield post office January 15, 1952, it was poignantly significant that his first customer was a spry octogenarian. A.B. Graham had ridden from Columbus to launch Ohio's ceremonies for the 4-H Club Jubilee in the city where it all began fifty years earlier.[2] The Springfield post office had prepared by hiring fifty extra workers for the heaviest single day flow in the city's history.

Over 400,000 of an initial printing of 110,000,000 4-H Club commemorative stamps received first day cancellations from the Springfield office. The green three-cent stamps featured portraits of a teenage boy and girl on the right and a group of typical farm buildings on the left with the 4-H clover symbol in the center and the club's motto, "To Make The Best Better," imprinted across the top. The 4-H Clubs were joining a distinguished company of individuals, organizations, and events which began in 1893 when the first U.S. commemorative stamp honored the Columbian Exposition celebrating the 400th anniversary of Columbus' discovery of America.

Springfield Postmaster Herbert A. Lannert opened the official ceremonies at the high school auditorium and Mayor Paul G. Miller welcomed an overflow crowd studded with local, state, and national dignitaries as well as hundreds of local 4-H members excused from school to attend. Assistant U.S. Postmaster General Osborne Pearson presented stamp albums to Graham, the Clark County Historical Society, the Springfield Chamber of Commerce, the Clark County 4-H Council, and the Ohio State University Agricultural Extension Service.

Many people throughout the audience shared the day's pride: Robert Grieser who had chaired the planning committee as president of the Clark County 4-H Council; George M. Barmann, a reporter for the *Springfield Sun* who had championed the commemorative stamp idea; fifteen members of Graham's boys' and girls' agricultural club in Springfield Township; and nine-year-old Barbara Baker, who attended the festivities in a red dress made by her grandfather. But the star of the day was A.B. Graham, who recalled Ponce de Leon's search for the Fountain of Youth and concluded that spiritually he himself had found such a fountain in his work with the youth of Clark County.[3]

At a luncheon in the Shawnee Hotel, Graham became the fourteenth American to receive the Fraternal Order of Eagles Civic Service Award, joining such previous recipients as Eleanor Roosevelt, Dwight Eisenhower, Francis Spellman, Babe Ruth, and J. Edgar Hoover. The citation presented by Grand Worthy President William P. Wetherald read, "To A.B. Graham, Citizen, Educator, Youth Leader, and Pioneer Spirit, Whose deep concern for the welfare and education of our rural boys and girls has led to the development of the 4-H movement which has inspired more than 15,000,000 young farmer citizens to become better farmers, homemakers, and community citizens, we present our Grand Aerie, Fraternal Order of Eagles, International Civic Service Award."[4]

The vigorous enthusiasm of the 84 year-old pioneer was generously shared throughout the afternoon in meetings with local 4-H Club leaders and state and county extension workers. Those who remember Graham that day saw what he meant when he said, "I'm still drinking from that fountain of youth and I'm still young." His enthusiasm was to be tapped again and again throughout the jubilee year as this master storyteller with the booming voice inspired celebrating 4-Hers and their leaders across the state. Governor Lausche proclaimed 1952 Ohio's 4-H Golden Anniversary Year.

During National 4-H Club Week in March the cover of the *National 4-H News* featured the 4-H commemorative stamp superimposed upon a photograph of Graham with fifteen alumni of his agricultural club who had attended the commemorative stamp ceremonies. Springfield celebrated again with a special pageant, "Pages of Progress," written by Eva Kinsey of the Ohio 4-H Club staff featuring five tableaux depicting milestones in the

4-H Club movement. The unique bond between education and agriculture was represented by guests Clyde Hissong, State Superintendent of Public Instruction, and H.S. Faust, State Director of Agriculture.[5]

The original group of boys and girls enrolled in agricultural projects in Clark County had evolved by the 1952 jubilee into a total of two million Ohio 4-H members and alumni who had been assisted by 275,000 volunteer leaders.[6] Even the celebrants had difficulty comprehending the scope of such growth.

In writing the history of the national 4-H movement Reck was certainly correct in beginning, "4-H Club work is too great a movement to be claimed by any one man."[7] But when the commemorative stamp was issued, controversy regarding the origins of the 4-H Club program intensified, and some resented the attention being given Graham by his ardent supporters. Few understood why Graham had been attempting for twenty years through internal U.S.D.A. memoranda to correct misinformation being disseminated regarding the club program's origins, but his reasons were significant. He was attempting to credit the partnership between land-grant universities and public school teachers which had developed in a number of states throughout the country well before the U.S.D.A. established a youth program.

An illustration of the misinformation is the statement regarding origins of boys' and girls' club work which is contained in the most current introduction to extension service records in the National Archives, a source virtually unknown to extension practitioners, but one accepted as fact by historical researchers.

> "Boys' and girls' club work appears to have been begun by W.B. Otwell, in 1900, in Macoupin County, Ill., and the first boys' club in the South was organized in 1907 in Holmes County, Miss. In 1909 Dr. Knapp undertook to systematize the boys' and girls' club work and made the State, district, and county agents responsible for its supervision and expansion. Girls' canning clubs were first organized in the South in 1910 in Aiken County, S.C., by Miss Marie Cromer, a rural school teacher. In the northern and western States boys' and girls' club work developed rapidly after 1912, when O.H. Benson, formerly with Dr. Knapp in the southern states, was transferred to the Office of Farm Management and placed in charge of that work. Mr. Benson is largely responsible for the broad principles and methods used in carrying on this work today."[8]

This statement ignores the early work of public school people from New York through the midwest who were responsible for tying the movement to the resources of land-grant universities. It implies that club work developed in the north and west after 1912, when in fact it had a decade of experience there. Ohio was one of several states which had networks of clubs in various counties operating in cooperation with their land-grant university long before 1912.

This misleading summary regarding 4-H origins contained in the official U.S.D.A. archives is an unfortunate example of department policy being perpetuated as historical fact.[9] There were excellent political reasons for emphasizing club programs in the south, although their origins were later than many of the northern states. The federal legislation making an appropriation for extension education was sponsored by Senator Hoke Smith of Georgia and Representative A.F. Lever of South Carolina, and southern congressmen often continued to hold key positions on agricultural committees.

It is equally unfortunate that the U.S.D.A. position continued to emphasize Otwell's corn growing contests held in conjunction with farmers' institutes as the predominant form of extension youth work when so many of the educational pioneers had organized diversified programs with far more of the 4-H program's enduring concepts. Otwell's dramatic display of "Farmer Boy Corn" at the Louisiana Purchase Exposition in St. Louis in 1904 was glowingly described in the U.S.D.A. Yearbook,[10] but his correspondence with Graham clearly identifies him as a businessman interested in selling farmers better quality seed corn.[11] Boys who won prizes for their accomplishments were excellent advertisements.

The perception of the movement by public school educators not directly associated with 4-H Clubs was different, although not necessarily more accurate. One cited Springfield Township, Ohio; Keokuk and Page Counties in Iowa; Natchitoches Parish, Louisiana; Winnebago County, Illinois; and Wexford County, Michigan as places "where boys' agricultural clubs have not only been the means of improving school conditions but by their success have led to similar work being introduced in other places."[12]

From the founding days of the program, the question was clearly drawn whether the focus was to be the development of youth through agricultural education or the promotion of agriculture by rewarding the accomplishments of youth. It is a question which remains unresolved as the organization attempts to accommodate both viewpoints.

Patterns of 4-H organization did evolve in varied forms across the nation. The Ohio structure led by volunteer leader-teachers outside the public schools was nurtured by William (Billie) Palmer, who became Ohio's first State Leader for Boys' and Girls' Club Work in 1916. He had retired after thirty-five years of service just before the jubilee celebration.

March 18, 1952 a state-wide recognition program for 4-H volunteer advisors was held in the new student union at Ohio State University, with certificates and pins presented to those who had served 5, 10, 15, 20, or 25 years.[13] A ceremony written for this occasion by Miss Kinsey entitled, "Flame of Gold," utilized lighting effects to show the budding and growth of 4-H from leaf to twig to branch. It was symbolism perhaps even more appropriate than she had envisioned. The 4-H movement had grown in so many places and many directions during its early history and the extensive celebrations in Ohio made little mention of other pioneers who shaped the movement in various ways. When a seed is planted in the ground it is difficult to pinpoint the precise moment when the first sprout appears, and impossible to determine how long that sprout has been pushing upward invisibly beneath the soil.

Counties were encouraged to use the jubilee year as an occasion for writing their own 4-H history or ceremony and this they did throughout the state all year long. A surprising number were able to enlist Graham's personal appearance. When Preble County kicked off its jubilee celebration in February, the *Eaton Register-Herald* was impressed by the remarks of the "charming and learned Mr. Graham."[14] Reporters frequently noted that Graham seemed to gain vigor from the celebrating youth. He told Franklin County celebrants on June 3rd that, "My joints are rusty but I'm sixteen tonight."[15]

As the summer wore on Graham crossed the state, celebrating with Belmont County in the east, Mercer County in the west, Mahoning County in the northeast and Montgomery County in the southwest. The pioneer was making an impression long remembered by many who heard him. The *Dayton Daily News* wrote, "His vigorous gait, his emphatic opinions, his ability to make an impromptu speech without hesitation, belie his age. He would rather you consider him 84½ years young."[16] Perhaps the most elaborate of the local pageants was the one September 3rd staged by a Van Wert County cast of 600 under the direction of

Mrs. Virgil Johnson. A series of local 4-Hers were featured in historical events from the Treaty of St. Marys, through Abraham Lincoln signing the Morrill Act, and Theodore Roosevelt appointing the Country Life Commission. But the pageant's real live star was A.B. Graham playing himself with a group of 4-H Club members. [17]

Some of the local celebrations, of course, held personal significance for Graham. His boyhood home, Miami County, celebrated July 18th and presented her famous son with a beautifully inscribed walking cane. One of the most personal moments among the local celebrations occurred September 24th in Butler County when first year 4-H member, Marilyn Graham, was given the opportunity to present her grandfather a token of appreciation from the Butler County 4-H Clubs. [18]

At the Clark County Fair August 13th, Graham began the day touring the exhibits in the youth building before participating in ceremonies unveiling a plaque listing 103 members of the agricultural club. It was a commemoration which significantly understated the total number of at least 145 youth who had participated during Graham's leadership from 1902 to 1904. [19] Graham accepted the honor by quoting Horace Mann, "Be ashamed to die until you have performed some good deed for humanity." [20] On this occasion twenty-three of the members whose names appeared on the plaque were present, and one of them, Theodore Spears, handed Graham a newspaper clipping which revealed some little known facts about that early club.

The article was from the magazine section of the *Pittsburgh Courier,* a newspaper which served the Negro community. It pictured Spears with the handsaw he had received from a Springfield hardware store as first prize for the best exhibit of corn grown by a club member in 1903. Theodore remembered that the courtroom was crowded by the time the judges made their decision and the applause was vigorous when he was asked to stand and again when his parents joined him. It was certainly one of the first instances of a Negro youth receiving recognition as a member of a racially integrated group. Fifty years later a Negro newspaper featured the story proudly. [21]

In writing a brief history of boys' and girls' club exhibits for the Ohio State Fair Junior Division Bulletin, Graham included one of the stories which so typified his speeches, "The hen lays an egg, she cackles to tell the world she has done something. The

world passes judgment as to its worth."[22] As usual, he combined it
with a little philosophy lesson, reminding readers that for many
early exhibits premiums were paid to the club group, not to individual members. He specifically mentioned the Locus Corner
Club of Morrow County, which received $10 and used it to buy
books for the school library. At age eighty-four, Graham had firm
opinions about right and wrong, and he seldom hesitated to
praise or criticize behavior according to his values. He applauded
group incentives and deplored what he saw as excessive individual rewards, just as he had forty years earlier.

Throughout his life Graham delighted in being thought provoking and his remarks during the jubilee celebrations were
sometimes calculated for maximum effect. In a prepared speech
to some 850 delegates attending the Ohio 4-H Club Congress in
September, he proposed that 4-H be made available to city boys
and girls as well as to farm youth, and that funding appropriations be made for such a program increase.[23] It was the same
theme he had stressed in the U.S.D.A. news release sixteen years
earlier and now in the post-war period both extension workers
and public officials were openly supporting the concept. Graham's stand was somewhat remarkable considering his background in country schools and long years of service to rural
Americans.

On September 18th Graham was one of five individuals and
three organizations receiving Ohio's highest award, the Governor's Award for the Advancement of Ohio's Prestige. Selected by
the Ohio Development and Publicity Commission, these awards
were presented at the banquet of the Ohio Newspaper Association. Other Columbus honorees that year were World War I flying
ace, Eddie Rickenbacker, and Battelle Memorial Institute.[24]

The last celebration of the jubilee year in which Graham is
known to have participated was a banquet honoring 4-H advisors
in Ottawa County on December 8th. Graham was the featured
speaker and accepted a county 4-H history prepared especially for
the occasion.

Across the nation, but especially in Ohio, the 50th birthday
celebration was a media event focusing much attention on the 4-H
club movement and its development. Graham's vigorous enthusiasm became attractive counterpoint amid the celebrations of
healthy young farm boys and girls. The attention was a mixed
blessing. The spotlight focused throughout this year upon Gra-

ham's influence on the 4-H club movement left his other educational achievements largely unknown, but without the attention of 4-H supporters, Graham himself would not have become known. Some friends of other 4-H pioneers whose contributions were less dramatically recognized may have been wounded. If Graham had remained in the public schools throughout his career or died twenty years earlier, he would not have earned such adulation for his contributions to the 4-H program. Graham was sensitive to this issue and always referred to his boys' and girls' agricultural experiment club as a forerunner of 4-H clubs. He was one of the first to research the history of the 4-H movement and his position in U.S.D.A. gave him access to information throughout the country. He was very proud to be one of its "pioneers," and tried diligently to see that student members of his club received as much recognition as their teacher leader.

Graham himself may have done the best job of placing the year long celebration into perspective. "A deep and lasting expression of appreciation is made by each of the members of the original club and their leader for the interest and effort by individuals and organizations in making 1952 a punctuation mark in the history of 4-H clubs — especially in Ohio."[25]

Chapter 11
Honors for a Humble Pioneer

"We should not forget the results of a well shaken barrel of potatoes. The large ones are elevated to the top. One important question arises. What are the other potatoes doing? There is but one answer. Holding the big ones up. Each individual potato or person has its own potency either in followership or leadership."[1]

It becomes interesting to contemplate why the Graham "potato" so often came to rest on top of the barrel. Honors are intended to reward achievement, yet we have all known individuals whose accomplishments are largely unrecognized. A.B. Graham is particularly interesting because his accomplishments were diverse. Some of them became well known and honored, others have remained relatively unknown and unrewarded.

There is an obvious answer which cannot be denied. Longevity and charisma are appealing providing they rest on a solid base of accomplishment. Everyone who knew A.B. Graham personally begins to smile when asked about him, and few can resist sharing one or more of their treasured memories. Throughout life he had an exuberant personality, packaged in a visage Dickens would have immortalized, expressed in the booming voice of a master storyteller. His greatest honors were received as a spry octogenarian whose twinkling eyes betrayed his keen wit. He was a delightful guest of honor, somewhat akin to a three-year-old flower girl who delights the audience at a wedding. A.B. Graham's joy of life could be disarmingly charming.

But charisma is a small part of the story. Graham's accomplishments as an educator might have won recognition by educational organizations associated with adult or parent education, agricultural or nature study groups, library associations, youth groups, or the communities in which he lived and worked. Most of the honors Graham received occurred a half century or more after the accomplishment. Most were granted because he kept detailed records of his activities, kept in touch with former students and colleagues, and gradually acquired a core of advocates who recognized that his accomplishments were extraordinary.

This is illustrated by the first major award Graham received January 22, 1932 in Springfield, Ohio. At a thirtieth anniversary banquet in the Central Christian Church, Lynn Gower unveiled a bronze plaque to be hung in the courthouse to commemorate the first agricultural club in the United States. By then A.B. Graham was in charge of extension specialists in the United States Department of Agriculture, youth clubs under the 4-H emblem enrolled about 850,000 members in 48 states, and pioneers like Graham were assembling the history of the movement. Twenty-one members of Graham's club were present at this reunion and nine made brief remarks. A "Graham Club" alumni group was organized with Lynn Gower as president and Eliza Trout, secretary.[2]

Speakers for the occasion included W.H. Palmer, Ohio 4-H Club Leader, and John F. Cunningham who, at that time, was farming in Moorefield Township of Clark County. More significantly, Cunningham was a 1897 graduate of Ohio State University who had been actively involved as a member of the Agricultural Student Union in the distribution of Agricultural Experiment Station seeds to the youth clubs Graham began. Later, as editor of the *Ohio Farmer* and as a trustee of the Ohio State University, he had worked closely with Supt. Graham during the developmental stages of agricultural extension. Four months later, in May of 1932, Cunningham was selected to replace retiring Dean Vivian as Dean of the College of Agriculture at the Ohio State University.[3] He had known of Graham's work for many years and was an influential supporter.

In accepting the tablet in January 1932 Graham responded to the honor "dedicated not to any man or club but to a cause that had spread to every state in the Union and to several foreign countries as a guide and beacon to more wholesome farm and home life." It was a statement he repeated over and over during the next twenty-eight years. One suspects that Graham was willing to stand in the spotlight, perhaps even sought the spotlight, because a youth movement deeply rooted in his affections shared the illumination. There is no doubt that many people and places shared glory through their association with him.

Clark County was not the only place which recognized Graham's contribution to the 4-H club movement, of course. The two national 4-H events both honored Graham and several times invited him to be a part of their program. At the National 4-H Camp in Washington, D.C. in 1941, a medallion and citation from the U.S.D.A. was given Graham in recognition of his accomplishments as, "Teacher, Extension Agent, and Philosopher."

At the 25th National 4-H Club Congress in Chicago in 1946, a plaque cited his "foresight, leadership, devotion and service in pioneering and building the 4-H Club movement." Graham was one of ten extension pioneers recognized on this occasion and he no doubt enjoyed the reunion with former colleagues such as C.B. Smith, O.H. Benson, and Gertrude Warren, but he may have regretted the omission of deceased pioneers such as O.J. Kern, Cap. E. Miller, and Jessie Field Shambaugh.[4]

In 1942, radio station WRFD at Worthington, Ohio marked the fortieth anniversary of the agricultural club's organization by recording Graham conversing with several former members of his Springfield Township club about their projects and activities.[5] This script was widely borrowed and many people throughout Ohio and the nation became aware of the historic concepts and organization of this group.

During his seventh decade Graham was a very active retiree, delighted to speak to a class of Columbus fourth graders, a leadership camp for 4-H teenagers, or conferences of extension workers in numerous states. But it was in his eighth decade, after the death of his wife of sixty years, that recognition of his accomplishments became an avalanche.

Some of the most valuable tributes which came his way were verbal commendations from colleagues whose judgments were prized. In remarks celebrating the 75th Anniversary of the Ohio State University, President J.L. Morrill of the University of Minnesota recalled that the first person he met as a student at Ohio State was A.B. Graham, "my long-time friend still happily among us, whose labors helped conspicuously to give form and future to the most extensive system of adult education in the world today — the agricultural extension service conducted by the Federal government and the States through their land-grant institutions."[6]

During National 4-H Week in 1951, Clark County's Senator C.I. Powell introduced Graham and twenty members of his agricultural club to the Ohio Senate where they were presented a scroll by President Pro Tempore, Roscoe Wolcutt.[7] The state officially recognized that this group was a foundation both for the 4-H club movement and for agricultural extension work in conjunction with the Ohio State University.

In October of the same year, the Clark County Historical Society celebrated Springfield's sesquicentennial at Memorial Hall. 4-H Club member, Jane Gordon, unveiled a plaque "In commemoration of the organization of the first boys' and girls' agricultural club in the United States by Albert B. Graham of Clark County, Ohio, resulting in the establishment of the 4-H Clubs of America."[8] Now embedded in the corner of Memorial Hall, home of the Clark County Historical Society, this plaque marks the site of memorabilia associated with those historic club meetings.

From the 4-H Golden Anniversary Jubilee described in the previous chapter, until Graham's death, recognition took many forms. One of his most cherished awards was bestowed June 12, 1953 during the Ohio State University commencement when he received the hood and diploma of an honorary Doctor of Laws. His nomination by Dean Rummell of the College of Agriculture and Secretary Fullen of the Ohio State Alumni Association recognized him as a "pioneer in agricultural education who has devoted more than half a century to the building of better citizens in rural America and to the extension of modern agricultural practices in Ohio and throughout the nation."[9] Specifically mentioned were the agricultural club which was the forerunner of the 4-H Club movement, the development of the agricultural extension service at Ohio State University, his drive for centralization of rural schools, and his instigation of agriculture and home economics teaching in high schools. It was an honor he treasured more than he could express, although he joked to friends about the university taking more than sixty years to be sure he had enough credits for a degree.[10]

Official alumnus status could not increase the loyalty Graham had already developed for the institution, but neither could it make him the typical Buckeye sports fan. Writing to a cousin the day after an Ohio State-Michigan football game attracted 82,000 fans he commented, "I wish I knew the game so I could take more interest in it. It must be great sport because so many are interested in it. I wish a class in history, geometry or civil government could elicit half as much interest."[11] It was a sentiment no doubt shared by more than one faculty member through the years.

In 1955, Marietta College presented him an honorary Doctor of Humanities degree, citing his organization of the agricultural club which was the forerunner of the 4-H Club movement, service as Ohio's first director *(sic)* of agricultural extension, membership on the N.E.A. committee recommending a structure for junior high schools, and a U.S.D.A. specialist in extension teaching methods.[12] No record of proceedings in regard to his nomination has been found but it is probable the President Irvine, a strong supporter of conservation education, knew and admired Graham's work.

That same summer Graham was honored at the Ohio State Fair when his portrait was hung in the newly dedicated youth building. A fund raising drive among 4-H members and friends for "Portrait Pennies" had been spearheaded by Mary Lou Pfeiffer, WRFD Womens' Director with the assistance of Jane Lausche, wife of the Governor, and Sam Cashman, Ohio State Fair Manager.[13] As an amateur artist-photographer Graham thoroughly enjoyed sittings with artist Charlotte Daniels. After the portrait was completed, he enjoyed sitting near it in the Youth Center lobby and encouraged startled State Fair youth exhibitors to pause for a chat about their projects.

A controversy behind this painting reveals much about the character of the subject. Columbus artist, Emerson Burkhart had originally been commissioned to do this portrait but the committee rejected his painting as uncomplimentary. Although angry at the selection committee's interpretation of art, Burkhart had filled a notebook with "Graham cracker notes" during their sittings and remained a great admirer of Graham personally. The "Graham Cracker" nickname originated with Graham himself, who encouraged its use among the youngsters in his Clintonville neighborhood who enjoyed visiting with him. Burkhart told a reporter, "The days we spent together were rich for me. I found A.B. Graham to have an understanding of human life possessed by few educators and fewer politicians."[14]

In the fall of 1957 two significant agricultural groups recognized Graham's contributions. At its annual meeting in Columbus the Ohio Farm Bureau, which had developed in conjunction with the first county extension agents, presented Graham with its award for outstanding service to agriculture.[15] A few days later, accompanied by Ohio Extension Director Wilbur B. Wood, the eighty-nine year old Graham flew to Chicago to receive the distinguished service award from the American Agricultural Editors, an organization representing seventy-five farm publications with a monthly circulation of more than twenty million subscribers.[16]

Sunday, December 15, 1957 was a very special day both for A.B. Graham and the Champaign County community where he attended school and began teaching. Members of the community were invited to the formal dedication of Graham High School east of St. Paris and were delighted to inspect the $700,000 building which had already opened with more than 400 students and a faculty of twenty. C.M. Bricker, Executive Head of the Graham local school district, and Harold Shank, high school principal, were proud to show the guest of honor the specialized facilities for fine arts, industrial arts, vocational home economics and agriculture. Some of those in attendance described Graham's sprightly address as the highlight of the day. "God the architect and Jesus the teacher did not build buildings, they built human souls. It is to the idea of building human souls that we should dedicate this building and ourselves."[17] Additional honors from the Graham High School students came the following spring when the class of 1958 elected him an honorary member and in 1959 when the F.F.A. chapter made him its first honorary member.[18] Remembering Graham's speech on "Fame" at his own high school graduation seventy-three years earlier, one can only suspect that this recognition in his home community must have exceeded his highest aspirations.

March 13, 1958 A.B. Graham observed his 90th birthday sharing a four-tiered cake with friends at radio WRFD. Gov. O'Neill had proclaimed this "A.B. Graham Day" and the station highlighted its programing with some of his thoughts and tributes from his admirers. *Agricola* magazine presented him its Golden Award for outstanding service to the youth of America. Newspapers joined personal friends in offering birthday congratulations on his keen mind and spirit, one editorializing, "Albert Graham, unlike so many who have dedicated themselves to the service of mankind, has lived to see the fruits of his pioneer efforts in agricultural education"[19] WRFD General Manager Joseph Bradshaw recognized Graham with a plaque for achievements in the development of better living through home and community improvement, and Mary Lou Pfeiffer recorded interviews which saved this educational pioneer's philosophy for generations to come.

Perhaps it was fitting that one of the last tributes Graham would receive in person should come from Roy Buck, President of the American Country Life Association, at its annual meeting which was held in Columbus during the summer of Graham's ninty-first year. The plaque reads simply and eloquently, "For His Outstanding Contributions to the Improvement of Rural Life."[20]

Six months after Graham's death the 4-Hers of Clermont, Hamilton, Montgomery and Warren counties dedicated their camp near Clarksville, Ohio in his honor. [21] If A.B. Graham had been with them perhaps he would have told them about his geology class from National Normal University exploring nearby cuts made by the Little Miami River, or a group of student astronomers awed by the lunar eclipse on a summer night in 1888. But the remarks July 10th, 1960 were made by John Mount, an Ohio State University Vice-President who had grown up in southwestern Ohio, been a member of the Ohio 4-H staff during the Golden Jubilee anniversary, and later an assistant dean counseling students in the College of Agriculture and Home Economics. A new generation had assumed educational leadership and still another was exploring the camp's nature trails and discovering their own wonders. These 4-H campers would never know A.B. Graham, but at Camp Graham they would have opportunities to learn from nature, one of his favorite classrooms.

March 10, 1968 St. Paris, Ohio celebrated "A.B. Graham Day", on the Sunday preceding the one hundredth anniversary of his birth.[22] Although never his hometown, he lived thirty years of his life within a few miles of this community and as student and teacher spent many a day with friends and relatives there. When the Graham Consolidated School District encompassed the town, he became one of its favorite sons. That same summer, Graham was inducted posthumously into the Ohio Agricultural Hall of Fame and his portrait was hung in the Rhodes Center gallery at the Ohio State Fairgrounds, an honor bestowed annually by the Ohio Agricultural Council on two farmers and two agricultural leaders.[23]

Four years later the Ohio Historical Society selected 149 native or adoptive Buckeyes who had made extraordinary contributions to all aspects of human endeavor and dedicated the

"Great Ohioans Hall of Fame" January 21, 1972. The selection committee made an effort to categorize these persons across occupations with titles such as trailblazers, builders, creators, reformers, and legends. One suspects A.B. Graham might have qualified in several of these categories, but his portrait was included among the twenty-five "organizers," in company with Harvey S. Firestone, William Rainey Harper, William C. Proctor, James N. Gamble, John D. Rockefeller, Amos I. Root and others.[24]

The nation's bicentennial brought historic tributes in communities across the land, and Springfield, Ohio created a visible monument to A.B. Graham by naming the building where the original agricultural club members met in his honor. July 3, 1976 Clark County Commissioner Howard Hahn, representing Springfield and Clark County's bicentennial committee, dedicated this county office building the A.B. Graham Memorial Building. Bronze plaques were placed on each side of the front entrance to call the attention of visitors to the county's 4-H heritage. The left pillar silhouettes a boy and girl, while the plaque on the right lists 103 members of Graham's club, six of whom were present for the ceremonies. Beside the ground floor meeting room, a portrait by local artist, Eunice Bronkar, features Graham with his granddaughter wearing the dress he made for her to attend 4-H commemorative stamp ceremonies in 1952.

A plaza at the Limestone & Columbia Street corner contains flagpoles for displaying the United States, Ohio and 4-H flags. Dean Roy Kottman of the Ohio State University College of Agriculture, Home Economics and Natural Resources spoke on the 4-H heritage, and A.B. Graham was represented by his daughter Helen and son Joseph. More than seventy years later, Graham's agricultural club members, current university extension leaders and local community officials were again united in paying tribute to a man and a movement which brought the city recognition.[25]

The Diamond Jubilee of this agricultural club was celebrated in 1977 with the Ohio 4-H Foundation establishing an "A.B. Graham Club" to recognize significant contributors. Retired 4-H staff member Beatrice Cleveland spearheaded a drive to raise a $750,000 endowment for educational programs. A 4-H Hall of Fame was inaugurated, inducting A.B. Graham posthumously along with six surviving members of his agricultural experiment club.[26]

April 10th, 1981 three members of Graham's agricultural club visited the Ohio capitol just as the group did in June of 1903. Blanche Bickle, Jenny Irie, and Theodore Spears saw Governor Rhodes and the Ohio 4-H Foundation unveil a tablet in the east rotunda entrance commemorating the contribution to the 4-H movement by the club organized in Springfield, Ohio on January 15, 1902. It was an enduring tribute to what the group had meant to these members personally as well as to the 4-H club program. In joint resolution the Ohio House and Senate again proclaimed "A.B. Graham Day"[27]

November 20, 1983 the dreams of many Ohio 4-H supporters culminated in the dedication of the Ohio 4-H Educational Center on the Ohio State University campus. Envisioned by Charles W. Lifer, Ohio's State Leader, 4-H as evidence of the renewed commitment between the land-grant university and rural youth, the center features exhibits which tell the story of 4-H development, provide a permanent display of the Ohio 4-H Hall of Fame members, and present a constantly changing review of current programs and projects. Its auditorium provides space for seminars for local volunteer leaders, 4-H members, extension faculty and staff.[28]

April 27, 1984 A.B. Graham was among eleven "Agricultural Achievers" inducted into the national Agricultural Hall of Fame at Bonner Springs, Kansas.[29] One suspects that Graham would be inordinately pleased that his name continues to focus a spotlight on the educational organizations he loved, the communities in which he worked, and the "students" with whom he kept in touch. Surely he would have some quip about the barrel full of potatoes.

Chapter 12
Living Memorials - A New Era for Rural Education

"One may live in perfectly still air but I prefer to feel the exhilarating effects of a good stiff breeze occasionally."[1]

Controversy held no fear for A.B. Graham, but he was deeply hurt by those who referred to him as an educational heretic. Perhaps he should have been honored. Although the term is more often applied in a religious or political context, by dictionary definition it does refer to one who challenges established doctrine and maintains unorthodox or controversial opinions. It was precisely because Graham spent so many years on the forefront of educational change for rural areas and spoke so eloquently regarding its issues that his example is memorable.

There never seems to have been any question that the Grahams would return to Ohio in retirement. Throughout the years they had been in close contact with various family members, sister Lettie Love at Piqua, brother-in-law and sister George and Minnie Lauer Stephenson at Rosewood, son Blair's family at Columbus, daughter Helen's family and son Joe's family, both at Middletown. But it was professional roots which led the Grahams back to Columbus. Although his twenty-two years in the U.S.D.A. had taken him to every state in the nation, Ohio was the educational arena in which Graham had made his mark.

It would be inaccurate and unfair to credit Graham individually for any one of the significant changes in rural education during the early part of the twentieth century. Part of his story is pure timing and luck which placed him at the cutting edge of progess for several decades. But the genius of Graham which deserves serious analysis, was his repeated success as an educational innovator interpreting theory into applications for both youth and adults. It is somewhat curious that such interpretive skill is only rarely recognized and rewarded by the educational establishment, and yet educational researchers consistently define synthesis and interpretation at the highest levels of cognitive reasoning.[2]

As the century began, educators had taken the early steps toward professionalism. The qualifications of teachers were receiving increasing attention both from the institutions which prepared them and the local jurisdictions which accredited them. Committees of the National Education Association were drawing attention to key issues which were in turn attracting local advocates. Then as well as now, education was perceived as the avenue by which individuals or groups could advance economically, socially, and culturally. As the twentieth century began, rural Americans were the largest and most widespread disadvantaged population. Nationally, half of the population lived in rural areas, and in some states the percentage was much higher. The social-cultural isolation of this lifestyle was being placed at the doorstep of the country school for solution.

No issue was more critical nor more controversial than the concept of school consolidation. Graham's early advocacy of the concept, his implementation of it as a rural superintendent, his state-wide surveys of progress, and reports on advantages and disadvantages offer an unusual opportunity to share the viewpoint of a participant in this movement. While everyone agrees that schools can be too small or too large for optimum education, it is the definition of optimum educational opportunity which remains as controversial today as when the issue was first raised. In actions and words, Graham often demonstrated his position on two of the most central issues: community participation and control.

Local control of public schools was a concept implanted in the minds of settlers who migrated west, and it became a key to social organization in the communities they established. It is not the intent of this biography to examine the conceptual organization of our society, but rather to look at one man's role as professional educators began to demand a share of the decision making in regard to curriculum and credentials. Graham's experiences teaching in one-room schools gave him a clear realization of the limitations imposed by township sub-district boards, usually composed of local farmers, who were solely responsible for hiring teachers, purchasing textbooks, and maintaining a school building. Very early in his career Graham began exerting his right as the teacher to participate in these decisions, and he was soon encouraging other teachers to do the same through his newspaper columns and by contacting legislators to request support for key issues such as tax funds for library books or transportation wagons.

But a key element in Graham's success, and one which few educators emulated vigorously, was his persistent involvement of the adults of the community in the business of the school. He envisioned professional educators as partners not dictators in matters of school policy. His evening meetings for parents considered a variety of relevant topics from supplementary reading materials to vocational guidance. Community businesses were encouraged to contribute to the educational process in a variety of ways from art for classroom walls to shrubs for landscaped playgrounds. Parents and community leaders were invited to participate in extracurricular activities by testing soil acidity with the boys' and girls' experiment club or touring the land-grant university and state government offices. School acomplishments were displayed not only in commencement orations and school exercises, but at the county fair exhibit hall.

To Graham, everything about education was a participatory experience. As a rural superintendent he frequently wrote about and photographed classes and playgrounds which provided group participation. "If a school is to prepare for life there should be enough children in the school room or on the school ground to make social life a reality. A child brought up in a home where it has no brother or sister to question its rights or a few children on a school ground where there is no particular right to be defended or duty to be performed, does not get a true notion of what community life is. Man is a gregarious animal. . . School games are no small part of school life; in these games there is an opportunity for fairness, justice and many other minor virtues to be displayed. Here is an opportunity for the moral precepts and examples of the school room, home and church to become a part of the life of the child."[3]

None of these ideas or actions seem the least revolutionary today when school buses regularly pass rural homes, parent-teacher organizations have a variety of programs throughout the year, curricula in rural districts offer challenging courses in chemistry, or Spanish, or word processing, and extracurricular options allow participation in dramatics, soccer or band. Some pioneers of school consolidation lived to see their innovative ideas become commonplace, and Graham, like others, began to raise questions about the size of school environments which encouraged students and parents to become spectators rather than participants. Some of his retirement correspondence reveals how distressed Graham was to learn of a parent-teacher organization serving as a school administrator's rubber stamp or a well maintained gymnasium floor reserved for the exclusive use of a championship basketball team. A concept designed to solve one problem was sometimes being implemented to the point where it created another.

Like many educational leaders of the 1890s and early 1900s Graham attempted to increase the teacher's role in decision making, but he tried to do this while enhancing parent and student participation until schools became community centers. It was a difficult challenge and many educators have concentrated on and accomplished much of the first part. It may be the second part which holds the long range key to educational quality.

One of the keys to Graham's success as an educational advocate was his ability to extract a single component of the educational challenge and present it in a manner which won support from a special interest group. It might be possible for a casual reader to dismiss Graham's focus on school libraries, pictures for classroom walls, landscaped playgrounds, school transportaion wagons, nature study and agriculture as diverse fragments without focus. But no careful reader will miss the fact that Graham always returned to the central theme: a consolidated school with a physical environment, diversified curriculum, and parent participation which facilitated learning and encouraged students to continue through secondary education which was relevant to their prospective life work. Today it sounds almost too obvious to mention, but in 1900 when 85% of the rural students in many states went no further than a one-room country school, it was often an impossible dream.[4]

Graham's contributions to the N.E.A. committee which recommended revising the basic eight-four year organizational structure to a six-three-three was not an isolated assignment but an integral part of this overall concept. A psychological breaking point was removed by providing the transitional component of a junior high school. When the committee analyzed options and made its recommendations in 1907 there were four schools throughout the country experimenting with some part of this concept. A decade later, Ohio reported just 34 junior high schools and the nation recorded 791,[5] but it became the standard educational structure throughout the country and endured conceptually to the present day.

Graham's focus on elementary nature study and the development of centralized township high schools was interwoven with his advocacy of secondary courses in agriculture, domestic science, and manual training. This linkage which Graham and others were emphasizing in Ohio, and in other states, led directly to the Smith-Hughes legislation providing federal support for vocational education a decade later. Much of the structure of the vocational education component which evolved persists to this day with approriations and supervision at state and federal levels. The linkage of domestic science with agriculture to meet the needs of farm wives at the beginning of the twentieth century has resulted in the continued inclusion of home economics within vocational education and in many states in persistent linkage of agriculture and home economics in teacher education components and in cooperative extension units of land-grant universities. This example of an incompatible union of disciplines rooted in diverse physical and social sciences, has in some instances been detrimental to both by preventing more mutually supportive research linkages. One wonders how the practitioners who solved an educational access problem would react to the institutionalization of their solution through funding procedures.

When the Springfield Township agricultural experiment club was organized in 1902 across school boundaries it was impossible for Graham to imagine the impact this concept would have. His relationship with the land-grant university, like his peers in states such as New York, Iowa, and Illinois, embedded this youth program within that institution, relying upon a subject matter base provided by university specialists. The popularity of this structure is demonstrated in Ohio where it is estimated that one of every six Ohioans is currently or was formerly a 4-H club member. Throughout the world, ten million youth in eighty-two countries participate in 4-H type programs.[6] The 4-H program has accommodated within its educational purpose and heritage, competitive goals which trace their origins to corn growing contests and livestock judging events supported by breed associations. Graham attempted unsuccessfully to resolve the incompatible goals of the Ohio State University and the Ohio Agricultural Commission and later raised similar questions about the formation of the Committee on Boys' and Girls' Club Work and its relationship to the youth program of the U.S. Department of Agriculture. In many ways the educational and competitive goals still remain incompatible. Perhaps it is too soon to state with certainty what forms of this youth program will prevail, and who will support and administer them.

Graham's experience demonstrates the degree to which agricultural extension education in Ohio evolved from popular support for the growing youth program. Ohio was not the only state, and this would not be the last time, that adult education found it politically expedient to ride a wave of political support created for youth education. The most significant fact is that Graham's experience in Ohio typifies the grassroots movement for agricultural extension prior to the Smith-Lever federal funding. Progressive farmers anxious for research results from agricultural experiment stations literally pushed university faculty into extension teaching methods. The fact that extension education was imposed upon university faculty members, rather than an idea born among them, dramatically influences the acceptance of extension educators as faculty peers to this day. The partnership which evolved between the U.S. Department of Agriculture, land-grant universities, and county governments for funding and administering this program became a model sought by developing countries around the world. But the Cooperative Extension Service evolved as a product of its time and culture. Attempts to create similar types of organizational structures to serve current social needs have been too diverse to succeed, and international efforts have required extensive modification to suit other governmental and educational forms.

Although some of these trends regarding historic significance were becoming evident within Graham's lifetime, it would be inaccurate to view his retirement years as a living monument to accomplishments in rural education. In the truest sense, he remained the professional educator he had always been. He was constantly in demand as a speaker, as delighted to meet a class of school children near his Clintonville home as to address a conference of extension staff members in a distant state. One high school reporter caught the essence of the Graham style. "A very old copy of music was produced from one of his pockets, and he explained to us how it was used. An old book on bees emerged from another pocket and its contents were read. . . In humor and historical facts, Mr. Graham excels and he held his youthful audience spellbound."[7]

A.B. Graham believed that the first requisite of a good teacher was knowledge. He had prepared to teach by earning a degree in science, and he was confident that if what you knew was important, then other people would need it and want to know also. This was the key to his successful missionary zeal, and that of his contemporaries whose educational leadership dramatically changed rural education in America. They began with content rather than process, but sought excellence in both. Their applied research in methodology contributed immeasurably to adult education.

Graham's educational philosophy was rooted in intellectual curiosity. A fascinating example of his own lifelong learning is revealed in a 1941 letter to a colleague. Speaking of new developments in chemistry, physics, and biology, he refers to chemurgy, atom smashing, and artificial insemination.[8] One doubts that many scientists, and certainly very few school teachers, active or retired, were discussing atom smashing six months prior to Pearl Harbor. But Graham did not fear change, and peers who tried to retain a position or a specific responsibility were often threatened by his readiness to move on to the next challenge. In the same letter he wrote, "No one expects life to be static, but it can be made to take on proportion and balance as it goes along the line of progress."

It is not a contradiction to say that Graham was both humble and proud regarding his accomplishments. Characteristically, a decade before his death he had his own tombstone inscribed and erected, leaving a record in his own words of the way he wished to be remembered, "A.B. Graham was a teacher and superintendent of rural schools. An early promoter of centralized schools in Ohio. Organizer of the first boys & girls agricultural club in the United States, 1902. The first Director of Agricultural Extension in Ohio, 1905. A member of the Committee that prepared for N.E.A. the first plan for Junior High Schools in the United States, 1907. Administrator of subject matter specialists, U.S. Department of Agriculture, 22 Years."[9]

Viewing Graham's life as an educational advocate one is acutely aware of his frequent references to Ralph Waldo Emerson's writings, as early as the 1890s and as late as the 1950s. Searching for the guidance Graham obviously found from this idol, one encounters a dramatic plea, "I will not dissemble my hope that each person whom I address has felt his own call to cast aside all evil customs, timidities, and limitations, and to be in his place a free and helpful man, a reformer, a benefactor, not content to slip along through the world like a footman or a spy, escaping by his nimbleness and apologies as many knocks as he can, but a brave and upright man, who must find or cut a straight road to everything excellent in the earth, and not only go honorably himself, but make it easier for all who follow him to go in honor and with benefit."[10]

A.B. Graham was a country schoolmaster who heard that call, and devoted his life's work to its answer.

THE END

43   Honorees and Extension leaders at National 4-H Club Congress 25th Anniversary, December 1946 —
A. B. Graham, 1st row, 2nd from right

44 Graham with fifteen members of the original agricultural club attending Golden Jubilee, January 1952; seated, l to r, Mrs. C. W. Irie, Mrs. Clyde Quick, Mrs. Frank Layton, Graham, Mrs. Jessie Butler, Mrs. Clara V. Read; standing, Theodore Spears, Albert Gray, Charles Schneider, J. W. Fenton, Earl Hyslop, Karl Hirtzinger, Harry F. Otstot, B. L. Tavenner, J. Lynn Gower, W. A. Shurr

45 4-H Commemorative Stamp issued at Springfield, Ohio,
January 2, 1952

46
Graham with Ohio
State Junior Fair
Board members in
front of Youth
Center portrait, 1956

47 Graham receiving LL.D. hood, Ohio State University Commencement, June 1953

48 Graham viewing Ohio Historical Society exhibit of 19th century schoolbooks with James Bieber, a 6th grade student

49
Graham with
90th birthday
cake at Radio
WRFD

50   Graham in sunroom of Clintonville home with retirement
     correspondence

51 Graham High School, Champaign County, Ohio

52 A. B. Graham Memorial County Building, Springfield, Ohio

Glossary

Association of American Agricultural Colleges and Experiment Stations (A.A.A.C.E.S.) — Organized in 1887 and known by this title until 1919, this organization evolved through a series of name changes into the current *National Association of State Universities and Land-Grant Colleges* (N.A.S.U.L.G.C.).

Boys' and Girls' Agricultural Experiment Club. This is the name of the original group of students with whom A.B. Graham worked in 1902-1904. The name "Boys' and Girls' Club Work" was used by U.S.D.A. until the adoption of the 4-H Club title and symbol. The possessive form is shown in this book, since that was the title in use in the early 1900s.

Domestic Science — Was a department affiliated with the Agricultural College when Graham came to Ohio State University. The name was changed to *Home Economics* in the 1911-12 academic year. Various titles underwent similar changes at different times in other states.

Ohio State Teachers' Association (O.S.T.A.) — Organized in 1847 this evolved into the *Ohio Education Association* (O.E.A.) which affiliated with the *National Education Association* (N.E.A.) in 1922.

Ohio Teachers' Reading Circle (O.T.R.C.) — Organized in 1883 as a department of O.S.T.A., this was a powerful voice in teacher education with its own Board of Control at the turn of the century. It passed out of existence as insitutions of higher education developed programs for teacher education.

State Commissioner of Common Schools — Established in 1853 by Ohio's second constitutional convention as a position controlled by the Governor and legislature, this was changed after the 1912 constitutional convention to the current politically independent *Superintendent of Public Instruction.*

Superintendent for Agricultural Extension — Graham's title from 1905 to 1914 changed to *Director of Agricultural Extension* with receipt of federal funding. Terminology varied somewhat from state to state. Ohio changed from Agricultural Extension to the *Cooperative Extension Service* in 1963.

United States Department of Agriculture (U.S.D.A.) — This was one of the largest federal departments prior to World War II. It began reporting on various state extension activities in 1907 under its Office of Experiment Stations. In 1915, after the Smith-Lever Act provided federal funding, it established the *States Relations Service* (S.R.S.) which evolved into the *Cooperative Extension Service* (C.E.S.) section in 1923.

Bibliographic Notes

Abbreviations for Manuscript Materials):

Clark County Historical Society (CCHS) File (#.)
National Archives (NA) Record Group (RG) Extension Service, 1907-1943 (33)
Account (#) Drawer (#).
Ohio Historical Society Archives (OHS) Manuscript Collection (MC) Albert B.
Graham (194) Box (#) File (#).
Ohio State University Archives (OSU) Record Group (RG) Albert B. Graham
(40/8) Box (#) File (#).

Introduction

1. Graham notation on newspaper clipping, "Grace Goulder's Ohio," *Cleveland Plain Dealer,* Pictorial Magazine, 23 Sept. 1951, pp. 5-6 (OSU RG 40/8/2/22)
2. *Oliver Brown et. al. v. Board of Education of Topeka,* United States Supreme Court, 17 May 1954.

Chapter 1

This chapter relies heavily on personal manuscript records of A.B. Graham. At the Ohio Historical Society (OHS MC 194) this particularly included "The Story of Joseph A. Graham's Life" (Box 3, Folder 5), "The Biography of My Mother, Esther Pownall-Reeder Graham," (Box 3, Folder 5), "History of the Lena-Conover Community," (Box 3, Folders 1-4) and letter from Graham 2 Feb. 1958 to Joseph and Cecilia Graham, re: burning of farm home (Box 3, Folder 5). At the Ohio State University Archives (OSU RG 40/8) this particularly included "The Story of My Life" by Graham 18 Aug. 1958 (Box 1) and a biographical letter from Graham to Orton Rust of the Clark County Historical Society, 19 Jan. 1950. Among manuscripts in the possession of Helen Graham Baker the authors used a group of Graham's boyhood memories, "Christmas Time," "Wearing Other People's Clothes," My First Train Ride," "Home Newspapers," "My First Circus," "The Old Rain Water Barrel," "Basket Making on the Farm," and "Wild Blue Pigeons."

The U.S. Census, Productions of Agriculture, Schedule 3, 1870, Champaign County, Ohio; Johnson Twp., p. 4, #35 provided specific data about the Graham farm. The U.S. Population Census for 1880, Miami County, Ohio; Brown Twp., pp. 38-40 provided data regarding the Graham family and the Lena-Conover community.

The *Miami Democrat* at Piqua and the *St. Paris New Era* were the newspapers which provided most helpful background regarding community organizations and events during this time period. The *Miami Democrat,* 8 Feb. 1879, p. 3, and 15 Feb. 1879, p. 4, contain accounts of the Graham home fire and Joseph Graham's death.

In addition to the Graham manuscript collections previously cited, Graham's school days are described by George C. Crout in "Albert B. Graham: School Days of a Schoolmaster," *Ohio History,* Vol. 86, (Spring, 1977), pp. 115-126.

Records regarding the Joseph Graham farm are found in the Champaign County Recorders Office Deed Records Vol. L, p. 341; Vol. 46, pp. 452-454; Vol. 54, pp. 354-355; and Mortgage Records Vol. M, p. 137 and Vol. O, p. 266; and in Probate Court Estate Files #O-2545, #10 and #92. J.W. Starr & J.N. Headington, *Atlas of Champaign County, Ohio* (Cincinnati: Strobridge & Co., 1874), p. 41 shows the specific location of the farm in Johnson Township. Records regarding the Esther Graham home in Lena are found in Miami County Deed Records: Vol. 61, p. 357, and Vol. 93, p. 436. A plat map showing survey lot numbers for the village of Lena is found in D.J. Lake, *Atlas of Miami County, Ohio* (Philadelphia: C.O. Titus, Publishers, 1871), p. 59.

For background material several county histories have proven helpful: *The History of Miami County, Ohio* (Chicago: W.H. Beers & Co., 1880), pp. 309-322; *History of Champaign County, Ohio* (Chicago: W.H. Beers & Co., 1881), pp. 438-456; Thomas C. Harbaugh, *Centennial History: Troy, Piqua and Miami County, Ohio* (Chicago: Richmond-Arnold Publishing Co., 1909); Evan P. Middleton, ed., *History of Champaign County, Ohio* (Indianapolis: B.F. Bowen & Co., Inc., 1917) pp. 297-309; Leonard U. Hill, ed., *A History of Miami County, Ohio, 1807-1953* (Columbus: F.J. Herr Printing Co., 1953), pp. 160-163.

Footnotes:

1. Graham manuscript, "The Story of Joseph A. Graham's Life," (OHS MC 194/3/5).
2. U.S. Census of Agriculture, 1870: Ohio, Champaign County, Johnson Township, p. 4, #35.
3. Graham manuscript, "My First Train Ride," (Graham Family collection).
4. Lining out was a common practice before all members of a congregation had hymnals. The minister or leader would read or sing a line and pause for the congregation to sing it before reading the next.
5. Graham manuscript, "History of the Lena-Conover Community" (OHS 194/3/1).
6. Playing marbles for keeps was considered gambling, an offense so serious that two boys in the Lena-Conover community were sent to the state juvenile correction institution for their continued indulgence.
7. Graham manuscript, "History of Lena-Conover Community" (OHS 194/3/2).
8. Miami County teacher examination, 17 May 1884 (OSU RG 40/8/2/44).

Chapter 2

This chapter relies heavily on the *Graham Genealogy, 1759-1946,* a nineteen page typed manuscript by A.B. Graham at the Ohio Historical Society; the box of correspondence used in compiling it and the 116 page Graham family photograph album with handwritten notations by A.B. Graham in the possession of Helen Graham Baker.

References for Archibald and Hannah Graham are the petition filed by Hannah for real estate partition (Bucks County, Pennsylvania Orphans Court, 5 Sept. 1823); obituary for Archibald Graham (Bucks County Historical Society, *Doylestown Democrat,* 5 Aug. 1823); D.A.R Record of Cora Davis Berry, Hastings, Nebraska, and Clara Maria Short, Gambier, Ohio #269330; and *Pennsylvania Archives,* 5th Series, Vol. II, pp. 472-474, and Vol. V, p. 329. Useful maps and background regarding Duer, Graham, Lauer, Reeder, and Pownall family origins are provided in the William H. Davis *History of Bucks County, Pennsylvania* (New York: Lewis Publishing Co., 1905).

The Joseph Graham Bible containing birth and marriage data for his siblings, his marriage to Maria Duer, and the births of their children is in the possession of Helen Graham Baker. Joseph Graham's will and property inventory are included in Champaign County Probate Court Estate Case File O-2545, Joseph and Maria Graham are buried on Lot 225, Fletcher Cemetery, Fletcher, Ohio. *The History of Champaign County, Ohio* (Chicago: W.H. Beers & Co., 1881) contains biographical sketches of his son George D. (pp. 751-752) and nephew Charles Slack (p. 766), son of sister Achsah Graham Slack. *The History of Miami County, Ohio* (Chicago: W.H. Beers & Co., 1880) contains biographical sketches of his brother William Graham (p. 484), son-in-law John Wolcott (p. 501), and various Duer and Anderson relatives. A detailed biographical sketch of William and Clementine (Middleton) Graham descendants is contained in *A Genealogical and Biographical Record of Miami County, Ohio* (Chicago: Lewis Publishing Co., 1900), pp. 594-596.

Graham manuscript sources cited in chapter one regarding Joseph A. and Esther R. Graham also provided data for this chapter. Reeder family sources included U.S. Census Records; 1850 Bucks Co., Pa., Solebury Twp., p. 170, #106; 1860 Miami Co., O., Brown Twp., p. 201, #61; and 1870, Miami Co., O., Brown Twp., p. 252, #68. John S. Reeder's will is recorded in Miami County Probate Court, Will Record, Vol. C, p. 529. A biographical sketch of the John S. Reeder family is included in *The History of Miami County, Ohio,* p. 495. Tombstone and burial records for Joseph A. and Esther R. Graham are found on Lot 225, Fletcher Cemetery.

In addition to the autobiographical sketches cited in chapter 1, the sources for Albert and Maud Graham rely heavily on personal correspondence, photograph inscriptions and manuscripts in the possession of Helen Graham Baker. This includes a biographical sketch of Maud Lauer written by A.B.G. 17 Sept. 1950; correspondence between A.B.G. & M.K.L. prior to their marriage; photographs and inscriptions of Lauer family members; and an eight-page letter from A.B.G. to his three living children 15 Jan. 1948 describing nearly fifty-eight years of marriage, homes lived in, and salary earned. The James D. Lauer family is found in U.S. Census Records; 1870, Preble Co., O., Eaton, p. 272, #106 and 1880, Miami Co., O., Conover, p. 40, #3. Obituaries for A.B. Graham appeared in numerous newspaper, e.g. *Columbus Dispatch,* 15 Jan. 1960, p. 15A; *New York Times,* Vol. 31, #1, 15 Jan. 1960, p. 31; *Piqua Call,* 15 Jan. 1960.

Helen G. Baker and Joseph R. Graham provided autobiographical sketches and have graciously responded to numerous questions regarding their parents, siblings, and children. Biographical sketches of E. Blair Graham and Walter Graham written by their father are in the possession of Helen Baker. An obituary for E.B. Graham appeared in the *Columbus Dispatch,* 29 Apr. 1955, Sec. B, p. 5.

Footnotes:

1. Graham, Commencement address, "Fame," Lena-Conover School, June 19, 1885 (OSU RG 40/8/1/22).
2. Champaign Co. Recorder, Deed Record, Vol. L, p. 341.
3. *Pennsylvania Archives,* 5th Series, Vol. II, pp. 471-474.
4. Letter, Esther H. Anderson to Bucks County, Pennsylvania relatives, 25 Oct. 1830 (OHS MC 194/3/2).
5. *Ibid.,* 23.Dec. 1834.
6. *Official Roster of the Soldiers of the State of Ohio in the War of the Rebellion, 1861-1866* (Cincinnati: Ohio Valley Press, 1888), Vol. 7, p. 224.
7. *Military History of Ohio* (New York: H.H. Hardesty, Publisher, 1886, Miami County Edition), pp. 10-11.
8. Champaign Co. Probate Court, Estate Case File O-2545.
9. Champaign Co. Recorder, Deed Record, Vol. 46, pp. 452-454.
10. Champaign Co. Probate Court, Estate Case File #10.
11. Letter, Graham to A.E. Bowman, Extension Director, Wyoming, 3 May 1927 (OSU RG 40/8/1/24).
12. Miami Co. Recorder, Deed Record, Vol. 95, p. 38.
13. Ibid., Vol. 99, p. 332.
14. These examples and those in the two succeeding paragraphs are taken from issues of *The Press-Republic* printed at Springfield, Ohio between October 1900 and June 1901, during Graham's first year as Springfield Township Superintendent.
15. Letter, Graham to Rev. Chas. O. Gill, 104 N. 3rd St., Columbus, Ohio, 29 Jan. 1915 (Graham Family collection).
16. Letter, Graham to Harry Manning, Minister, Lena Baptist Church, 2 Apr. 1944 (Graham Family collection).
17. During a six month period in 1903 Graham's journal mentions attendance at the 3rd Lutheran, 1st Presbyterian, Blessed Hope Baptist, Clifton Ave. M.E., Jewish Synagogue, High St. Methodist, 2nd Presbyterian, 1st Lutheran, Universalist, 3rd Presbyterian, and Episcopal congregations (CCHS, Folder #4331).
18. *Official Roster of Ohio Soldiers, Sailors and Marines in the World War, 1917-1918* (Columbus: F.J. Heer Printing Co., 1926) Vol. VII, p. 6363.

Chapter 3

Graham's teaching certificates for Miami, Champaign, and Shelby counties for the years from 1884 to 1899 show the scores attained and subjects in which he was certified. (OSU RG 40/8/2/44). A seven page letter from Graham to his three surviving children written 15 Jan. 1948 (Graham Family collection) describes his various teaching positions, salary, and family living arrangements.

Background information on Johnson Township schools is contained in Evan P. Middleton, ed., *History of Champaign County, Ohio* (Indianapolis: B.F. Bowen & Co., Inc., 1917, Vol. I), pp. 297-309, and Adams Township schools on pp. 320-333. The J.W. Starr & J.N. Headington, *Atlas of Champaign County, Ohio* (Cincinnati: Strobridge & Co., 1874), p. 41 shows the location of Carmony School in Section 31,

SE 1/4, and p. 43 the location of Cook School in Section 26, NW 1/4. A history of
Carmony School was published by retired editor L.E. Brown in the *St. Paris
News-Dispatch*, 14 Sept. 1933, p. 5.

L.H. Everts, *Illustrated Historical Atlas, Miami County, Ohio, 1875* (Evans-
ville, Ind.: Unigraphic, Inc., 1973) p. 47 and *The County of Miami, Ohio — Imperial
Atlas and Art Folio* (Richmond, Ind.: Rerick Brothers, 1894), Brown Township
show the location of Allen's School(#6) and later Lena-Conover School in Section
1, SW 1/4, and New Hope School (#2) in Section 24, NE 1/4.

Background on Greene Township schools is provided in *History of Shelby
County, Ohio* (Philadelphia: R. Sutton & Co., 1883, reprinted in 1968 by Shelby
County Historical Society), p. 182 and in A.B.C. Hitchcock, *History of Shelby
County, Ohio* (Chicago: Richmond-Arnold Publishing Co., 1913), p. 266. The *Atlas
& Directory of Shelby County, Ohio* (Cleveland: The American Atlas Co., 1900), p.
9 shows Brush School (#1) in Section 23, SW 1/4.

Annual Reports of the Ohio Commissioner of Common Schools for the period
between 1885 and 1895 provide statistical data regarding teacher experience and
salaries. Specific data for each county varies from year to year but examples of
examination questions and numbers of certificates granted and applicants
rejected are available for both Champaign and Miami Counties. James J. Burns,
Educational History of Ohio (Columbus: Historical Publishing Co., 1905) provides
a broad perspective regarding early educational developments in Ohio.

The Graham manuscripts are supplemented by background data on National
Normal University taken from Karl J. Kay, *History of National Normal University* (Wilmington, O.: Wilmington College, 1929) and *32nd Catalogue of Teachers
and Students* (Lebanon, O.: National Normal School, 1887).

More complete sources regarding country schools are cited for chapter seven,
but Fletcher B. Dresslar, *Rural Schoolhouses and Grounds* (Washington, D.C.:
U.S. Bureau of Education, Bulletin No. 12, 1914) and Wayne E. Fuller, *The Old
Country School: The Story of Rural Education in the Middle West* (Chicago: The
University of Chicago Press, 1982) provide helpful context in which to view
Graham's experience during this decade.

Footnotes:
1. A.B. Graham, "Beautify the Country Schools," *Agricultural Extension Bulletin*, Vol. 2, #1 (Sept. 1906), p. 12.
2. Leroy D. Brown, *Thirty-Second Annual Report of the State Commissioner of
Common Schools* (Columbus: 1885), pp.88-89.
3. *Ibid.*, pp. 220-221.
4. Graham manuscript, "My First Job" (OSU RG 40/8/2/27).
5. Brown, *1886 Ohio School Report*, p. 12.
6. National Normal University certificate for Albert B. Graham showing
grades in subjects completed (OSU RG 40/8/2/38).
7. Certification from Marguerite Mitchell, Registrar, Wilmington College, 24
Feb. 1942 *(OSU RG 40/8/2/44)*.
8. F.L.B., "One Night in Lebanon, Scenes and Incidents in the City of Cedars,"
The Western Star, Lebanon, Ohio, Thursday, 23 Aug. 1888, p. 1.

Chapter 4

A folder on Terre Haute School is included in the Graham manuscripts (OSU RG 40/8/2/45), and Middleton's *History of Champaign County,* pp. 542-546, contains background on Mad River Township schools. This chapter relies significantly, however, on local newspapers during the 1896-1900 period. The Republican *Urbana Citizen & Gazette,* published semi-weekly, offers detailed reports of educational meetings, with summaries of speeches and names of those in attendance or elected to leadership roles. The weekly *Champaign Democrat* was more likely to carry Graham's lengthy educational editorials on current issues, sometimes accompanied by photographs, most unusual for a paper of its size in this time period. While there is much repetition between these and the St. Paris papers, most families probably subscribed to only one and the Champaign County teachers obviously gave each the same information. During the period from Sept. 1897 to June 1900 when Graham served as educational editor, columns did not carry his byline, but columns reporting a speech at local teachers' meetings quoted the speaker and those written by someone other than Graham are clearly identified, (e.g. "The Kindergarten, Work and Philosophy," by Miss Mabel Smith, *Urbana Citizen & Gazette,* 7 Apr. 1898.) Because the majority of the educational columns were written by Graham without a byline, they have received little notice, but his style is clearly recognizable, and their existence demonstrates how early Graham was speaking out on nationally recognized educational issues.

Background on the National Education Association in this time period has been gleaned from Edgar B. Wesley, *N.E.A.: The First Hundred Years, The Building of the Teaching Profession* (New York: Harper & Brothers, 1957) and contemporary *Reports of Proceedings of N.E.A. Annual Meetings.*

Background on Ohio educational issues during this time period has been derived largely from *Annual Reports of the Commissioner of Common Schools* and from the *Ohio Educational Monthly,* the official organ of the Ohio State Teachers Association, during 1896-1900. The Ohio organization is described in Harvey C. Minnich, *Centennial History of the Ohio Education Association* (Columbus: Ohio Education Association, 1947).

Legislation relating to pupil transportation, the forerunner of consolidation, is summarized in Nelson L. Bossing, "The History of Educational Legislation in Ohio from 1851 to 1925," *Ohio Archaeological and Historical Society Publications,* Vol. 39, pp. 78-399, and A.C. Monahan, *Consolidation of Rural Schools and Transportation of Pupils at Public Expense* (Washington, D.C.: U.S. Bureau of Education, Bulletin No. 30, 1914).

Footnotes:

1. Educational column, A.B. Graham, ed., *Champaign Democrat,* 16 Nov. 1899, p. 1.
2. Ginn & Co. advertisement, *Ohio Teacher,* March, 1900.
3. Series of articles on Mad River Township schools, *Urbana Citizen,* 23 March 1938 (OSU RG 40/8/2/36).
4. Terre Haute News, *Champaign Democrat,* 4 May 1899.
5. Interview with A.C. Neff, *The Springfield Sun,* 30 Dec. 1935 (OSU RG 40/8/2/2).
6. Terre Haute News, *Champaign Democrat,* 16 March 1899.

7. *Ibid.*; 30 March 1899.
8. Report on Champaign County Teachers' Insitute, *Champaign Citizen & Gazette*, 6 Sept. 1897.
9. Educational columns, A.B. Graham, ed., *Champaign Democrat*, 14 Oct. 1897.
10. *Ibid.*, 23 Feb. 1899.
11. *Ibid.*, 31 Aug. 1899.
12. Lewis D. Bonebrake, *46th Annual Report of the Commissioner of Common Schools* (Columbus: J.L. Trauger, State Printers, 1900), pp. 334 & 346-355.
13. Terre Haute News, *Champaign Democrat,* 29 June 1899.

Chapter 5

Materials relating to Supt. Graham's work in Springfield Township are deposited in the archives of the Ohio Historical Society, The Ohio State University, and the Clark County Historical Society. The most complete and carefully organized collection of records regarding the agricultural experiment club is in the Ohio Historical Society Manuscript Collection #194, Box 1, which was organized by Graham personally after his retirement with staff assistance from the Ohio Cooperative Extension Service 4-H Club office.

The most complete data regarding Springfield Township Schools during Graham's tenure are his 1902 and 1904 annual reports. The first is a typescript manuscript dated 24 Oct. 1902 (OHS MC 194/1/9). The latter was printed with photographs when Graham resigned to go into the Springfield City system late in November 1904 (OHS MC 194/1/5). The latter is also available at OSU and CCHS. A concise summary of Graham's work in Springfield Twp. was incorporated in James J. Burns, *Educational History of Ohio* (Columbus: Historical Publishing Co., 1905) pp. 206-208 as an example of the role of the township superintendent at the turn of the century.

The most valuable material at the Clark County Historical Society is the original journal Graham kept as a record for his monthly and annual reports to parents and the school board. Folder #4331 contains these pocket sized journals for the period Sept. 1900 through Nov. 1904. There are no entries during the summer months and on weekends. Entries were usually made only for school related meetings. These are not diaries of personal or family activities, just his daily schedule and data for official reports. When quotations are given in the text by date without footnote, they are taken from these journals.

Background on the City of Springfield, Springfield Township, and Clark County has been taken primarily from Benjamin F. Prince, ed., *The Centennial Celebration of Springfield, Ohio* (Springfield: Springfield Publishing Co., 1901); William M. Rockel, *20th Century History of Springfield and Clark County, Ohio* (Chicago: Richmond & Arnold Publishers, 1908); and from the *Springfield Press-Republic* for the 1900-1905 period, which is available both at the Ohio Historical Society and the Clark County Historical Society. Many of the Springfield newspapers for this period are no longer available.

Background on Ohio schools and teachers during this time period has been taken primarily from annual reports of the Commissioners of Common Schools, 1900 to 1905, and from the *Ohio Educational Monthly*. Vol. 50 to 54, the official organ of the Ohio State Teachers Association, edited by O.T. Corson, Ohio Commissioner of Common Schools from 1892 to 1898. Local educational issues and leaders have been gleaned from J.R. Clarke, *A Semi-Centennial History of the Western Ohio Superintendents' and Principals' Roundtable, 1883-1940* (Columbus: J.R. Clarke, 1941).

Footnotes:
1. Graham Report, 1902.
2. Lewis D. Bonebrake, *47th Annual Report of the State Commissioner of Common Schools to the Governor of Ohio for the Year Ending August 31, 1900* (Cincinnati: C.J. Krehbiel Press, 1901).
3. *Ibid.*, pp. 42 & 48.
4. Rockel, *20th Century History*. pp. 309-317.
5. Prince, *Centennial Celebration*. p. 93.
6. Bonebrake, *Report*. 1900, p. 120.
7. Comparison of October enrollments in 1900, 1901 and 1902 in Graham Report,1902.
8. Graham's Journal for 1900-01 contains in the back his handwritten enrollment, naming students by grade in each district. The figures total: #1, 20 (1-8); #2, 31 (1-8); #3, 23 (1-8); #4, 35 (1-8); #5, 35 (1-4) and 21 (5-8); #6, 40 (1-8); #7, 34 (1-4) and 28 (5-8); #8, 31 (1-8); #9 47 (1-2) and 51 (3-5) and 22 (6-8); #10, 40 (1-4) and 23 (5-8); #11, 45 (1-8); #12, 34 (1-8). During subsequent years as many as nineteen classrooms were in use and pupils were transported from one subdistrict to another.
9. Graham in Burns, *Educational History*, p. 206.
10. Graham Journal, 4 Sept. 1900.
11. Graham Report, 1904, p. 36
12. Graham Journal, 21 Dec. 1903.
13. Graham Report, 1904, p. 31. An itemized list of these books by subject and grade level is contained in A.B. Graham, "Rural School Libraries, " *The Tenth Yearbook of the National Society For the Study of Education* (Chicago: University of Chicago Press, 1911), Part II, pp. 34-43.
14. Graham Journal, 28 Feb. 1902. For status on school libraries in Ohio see Charles B. Galbraith, "The State Library and Public Schools," *Ohio Educational Monthly,* Vol. 46 (Sept. 1897) pp. 468-472 and Vol. 49 (Oct. 1900) pp. 490-495 and Frederic D. Aldrich, *The School Library in Ohio with Speical Emphasis on its Legislative History* (New York: Scarecrow Press, 1959), pp. 86-95.
15. Prince, *Centennial Celebration,* p. 119.
16. The Ohio Township Superintendents Association was formed in 1893 as a forum for the pioneers in this position to exchange ideas. *O.S.T.A. Proceedings* in the late 1890s suggest a membership between 50 and 100.
17. Graham Journal, 19 Feb. 1904. Since Ohio did not have an elected State Board of Education until 1955, it is probable that Graham's entry referred to the State Board of School Examiners, a very influential group of educators.
18. Principal's Certificate, Second Class (3 yr.), Springfield City Board of Examiners, 28 Aug. 1902 (OSU RG 40/8/2).
19. Graham Journal, 1 Mar. 1901.
20. *Springfield Press-Republic,* 5 June 1903.
21. Graham Report, 1904, p. 33.

22. Poem by Fern Haley, Possum School (OHS MC 194/1/23).
23. Graham Report, 1904, p. 35.
24. Graham Journal, 8 Apr. 1904.
25. Graham Report, 1904, p. 41.
26. *Ibid.*
27. Graham Report, 1904.
28. Graham Journal, 15 Jan. 1902.
29. Graham's Journal for 1902 shows the following Saturday entries: Jan. 4, Examination day for teachers; Jan. 11, no entry; Jan. 18, AM joint meeting at New Carlisle, PM regular teachers meeting; Jan. 25, Twp. Supts. Assn.; Feb. 1, no entry; Feb. 8, no entry; Feb. 15, regular teachers meeting; Feb. 22, Twp. Supts. Assn.; Mar. 1, Co. Teachers Exam.; Mar. 8, no entry; Mar. 15, no entry; Mar. 22, regular teachers meeting; Mar. 29, Co. Teachers meeting. It appears that the first Saturday of the month was the regular day for examinations for teacher candidates, the third Saturday the regular meeting of the Springfield Township teachers, and the fourth Saturday the county teachers or township superintendents meeting. Both Graham and members of the original club described Saturday meetings, but Graham was obviously being scrupulous in citing Jan. 15, 1902, the earliest date for which he could provide a written record as the organization date for the agricultural club.
30. L.H. Bailey letter to Graham, 21 Jan. 1903 (OSU RG 40/8/1).
31. *Springfield Press-Republic,* 26 Jan. 1903.
32. *Ohio Teacher,* Vol. 25 (Mar. 1905), pp. 296-297.
33. George M. Barmann, "4-H Club Jubilee Points Up Value of the Vast Movement," *Pittsburgh Courier,* (Magazine Section), 2 Aug. 1952, p. 6.
34. An undated Graham manuscript (OSU RG 40/8/1/11) names 69 members, 5 of them girls, of the 1902 "boys' and girls' agricultural club." The names are listed by school district with eleven of the twelve township schools represented and four boys from outside the township. The "girls' garden club" for 1902 lists 18 members, four of them boys. Since three boys and one girl belonged to both groups, it appears that 83 individuals were participating by the spring planting season of 1902. This basically coincides with Graham's later references to 85 members in the 1902 group, the difference is probably due to the duplicate membership between the two groups or the discovery of an omission or two. In 1904 agricultural club lists throughout the state were sent to Ohio State University for the first time for the Ohio Federation of Rural School Agricultural Clubs. The Springfield Township club listed 101 members including Elliott Goodfellow, president, and Abbie LeFevre, secretary (OHS MC 194/2/1). The names suggest that 33 of these members were girls. No official list has been found for 1903, but lists for specific meetings include additional names, and it is almost certain that additional members participated during that season. Thirty-nine of the 1902 club members were also listed in 1904, so with duplications eliminated, the best available evidence provides the names of at least 145 individuals who were members of the Springfield Township agricultural club during Graham's leadership.
35. Letter, Graham to J.R. Clarke, 30 Mar. 1917 (OSU RG 40/8/2/1). This letter was written near the time that Boys' and Girls' Club Work in Ohio reverted from the Board of Agriculture to the university and W.B. Palmer was given leadership. Clarke was an agricultural supervisor with the state department

of education and had written Graham a few days earlier requesting information on the history of the Springfield Township club. In his reply Graham
indicated that 88 members had signed up to participate before the close of the
1902 school year, evidently not eliminating duplicate memberships.

36. U.S. Population Census for Springfield Township, Clark County, Ohio enu-
     merated 387 households, 42 of them black, in June 1900.
37. Graham Journal, 7 Oct. 1903.
38. Letter, William McK. Vance to Graham, 6 Nov. 1903 (OSU RG 40/8/1/28).
39. Graham Journal, 15 Jan. 1904.
40. Graham Journal, 3 Feb. 1904.
41. Letter, Homer C. Price to A.C. True, Office of Experiment Stations, U.S.D.A.,
     22 Nov. 1904 (OSU RG 40/8/1/28). The membership lists for 15 of these
     groups and the officers of the 16th are in (OHS MC 194/2/1) and were
     included in the mimeograph, *Ohio Golden Anniversary, 1902-1952*, by the
     Ohio 4-H Club Office.

Chapter 6

Data on the development of agricultural clubs in Ohio are contained in
Thomas F. Hunt, *Rural School Agriculture* (Columbus: Ohio State University
Bulletin, 1903), Series 4, No. 22 and Homer C. Price, *Agricultural Clubs in Rural
Schools* (Columbus: Ohio State University Bulletin, 1904), Series 8, No. 10, both of
which rely heavily on significant contributions from Graham (OHS MC
194/1/11).

A.B. Graham Manuscript Collection 194, Box 1 in the Ohio Historical Society
archives contains numerous examples of various report forms for the Ohio Federation of Rural School Agricultural Clubs, membership lists for the 1904-05 period,
and letters to Graham from participating students. Most of the correspondence
between A.B. Graham and Homer C. Price is deposited in the Ohio State University archives Record Group 40/8, Box 1.

Issues from the monthly *Agricultural Student* published at Ohio State and the
bi-monthly *Ohio Farmer* published in Columbus for the autumn of 1904 and
winter/spring of 1905 provide background on the viewpoint of the agricultural
press regarding boys' and girls' agricultural clubs and the evolution of an agricultural extension department at the university.

The development of the 4-H club movement throughout the country is sum-
marized in Franklin M. Reck, *The 4-H Story: A History of 4-H Club Work* (Ames:
Iowa State University Press, 1951) pp. 3-47. The more recent Thomas and Marilyn
Wessel, *4-H: An American Idea, 1900-1980* (Washington, D.C.: National 4-H
Foundation, 1981) relies on Reck for historical development of the movement.
Roy V. Scott, *The Reluctant Farmer, The Rise of Agricultural Extension to 1914*
(Urbana: University of Illinois Press, 1970) provides helpful analysis regarding
conceptual development of boys' and girls' club work. A.B. Graham and J. Phil
Campbell, "Boys' and Girls' Agricultural Clubs," *Agricultural History*, Vol. 15,
(Apr. 1941), pp. 65-71 and correspondence from the 1920s and 30s between A.B.
Graham and other 4-H pioneers such as L.H. Bailey, O.J. Kern, O.H. Benson, and
Jessie Field Shambaugh (OSU RG 40/8/1) were most helpful in placing events in
perspective.

Footnotes:
1. Graham Report, 1904, p. 38.
2. Letter, Graham to Guy L. Noble, National Committee for Boys' and Girls' Club Work, 25 Oct. 1951 (OSU RG 40/8/1/24).
3. *Journal of Proceedings and Addresses of the 41st Annual Meeting* (Minneapolis: National Education Association, 1902), p. 55.
4. Letters to Graham from Agricultural Club members (OHS MC 194/1/23).
5. Letter, Price to Graham, 25 Sept. 1903 (OHS MC 194/1/9).
6. Letter, Graham to Price, 11 Feb. 1904 (OSU RG 40/8/2/16).
7. Agricultural Club Membership Records (OHS MC 194/1/8). The discrepancy between these records and Dean Price's report to Washington in Nov. 1904 of 664 members in 16 clubs is further evidence of the fluid status of membership during early stages of the organization.
8. Testimonial advertisement, Ginn & Co., Publishers, 219 E. Town St., Columbus, Ohio (OHS MC 194/1/4).
9. *The Agricultural Student,* Vol. XI, #1 (Oct. 1904), #2 (Nov. 1904), #3 (Dec. 1904) (OHS MC 194/1/3).
10. *Ohio Farmer,* Vol. CVII (4 Feb. 1905), p. 24.
11. Letter, Price to Graham, 19 Apr. 1904 offers $600 "while working for your degree" (OHS MC 194/2/16).
12. Graham Journal, 28 Nov. 1904 and Rockel, *History of Springfield,* p. 462.
13. Letter, Graham to his children Blair, Helen, and Joseph, 15 Jan. 1948, (Graham Family collection).
14. *O.S.U. Trustee Proceedings,* 13 Apr. 1905, p. 55.
15. Prince, *Springfield Centennial,* pp. 116-119.
16. Letters to Graham from Agricultural Club members (OHS MC 194/1/12-15).
17. Letter, P.G. Holden to Graham, 3 Apr. 1934 (OSU RG 40/8/3/10).

Chapter 7

Primary resources for this chapter are the *Annual Reports of the Board of Trustees of the Ohio State University to the Governor of Ohio* for the years ending June 30, 1904 through June 30, 1914, (Springfield, Ohio: Springfield Publishing Co.) and the *Record of Proceedings of the Board of Trustees of the Ohio State University,* for the same period (Columbus: The Champlin Press). For descriptive background the *History of The Ohio State University,* edited by Thomas C. Mendenhall is invaluable. The years from 1870 to 1910 were authored by Alexis Cope as volume one (Columbus: The Ohio State University Press, 1920) and the years from 1910 to 1925 by Osman C. Hooper as volume two (Columbus: The Ohio State University Press, 1926). More specific histories which provide insight to the university are William A. Kinnison, *Building Sullivant's Pyramid* (Columbus: The Ohio State University Press, 1970) and H.G. Good, *The Rise of the College of Education of the Ohio State University* (Columbus: The Ohio State University College of Education, 1960).

The most comprehensive sources of information regarding national educational programs and policies are the *Journals of Proceedings and Addresses of the Annual Meetings of the National Education Association* for the period from 1895 to 1915. Several committee reports of particular value to this biography are footnoted individually. Edgar B. Wesley, *NEA: The First Hundred Years, The*

Building of the Teaching Profession (New York: Harper & Brothers, 1957) gives valuable insight into perceptions of professionalism during Graham's period of active committee participation.

The most helpful analyses of country schools written during the period Graham was at Ohio State are probably O.J. Kern, *Among Country Schools* (Boston: Ginn & Co., 1906) and Mabel Carney, *Country Life and the Country School* (Chicago: Row, Peterson & Co., 1912) although both strongly advocate the conventional wisdom of professional educators. A.C. True, "Some Problems of the Rural Common Schools," *Yearbook of Agriculture* (Washington, D.C.: U.S. Department of Agriculture, 1901) pp. 133-154 provides an agricultural perspective. Wayne E. Fuller, *The Old Country School: The Story of Rural Education in the Middle West* (Chicago: The University of Chicago Press, 1982) gives a broader historical perspective although it is nostalgic and idealistic regarding local control of schools.

Specific resources which provide helpful background on the consolidation issue which deeply concerned Graham are A.C. Monahan, *Consolidation of Rural Schools and Transportation of Pupils at Public Expense* (Washington D.C.: United States Bureau of Education, #30, 1914); Julius B. Arp, *Rural Education and the Consolidated School* (Yonkers-on-Hudson, N.Y.: World Book Co., 1920); Clayton S. Ellsworth, "The Coming of Rural Consolidated Schools to the Ohio Valley, 1892-1912," *Agricultural History*, XXX (Apr. 1956), p. 119-128.

The earliest useful references relating to junior high schools other than N.E.A. reports are G. Vernon Bennet, *The Junior High School* (Baltimore: Warwick & York, Inc., 1919) and Thomas H. Briggs, *The Junior High School* (Boston: Houghton Mifflin Co., 1920). The Ohio Department of Education first printed a manual of guidelines relating to junior high schools in 1920.

Nelson L. Bossing, "The History of Educational Legislation in Ohio from 1851 to 1925," *Ohio Archaeological and Historical Society Publications*, XXXIX, pp. 78-399 provides a useful summary of dates and legislation from which to access General Assembly arecords. Frederic D. Aldrich, *The School Library in Ohio with Special Emphasis on its Legislative History* (New York: The Scarecrow Press, 1959) provides a similar background on this issue of special concern to Graham. While much has been written, William L. Bowers, *The Country Life Movement in America, 1900-1920* (Port Washington, N.Y.: National University Publications, Kennikat Press, 1974) provides an excellent overview of this movement.

The annual reports of Ohio's Commissioners of Common Schools, Edmund A. Jones, 1905-1909; Frank Miller, 1909-1911; and John W. Zeller, 1911-1913 are primary resources for statistical information, background on issues, and participation of Ohio State University faculty in county teachers' insitutes. Burns, *Educational History of Ohio* cited in chapter 5 also provides invaluable perspective for this chapter.

Bound originals of *The Agricultural College Extension Bulletin,* beginning with Volume I, Number 1 in October 1905 are in the Education Library of the Ohio State University. These include Graham's widely reprinted "Centralized Schools in Ohio," "Township High Schools of Ohio," and "The Country Schools of Ohio."

Footnotes:
1. Graham, "Centralized Schools in Ohio," *Extension Bulletin*, Vol. 1, No. 5, (Feb. 1906) p. 16.

2. Letter, William O. Thompson to Graham, 25 Jan. 1905 (OSU RG 40/8/1/26).
3. Letter, Homer C. Price to Graham, 1 Feb. 1905 (OSU RG 40/8/2/16).
4. *O.S.U. Trustees Proceedings,* June 30, 1904 to July 1, 1905, pp. 44-45 & 55.
5. Letter, Graham to Price, 2 Feb. 1905 (OSU RG 40/8/2/16).
6. A.B. Graham, "Elementary Agriculture," *Ohio Educational Monthly,* Vol. 54 (June 1905), pp. 290-295, and "Should Agriculture be Made a Part of the Course of Study for Country Schools?", the paper presented to O.S.T.A. on 27 June, (July 1905), pp. 363-367.
7. Statistics in this section are taken from the annual reports of university administrators presented through the Board of Trustees, June 30, 1904; *34th Report.* Descriptive background is drawn from the *History of the Ohio State University* edited by T.C. Mendenhall, primarily from the first volume written by Alexis Cope, who was serving as Secretary to the Board of Trustees when Graham came to the university.
8. O.S.U. Trustees *34th Report,* and O.S.U. College of Agriculture and Domestic Science, *Bulletin for 1905-06,* Series 9, No. 12.
9. In addition to the report and history cited above, a copy of the *Dedication of Townshend Hall,* (Columbus: Champlin Printing Co., 12 January 1898) is available at the Ohio State University library. See also, Alfred C. True, *A History of Agricultural Education in the United States, 1785-1925,* U.S. Department of Agriculture Misc. Pub. #36, 1929, pp.72-73 & 225.
10. O.S.U. Trustees, *34th Report,* 1905, pp. 24-25.
11. *Ibid.,* p. 19
12. *O.S.U. Trustees, Proceedings,* 30 June 1905, p. 35.
13. Memorandum, Graham to Thompson, 2 July 1905, "A General Plan for Agricultural Extension," reproduced as a two-page mimeograph, May 1957, for Agricultural Education Course 526 (OSU RG 40/8/3/15).
14. O.S.U. Trustees, *44th Report,* 1914, p. 66. For an analysis of the influence of the extension bulletin see also the *Report to the Governor of Ohio by Ohio State School Survey Commission,* Horace L. Brittain, Director (Columbus: F.J. Heer Printing Co., 1914), pp.251-252.
15. *Commissioner's Reports,* 1905-1913. The annual reports during this time period contain a complete listing of teachers' institute speakers arranged alphbetically by counties. During his tenure at Ohio State Graham addressed institutes representing city and village districts as well as some of Ohio's most rural counties: Carroll, Clermont, Coshocton, Darke, Erie, Geauga, Jackson, Lake, Logan, Medina, Meigs, Miami, Monroe, Pike, Putnam, Seneca, Stark, Trumbull, Van Wert, Vinton, Wayne, Wood, and Wyandot.
16. O.S.U. Lecturers at County Teachers' Institutes:

	1905	1906	1907	1908	1909
W. W. Boyd	2	4	3	-	-
J. V. Denney	1	3	1	1	2
A. B. Graham	3	3	6	3	6
D. R. Major	1	-	1	-	-
W. O. Thompson	-	-	1	3	1

17. "Teachers' Institute," *Bellefontaine Examiner,* 30 Aug. 1907, p. 8, Graham was an administrative member of the university, not an academic faculty member, but such distinctions were lost on local reporters who often referred to local principals and superintendents by the title "Professor."

18. *Extension Bulletin,* Vol. 1, No. 2, p. 7.
19. *Extension Bulletin,* Vol. 1, No. 2, p. 10.
20. *Extension Bulletin,* Vol. 1, No. 3, p. 14.
21. *Extension Bulletin,* Vol. 1, No. 6, p. 12.
22. *Extension Bulletin,* Vol. 1, No. 3, p. 14.
23. A.B. Graham, "Of What Use to Plants are Roots?" *Ohio Educational Monthly,* 55 (Oct. 1906), pp. 565-567, and "Relation of Air and Heat to Soil," (Dec. 1906) pp. 693-695.
24. A.B. Graham, "Nature Study in Agriculture," *Ohio Educational Monthly,* 55 (Sept. 1906), pp. 513-516.
25. W. O. Thompson, "The State and Higher Education in Ohio," speech to the Allied Education Association, 28 Dec. 1905, O.S.U. Trustees, *35th Report,* Vol. X, Supplement No. 5, pp. 26+.
26. "Summer Term, 1906," *O.S.U. Bulletin,* Vol. X, No. 5, Jan. 1906.
27. O.S.U. Trustees, *36th Report,* pp. 29-30
28. *O.S.U. Bulletin,* Vol. XI, (Apr. 1907), p. 5.
29. H.G. Good, *The Rise of the College of Education of the Ohio State University,* (Columbus: The Ohio State University College of Education, 1960).
30. "Report of the Committee on Instruction in Agriculture," A.C. True, Chairman, *A.A.A.C.E.S. Proceedings,* 1912, pp. 19-42.
31. O.S.U. Trustees, *47th Report,* p. 80.
32. A.C. True, "Some Problems of the Rural Common School," U.S. Department of Agriculture, *Yearbook of Agriculture* (Washington, D.C.: Government Printing Office, 1901), pp. 133-155.
33. Wayne E. Fuller, *The Old Country School, The Story of Rural Education in the Middle West* (Chicago: The University of Chicago Press, 1982).
34. "Report of the Committee of Twelve on Rural Schools," to the National Council of Education *N.E.A. Proceedings,* (Milwaukee: July 1897, pp. 385-583) p. 424.
35. Nelson L. Bossing, "The History of Educational Legislation in Ohio From 1851 to 1925," *Ohio Archaeological and Historical Society Publications,* XXXIX, pp. 78-399.
36. A.C. Monahan, *Consolidation of Rural Schools and Transportation of Pupils at Public Expense* (Washington, D.C.: U.S. Bureau of Education, Bulletin No. 30, 1914).
37. A.B. Graham, "Centralization of Rural Schools," *Ohio Teacher,* XXIII (Oct. 1902), pp. 67-70.
38. A.B. Graham, "Centralized Schools in Ohio," *Extension Bulletin,* Vol. 1, No. 5, pp. 21-22.
39. Commissioner Jones in his annual reports was recording 58 consolidations in 1904, 101 in 1905, and 160 in 1906. There is some inconsistency in the use of the terms "centralized" and "consolidated", but some early educators, including Graham, used "centralized" to describe a planned school at a central location in the township and "consolidated" to describe abandonment of an existing school and transportation of pupils to another nearby school.
40. A.B. Graham, "Centralized Schools in Ohio," *Extension Bulletin,* Vol. 1, No. 5, p. 18
41. O.J. Kern, "The Consolidated School and the New Agriculture," an address

to the Department of Superintendence, *N.E.A. Proceedings*, Chicago, 1907, pp. 277-279.

42. Editorial, *Ohio Teacher*, June 1906.
43. Monahan, *op. cit.*
44. Mabel Carney, *Country Life and the Country School* (Chicago: Row, Peterson & Co., 1912).
45. O.S.U. Trustees, *44th Report*, p. 65
46. A.E. Winship, editorial, "A.B. Graham's Remarkable Work," *Journal of Education*, LXX (Dec. 1909) p. 637.
47. A.B. Graham, "Centralized Schools in Ohio," *Ohio Teacher*, XXVI (June 1906), pp.486-490.
48. A.B. Graham, "Township High Schools of Ohio," *Extension Bulletin*, Vol. III, No. 6.
49. A.B. Graham, "The Country Schools of Ohio," *Extension Bulletin*, Vol. VIII, No. 2, Supplement No. 1.
50. E.A. Jones, *54th Ohio School Report*, 1907, pp. 20-21 and A.B. Graham, "Early Boys and Girls Club Exhibits," *1952 Ohio State Fair Junior Division Premium List*, pp. 31-32 (OHS MC 194/1/33).
51. A.B. Graham, "Rural School Problems," *Ohio Educational Monthly*, 56 (June 1907), pp. 279-286 featuring L.D. Brouse, West Elkton; C.B. Stoner, Mt. Gilead; J.J. Richeson, Lee's Creek; William Walter, Lancaster; Ed A Zinninger, Canton; J.W. Moore, Leetonia; Ralph Lockman, Mt. Vernon; F.E. Cunningham , Steubenville; A.W. Shinn, Bartlett; A.B. Jones, Waldo.
52. "Report of the Committee on an Equal Division of the Twelve Years in the Public Schools Between the District and High Schools," *N.E.A. Proceedings*, Los Angeles, July 8-12, 1907, pp. 705-710. Further discussion of this report occurred at the Cleveland meeting in 1908. Photographs of the five committee members appear on a reprint titled, *Report of The Committee on Junior High Schools*, printed by L.E. Brown of St. Paris, Ohio, in July 1932.
53. City of Columbus, "Annual Report of the Board of Education for the Year ending Aug. 31, 1909", pp. 29 & 46. Alma Jagsch, "Some Significant Events in the History of Public Education in the Nation, State and Community," a report prepared by teachers of West Junior High School, Columbus, Ohio, Dec. 1935 (OHS P.A. Box 124, No. 5).
54. *N.E.A. Proceedings*, Boston, July 2-8, 1910, pp. 480-483.
55. *Extension Bulletin*, Vol. 1, No. 4, p. 15.

Chapter 8

Like the preceding chapter, this one relies heavily on the annual reports of the Ohio State University trustees. These include statistical as well as narrative reports and it was not unusual for Supt. Graham, Dean Price, and Pres. Thompson to include facts about agricultural extension, or for all three of them to comment upon its results within the same annual report.

President Thompson's papers in the Ohio State University Archives contain a file (Record Group 3/e/2-#1) for the period Oct. 1910 to Apr. 1915 of correspondence, reports, and news clippings relating to the Agricultural Commission and the removal of Dean Homer C. Price from the College of Agriculture.

A.B. Graham personally prepared two manuscripts which are invaluable in understanding the development of agricultural extension during its early years.

The first, entitled "Some Agricultural Extension Firsts," was written shortly after his retirement and presented during the Ohio 25th Anniversary celebration 10 Oct. 1939 (OSU RG 40/8/3/2). The second, "Agricultural Extension in its Infancy in Ohio," was reproduced as a seven page mimeograph for Graham's presentation to an Ohio State class, Agricultural Education 526, 5 Oct. 1955 (OSU RG 40/8/3/15). The only published history of agricultural extension work in Ohio, Carlton F. Christian, *History of Cooperative Extension Work in Agriculture and Home Economics in Ohio* (Columbus: Ohio State University Cooperative Extension Service, 1959) is not particularly detailed for the years prior to Smith-Lever funding.

The most detailed record of the formative years of agricultural extension work nationally is Alfred C. True, *A History of Agricultural Extension Work in the United States, 1785-1923* (Washington, D.C.: U.S. Government Printing Office, 1928). It provides a very helpful framework from which to analyze Ohio programs. Roy V. Scott, *The Reluctant Farmer, The Rise of Agricultural Extension to 1914* (Urbana: University of Illinois Press, 1970) provides an interpretive analysis of this period.

Footnotes:

1. "An Opportunity in Rural Schools," manuscript included among Graham speeches and articles 1905-1912 (OSU RG 40/8/3/4).
2. Senate Bill 50, *Ohio Senate Journal, 78th General Assembly* (Columbus: F.J. Herr, State Printers, 1909), pp. 79, 85, 117, 140-141 & 192; *Journal of the House of Representatives,* pp. 195, 244, 272, & 315.
3. Letter, Carl E. Steeb, Secretary, Board of Trustees to Graham, 12 Apr. 1909 (OSU RG 40/8/1/24); *Record of Proceedings of the Board of Trustees of Ohio State University* (Columbus: Champlin Printing Co., 1909) p. 55.
4. Graham, "Agricultural Extension Firsts," remarks made at Ohio Agricultural Extension 25th Anniversary, 10 Oct. 1939 (OSU RG 40/8/3/2).
5. W.J. Warrener, "First Extension School Under Alsdorf Act," *Athens Messenger,* 8 Sept. 1909, p. 6; 9 Sept. pp. 1 & 6; 10 Sept. pp. 1 & 4; 11 Sept. p. 6; 12 Sept. p. 3; 13 Sept. p. 2.
6. Thompson, *39th O.S.U. Report,* 1909, p. 15.
7. Graham, *44th O.S.U. Report,* 1914, p. 64.
8. *45th Annual Report of the Ohio State Board of Agriculture* (Columbus: The Westbote Co., 1891) pp. 292-316; John Hamilton, *Farmers' Insitutes and Agricultural Extension Work in the United States in 1913* (Washington, D.C.: U.S.D.A., Experiment Station Bulletin, No. 83, 1914), p. 27; Graham, *43rd O.S.U. Report,* 1913, pp. 83-84.
9. Graham, *44th O.S.U. Report,* 1914, pp. 63-64.
10. *Ibid.,* p. 65.
11. Alexis Cope, *History of the Ohio State University,* Thomas C. Mendenhall, ed. (Columbus: The Ohio State University Press, 1920).
12. "Country Church Conference," *Ohio Farmer,* Aug. 5 and Aug. 26, 1911.
13. Manuscript folder, Agricultural Trains, 1908-1913 (OSU RG 40/8/2/46); "Agricultural Trains in Ohio," *Ohio Farmer,* Vol. 129, No. 9 (Mar. 2, 1912) pp. 14-29; True, *History of Agricultural Extension,* p. 28; and J. Hamilton, *The Transportation Companies as Factors in Agricultural Extension* (Washington, D.C.: U.S.D.A. Office of Experiment Stations, Circ. 112, 1911).

14. Graham comment during discussion following presentation on agricultural trains as an extension teaching method. *Proceedings, 26th Convention, A.A.A.C.E.S., Atlanta, 1912* (Burlington, Vt.: Free Press Printing Co., 1913).
15. Graham manuscript, Agricultural Trains (OSU RG 40/8/2/46).
16. Manuscript folder and photographs, Agricultural Trains (OSU RG 40/8/2/46).
17. W.E. Mann, *41st O.S.U. Report,* 1911, pp. 118-119.
18. Homemakers' Reading Course, *The Agricultural College Extension Bulletin,* Vol. VI, Supplements Oct. 1910 to Feb. 1911; Farmers' Reading Course, Vol. VI, Supplements Oct. 1910 to Mar. 1911.
19. Thompson, *45th O.S.U. Report,* 1915, pp. 94-95.
20. Graham, *44th O.S.U. Report,* 1914, p. 63.
21. *Ibid.,* pp. 63 & 66.
22. "Agricultural Extension Work," *The Ohio State University Bulletin,* Vol. XVI, No. 1 (July 1911).
23. Thompson, *41st O.S.U. Report,* 1911, p. 14.
24. Legislation related to extension funding was regularly introduced in Congress from 1909 until its passage, but there were significant differences between extension departments in land-grant universities and advocates of more local control. Pres. Taft, of Ohio, was supportive of the effort to secure federal funding. True, *History of Agricultural Extension,* p. 103, and Scott, *Reluctant Farmer,* p.292.
25. J.R. Clarke, *A History of the Western Ohio Superintendents and Principals Round Table, 1883-1940* (Columbus: privately printed, 1941). Clarke was a part-time superintendent in German Township of Clark County at the same time Graham was in Springfield Township. He later became a supervisor of agricultural education in the state department of public instruction. He and Graham were opponents in regard to the Cahill legislation.
26. Graham manuscript, "The Transition From Boys' and Girls' Agricultural Clubs to Vocational Agriculture and Home Economics in Ohio," 21 May 1948 (OSU RG 40/8/1/11) and Brittain, *Ohio School Survey,* 1914, p. 251.
27. A.B. Graham, "The Function and Value of An Agricultural Course in the High School," *Ohio Educational Monthly,* 56 (Sept. 1907) pp. 514-518.
28. Frank W. Miller, *58th Ohio School Report,* 29 Dec. 1911, pp. 48-49.
29. Graham and Clarke manuscripts, op. cit.
30. Mendenhall, *History of Ohio State University; 49th O.S.U. Report,* p. 80 shows the first course listing by the Agricultural Education Department.
31. Memoranda, Price to Thompson with comparative charts on enrollments and budget appropriations for the period 1909 to 1914 (OSU RG 3/e/2/1). Dean Price may have been working from preliminary figures for the *44th O.S.U. Report,* p. 10 lists 1,247 students in the College of Agriculture (including Home Economics) and 3,829 students in the university for the year ending June 30, 1914.
32. James K. Mercer,*Ohio Legislative History, 1909-1913* (Columbus: Edward T. Miller Co., 1913), p. 79. *First Report to the Governor of the Acts and Investigations of the Agricultural Commisssion of Ohio* (Springfield: The Springfield Publishing Co., 1915), pp. 198-224 contains this legislation in its entirety.

33. *O.S.U. Trustees Proceedings,* 5 Aug. 1913, p. 27.
34. Graham, *The Agricultural College Extension Bulletin,* Vol. II, (Mar. 1907), p. 9.
35. *Proceedings, 25th Convention, A.A.A.C.E.S., Columbus, 1911* (Montpelier Vt.: Capital City Press, 1912), pp. 220-221.
36. *Ibid.;* F.W. Howe, *Boys' and Girls' Agricultural Clubs* (Washington,D.C.: U.S.D.A. Farmers' Bulletin, No. 385, 1910), p. 5 defines a "club" as "an association of boys who enter into a competition to determine who can grow the most or best corn on a certain area of ground under definite rules of planting, cultivation, and exhibit." It was exactly this concept which Graham was trying to convince his peers was not educational because it did not ask and attempt to answer the "why" questions.
37. "Corn Boys and Girls Home After Big Trip," *Columbus Dispatch,* 7 Dec. 1913, pp. 3 & 11; A.B. Graham's ticket confirms he attended although he did not arrange this trip (OSU RG 40/8/2/27).
38. W.H. Palmer, "Corn Growing Contests," *Ohio Golden Anniversary, 1902-1952,* p. 34 (OHS MC 194/2/4).
39. Graham, *A.A.A.C.E.S. Proceedings,* 1912, p. 223.
40. True, *History of Agricultural Extension,* pp. 46-47.
41. Hamilton, *Farmers' Institutes,* op. cit.; Cope, *History of Ohio State University,* pp. 477-478.
42. True, *History of Agricultural Extension,* p. 26.
43. *Ibid.,* p. 48.
44. *Ibid.,* p. 57.
45. *Ibid.,* pp. 100-115.
46. *Agricultural Commission Proceedings,* 26 Mar. 1914, p. 84; *O.S.U. Trustees Proceedings,* 1914, p. 80.
47. Letter, Graham to Thompson, 11 May 1914)OSU RG 40/8/1/24).
48. Price's recommendation to Thompson has not been preserved, but a copy was sent by Graham to Congressman Willis, 29 June 1914 in explaining his own resignation (OSU RG 40/8/1/25) and the *Proceedings of the Agricultural Commission* 14 July 1914, pp 122-127 show the establishment of the structure Price proposed.
49. Thompson, *44th O.S.U. Report,* 1914, p. 19.
50. *Ibid.,* p. 20.
51. Letter, Graham to O.H. Benson, U.S. Department of Agriculture, 24 May 1914 (OSU RG 40/8/1/25).
52. Letter of resignation, Graham to President Thompson and Ohio State University Board of Trustees, 24 June 1914 (OSU RG 40/8/1/25).
53. *O.SU. Trustees Proceedings,* 1 July 1913 to 30 June 1914, p. 159; 1 July 1914 to 30 June 1915, p. 10.
54. Price, *44th O.S.U. Report,* 1914, p. 29.
55. James K. Mercer, *Ohio Legislative History, 1913-1917* (Columbus: F.J. Herr Printers, 1918) pp. 185-186.
56. *O.S.U. Trustees Proceedings,* 1 July 1914 to 30 June 1915, p. 77.
57. Thompson manuscripts (OSU RG 3/e/2/1): Letter of resignation from Price to Thompson, 27 Apr. 1915; "Politics at Ohio State University," an open letter from Thompson to the press, 20 May 1915; Letter, Thompson to E.S. Bayard, Editor, *National Stockman & Farmer,* Pittsburgh, Penna., 24 May, 1915;

Columbus Dispatch, 11 June 1915, p. 1; 15 June, p. 15, and 16 June, p. 1.
58. *45th O.S.U. Report,* pp. 98-100.
59. *Report to the Governor of Ohio by Ohio State School Survey Commisssion,*
    Horace L. Brittain, Director (Columbus: F.J. Herr Printing Co., 1914).
60. Price, *44th O.S.U. Report,* p. 30.
61. Thompson, *45th O.S.U. Report,* p. 18.
62. Program, "25th Anniversary of Cooperative Extension Work in Ohio," 10
    Oct. 1939 (OSU RG 40/8/3/2); A plaque commemorating this event is
    embedded on the south side of the front entrance to Townshend Hall.

Chapter 9

The most valuable source of materials regarding Graham's work in the U.S.
Department of Agriculture is National Archives Record Group 33, which contains
Extension Service Records for the period 1907 to 1943. The preliminary inventory
of this record group compiled by Virgil E. Baugh and published by the National
Archives in 1955 (No. 56-1) is quite inadequate for efficient research, but is the only
index available for records in which the general correspondence alone requires
402 feet. The "author index to correspondence" contains only A.B. Graham's
personnel card, but hundreds of his letters and memoranda are included in this
collection. Since correspondence and reports are filed chronologically and then
alphabetically by states, researchers would be well advised to know that the
States Relations Service, 1915-23 and the Extension Service, 1924-43 are filed
under the District of Columbia. Useful material is filed in the papers of individual
staff members A.C. True, C.W. Pugsley, C.W. Warburton, C.B. Smith, and A.B.
Graham as well as unit files for States Relations Service North and West, Extension Specialists, and Smith-Lever Inspection Reports. There are doubtless good
materials related to Graham scattered among the correspondence of individual
state extension directors, but the resources of the authors did not permit such an
extended search. We are confident, however, that the review of Washington, D.C.
correspondence and reports presents a fair example of Graham's work during
these twenty-two years.

The Ohio State University Archives, Record Group 40/8, contains Graham's
personal files from the U.S.D.A. which he retained in retirement. This includes
photographs of colleagues, correspondence regarding the "Pride of the Land"
march, papers from specialist staff conferences for 1922-26 and 1929-32, and
separate folders for each of the 23 northern and western states describing their
extension activities during 1915-17.

The most comprehensive histories of pre-extension and early extension activities are True, *History of Agricultural Extension,* and Scott, *The Reluctant Farmer,*
cited in chapter 8. True's *History of Agricultural Education,* also mentioned
earlier, is an excellent reference for placing the development of agricultural extension into the broader perspective of agricultural education. Although limited in its
historical perspective by their U.S.D.A. employment at the time of publication,
Smith and Wilson, *Agricultural Extension System,* offers the perceptions of two of
Graham's long-time colleagues.

A complete bibliography of agricultural extension literature would not be
appropriate nor helpful to readers of this work, although the authors' experiences

perhaps draw upon works unnamed. Two publications supported by the extension professional fraternity should be noted for the particular contribution they make to an understanding of the pioneers of the profession: *The Spirit and Philosophy of Extension Work*, R.K. Bliss, ed. (Washington, D.C.: U. S. Department of Agriculture and Epsilon Sigma Phi, 1952) and *The People and the Profession*, R.L. Reeder, ed. (Epsilon Sigma Phi, 1979).

Footnotes:
1. Memo, Graham to Director Warburton, Dr. Smith, and Mr. Brigham, one week after his retirement, 8 Apr. 1938 (OSU RG 40/8/1/24).
2. Letter, Graham to Lowry F. Sater, President, O.S.U. Alumni Association, 22 July 1914 *(Graham Family collection)*.
3. Letter, Graham to William O. Thompson, 25 Mar. 1915 (OSU RG 3/e/24/44).
4. Letter, Graham to A.S. Neal, Manhattan, Kansas, 20 Sept. 1915 *(Graham Family collection)*.
5. Letter, T.L. Wheeler, Editor, *The Farmer's Guide,* Huntington, Ind. to Dr. Cardiff, Washington State Univ., 16 Nov. 1915. *(Graham Family collection)*.
6. Letter, W. O. Thompson to C. B. Smith 6 Nov. 1915 (NA RG 33/702/10).
7. Letter, C. B. Smith to Graham, 22 Nov. 1915 *(Graham Family collection)*.
8. Graham U.S.D.A. employment card *(NA RG 33, Author Index to General Correspondence, 1907-43)*.
9. Letter, A. A. Johnson to Graham, 28 Mar. 1916 (OSU RG 40/8/1/27).
10. True, *History of Agricultural Extension,* pp.124-174.
11. Illinois Extension Materials, 1916-17 (OSU RG 40/8/3/30).
12. Maine Extension Materials, 1916 (OSU RG 40/8/3/34).
13. Massachusetts Extension Materials, 1915-17 (OSU RG 40/8/3/35).
14. Memo, Graham to L. A. Clinton and C. B. Smith, 1916 (NA RG 33/702/11).
15. Letter, Graham to Lester Schlup, Information Services, U.S.D.A., 5 Apr. 1953 (OSU RG 40/8/1/25).
16. Memo, Graham to C. B. Smith, 21 Aug. 1920 (NA RG 33/702/89).
17. Graham, "Some Thoughts on Teaching Subject Matter to Adults," undated U.S.D.A. mimeograph. (OSU RG 40/8/3/6).
18. Graham speech, "Selling Notions," undated typed mss. (OSU RG 40/8/3/25).
19. Graham speech, "The Extension Specialist and His Work," Central States Extension Conference, Chicago, Ill., 22-23 Mar. 1921 (NA RG 33/702/89).
20. Letter from C. W. Pugsley, Asst. Sec., U.S.D.A. to State Extension Directors with Extension Service organization chart attached, 29 June 1922 (OSU RG 40/8/3/23).
21. Letter, Graham to Lester A. Schlup, 26 Dec. 1952 (OSU RG 40/8/1/25). This handwritten, 29 page letter to a close U.S.D.A. colleague contains some of Graham's frank opinions on personnel and internal office relationships.
22. *Ibid.,* Graham indicates that Crocheron of California, Johnson of the Washington State Experiment Station but formerly director in Kansas, Burrett of New York, and Christie of Indiana turned the position down.
23. *Ibid.,*
24. Memo, Graham to C. W. Warburton & C. B. Smith, 23 Sept. 1924 (NA RG 33/702/147).
25. C.B. Smith, "Ten Years of Extension Work Under the Smith-Lever Act," *Association of Land-Grant Colleges Proceedings* (Burlington, Vt.: Free Press Printing Co., 1925), pp. 270-280.

26. Memo, Graham to C. B. Smith reporting on examination of Smith-Lever accounts in six New England States, 24 Sept. 1925 (NA RG 33/702/163).
27. Memo, Graham to C.B. Smith, 19 June 1926 (NA RG 33/702/163).
28. Memo, Graham to J.A. Evans, Asst. Chief, Office of Extension Work, re: Virginia Project, 30 Aug. 1928 (NA RG 33/702/187).
29. Memo, Graham to C.B. Smith, 19 June 1929 (NA RG 33/702/187).
30. Graham presentation, transcript of specialists' meeting, 24 Sept. 1924 (OSU RG 40/8/3/7).
31. Transcript, 11 Feb. 1925 (OSU RG 40/8/3/24).
32. Transcript, 19 Feb. 1924 (OSU RG 40/8/3/8).
33. Transcript, 6 Jan. 1926 (OSU RG 40/8/3/9).
34. Transcript, 23 Oct. 1926 (OSU RG 40/8/3/9).
35. Transcript, 18 Nov. 1931 (OSU RG 40/8/3/10).
36. Transcript, 15 Jan. 1924 (OSU RG 40/8/3/8).
37. Transcript, 11 Mar. 1924 (OSU RG 40/8/3/8).
38. Transcript, 22 Oct. 1925 (OSU RG 40/8/3/9).
39. Transcript, 7 Oct. 1925 (OSU RG 40/8/3/9).
40. Transcript, 7 Nov. 1925 (OSU RG 40/8/3/9).
41. Interoffice memo re: meeting, 10 May 1937 (NA RG 33/2140).
42. Transcript, 8 Apr. 1925 (OSU RG 40/8/3/9).
43. Transcript, 24 Feb. 1926 (OSU RG 40/8/3/9).
44. Transcript, 23 Apr. 1930 (OSU RG 40/8/3/10).
45. Interoffice memo re: 16-17 Dec. 1936 meeting (NA RG 33/2140).
46. Memo, Graham to C.B. Smith, 5 Apr. 1928 (NA RG 33/702/181).
47. Graham speech, Conference of Extension Workers, St. Paul, Minn., 1 Oct. 1923 (OSU RG 40/8/3/7).
48. A.B. Graham, *Some Fundamentals of Extension Teaching* (Washington D.C.: U.S.D.A., Extension Service Circular 19, July 1926).
49. Memo, Graham to C.B. Smith, 13 Mar. 1933 (NA RG 33/702/214).
50. Memo, Graham to C.B. Smith, 5 Dec. 1934 (NA RG 33/1904).
51. Graham, *Let's Pretend,* privately printed, 1932 (OHS PA Box 10, #14). Graham describes the origin of this brochure in a letter to his cousin, Edith Bradley Reeder of Fletcher, O., 21 Nov. 1954 (OSU RG 40/8/1/25).
52. Milton Eisenhower's title was "Director of Information" on the April 15, 1934, U.S. Department of Agriculture table of organization.
53. Letter, L.A. Schlup to Graham, 17 Dec. 1934, re: Farmers' Bulletin #1738 (NA RG 33/1904).
54. Memo, Graham to C.B. Smith, 21 Apr. 1937 (NA RG 33/2140).
55. Memo, C.B. Smith to Graham, 21 July 1932 (NA RG 33/702/214).
56. Memo, Graham to C.B. Smith, 11 Apr. 1928 (NA RG 33/702/181).
57. Letter, Graham to Prof. Working, re: New York Smith-Lever projects, 8 July 1918 (NA RG 33/702/43).
58. Memo, Graham to C.B. Smith, 4 Nov. 1922 (NA RG 33/702/121).
59. Memo, Graham to G.E. Farrell, 21 Aug. 1923 (NA RG 33/702/134).
60. Memo, G.E. Farrell to Graham, 16 Oct. 1923 (NA RG 33/702/134).
61. Memo, Graham to C.B. Smith, 4 Mar. 1927 (NA RG 33/702/173).
62. Memo, Graham to C.B. Smith, 14 Dec. 1932 (NA RG 33/702/214).
63. Memo, Graham to C.B. Smith, 3 Nov. 1934 (NA RG 33/1904).
64. Letter, Graham to E. F. Goldman, 31 July 1933 (OSU RG 40/8/2/4). *Pride of*

the Land sheet music (OSU RG 40/8/2/18). "A Man and An Idea," *Washington Herald,* 15 July 1934 (OSU RG 40/8/1/17).

65. Graham speech, "The Importance of Vision," National 4-H Camp, 19 June 1935, mimeograph, Extension Service, U.S.D.A., Washington, D.C., 7 pp. (OSU RG 40/8/2/43).
66. Memo, C.B. Smith to Graham, 20 Feb. 1935 (NA RG 33/1904).
67. Graham U.S.D.A. employment card (NA RG 33, Author Index to General Correspondence, 1907-43) and Graham annual salaries, 1916-1938 (OSU RG 40/8/2/26).
68. *O.S.U. Trustees Proceedings,* 15 June 1936, pp 134 & 201.
69. Letter from R.J. Baldwin, Director, Michigan State College, requesting Graham as Annual Extension Conference speaker, 7 Oct. 1936 (NA RG 33/2140).
70. *Columbus Dispatch,* 27 Dec. 1936, Sec. A. p. 5.
71. *Washington Star,* 27 Dec. 1936, Sec. B, p. 5.
72. *Boston Globe,* 31 Dec. 1936, p. 6.
73. *Philadelphia Bulletin,* 31 Dec. 1936. All of these newspaper clippings are in (OSU RG 40/8/2/1).
74. U.S.D.A. news release regarding 30th Anniversary celebration of Boys' and Girls' Agricultural Club movement during the 1932 National 4-H Camp (OSU RG 40/8/2/3).
75. Memo, Graham to Editor Brigham re: Gertrude Warren's circular letter, 15 May 1925 (NA RG 33/702/147).
76. Memo, Graham to Gertrude Warren, 24 Oct. 1934 (NA RG 33/1904).
77. Memo from twenty-one extension specialists to Director Warburton, 5 Oct. 1937 (NA RG 33/2140).
78. Graham retirement luncheon program, 12 Mar. 1938 and C.B. Smith, "A.B. Graham Retires," *Extension Service Review* clipping (OSU RG 40/8/1/9).

Chapter 10

The most complete collection of materials on the 1952 4-H Jubilee Anniversary is included in the Graham manuscripts at the Ohio Historical Society, Manuscript Collection 194. This includes numerous materials from county celebrations throughout the state in the course of the year. The authors found local newspapers the best source for supplementing this manuscript material.

Volumes 35 and 36 of the *Ohio Extension Service News* are deposited in the rare books collection of the Ohio State University Library.

The most complete published data regarding 4-H Club origins are the works of Reck, Scott, and Wessel cited in chapter 6.

Footnotes:
1. Graham's remarks at 50th Anniversary luncheon, 15 Jan. 1952, Springfield, Ohio (OHS MC 194/1/28).
2. First day issue and cover (OHS MC 194/1/29). Copies are also deposited at CCHS.
3. *Ohio Extension Service News,* Vol. 35 (Jan. 1952), p. 1. "Ohio Man Honored For Early Youth Work," *National 4-H News,* Vol. XXX (Mar. 1952, p 21. *Springfield Daily News,* 15 Jan. 1952, p. 1. *Columbus Dispatch,* 13 Jan. 1952).

4. Herman Higgins, "Salute - The 4-H Story," *Eagle*, Vol. 40, No. 6 (June 1952), pp. 10-11; and photograph of plaque inscription (OHS MC 194/1/28). *Columbus Dispatch*, 16 Jan. 1952, Sec. A, p. 2.

5. Eva Kinsey, "Pages of Progress," typescript manuscript (OHS MC 194/1/28). *Springfield News-Sun*, 9 Mar. 1952, p. 1. Lois Winterberg, "50 Years of 4-H in Ohio," *National 4-H News*, Vol. XXX, No. 5 (May 1952) pp. 30-31.

6. *Ohio's Golden Anniversary, 1902-1952*, Ohio 4-H Club Office, Ohio Agricultural Extension Service (OHS MC 194/2/4).

7. Reck, *4-H Story*, p. 3.

8. Virgil E. Baugh, *Preliminary Inventory of the Records of the Extension Service* (Washington, D.C.: National Archives, General Services Administration, 1955) p.3.

9. C.B. Smith and M.C. Wilson, *The Agricultural Extension System in the United States* (New York: John Wiley & Sons, Inc., 1930), pp.33-35.

10. Dick J. Crosby, "Boys' Agricultural Clubs," *Yearbook of the United States Department of Agriculture, 1904* (Washington, D.C.: Government Printing Office, 1905) pp. 489-496.

11. Otwell exchanged letters with Graham during 1930 when his stationery letterhead was promoting "Farmer Boy Seed Corn" (OSU RG 40/8/2/25).

12. Benjamin M. Davis, "Agricultural Education: Boys Agricultural Clubs," *Elementary School Teacher*, Vol. XI (Mar. 1911), pp. 371-380.

13. Eva Kinsey, "Flame of Gold," typescript manuscript (OHS MC 194/1/30).

14. *Eaton Register-Herald*, 5 Mar. 1952, Sec. A, p. 2.

15. Ben Hayes, *Columbus Citizen-Journal*, 5 June 1952, p. 11. Bill Zipf, *Columbus Dispatch*, 8 June 1952, Sec. F, p. 18.

16. *Dayton Daily News*, 1 Sept. 1952.

17. Program and manuscript of Van Wert County pageant (OHS MC 194/1/34).

18. *Hamilton Journal and Daily News*, 25 Sept. 1952, p. 40.

19. *Springfield News-Sun*, 14 Aug. 1952, pp. 1-2.

20. See chapter 5, footnote 34 regarding club membership. Sixty-five of the 145 members appearing on Graham's 1902 and 1904 club lists are not named on this commemorative plaque. It is possible that misinterpretations of handwriting or spelling created minor discrepancies, but the authors have no explanation for such a large number of omissions.

21. George M. Barmann, "4-H Club Jubilee Points Up Value of the Vast Movement," *Pittsburgh Courier*, 2 Aug. 1952, Magazine Section, p. 6.

22. A.B. Graham, "Early Boys' and Girls' Club (4-H) Exhibits," *Ohio State Fair, Junior Division Premium List*, 22-29 Aug. 1952, Columbus, Ohio pp. 31-32.

23. "Adjusting Our Patterns," *Ohio Extension Service News*, Vol. 36 (Sept. 1952), p. 1.

24. Ohio Newspaper Association Banquet Program (OHS MC 194/2/3). *Columbus Dispatch*, 19 Sept. 1952, Sec. B, p. 2.

25. A.B. Graham, "Review of Golden Anniversary Year," *Ohio Extension Service News*, Vol. 36 (March 1953), p. 1.

Chapter 11

Plaques and portraits displayed in public locations are noted in the text. Most of the personal tributes to Graham, such as certificates and awards are currently in the possession of his daughter Helen Graham Baker.

There are frequently several newspaper or magazine accounts relating to each of Graham's awards. Readers must carefully weigh conflicting data since some of these accounts, written by reporters with only casual knowledge of Graham, contain significant inaccuracies. The footnotes attempt to suggest the most readily available and reasonably accurate sources.

Footnotes:

1. Letter, Graham to C.M.Ferguson, Director, Federal Extension Service, 13 June 1954, sending regrets that he cannot attend National 4-H Camp (OSU RG 40/8/1). This was a favorite Graham illustration and variations frequently appear in his speeches.
2. *Springfield Daily News*, 23 Jan. 1932, p. 4.
3. John F. Cunningham biographical sketch, *Extension Service News*, Vol. XVII, (May 1932), p. 1.
4. "25th National 4-H Club Congress Recognizes Ten 4-H Pioneers," *National 4-H Club News*, Vol. XXV (Jan. 1947), p. 34. The fact that two of these ten pioneers are not mentioned in Reck's *4-H Story*, published four years later by this same national committee leads one to suspect the criteria for this award included personal presence for acceptance.
5. Typescript manuscript (OHS MC 194/1/2).
6. Remarks, J. L. Morrill at the Ohio State University, 29 Oct. 1948 (Graham Family collection).
7. *Springfield Daily News*, 7 Mar. 1951, p. 4; *Columbus Dispatch*, 7 Mar. 1951, Sec. B, p. 4; *Ohio Extension Service News*, Vol. 34 (Mar. 1951), p. 1.
8. *Springfield Daily News*, 6 Oct. 1951, pp 1 & 4.
9. *Ohio State University Convocation Program*, 12 June 1953. Minutes of Committee on Honorary Degrees (OSU RG 35/C-2/2).
10. This reflects Graham's famous sense of humor and refers to his brief enrollment as an OSU student during 1899-90. Quoted by Grace Goulder, *Cleveland Press*, (Magazine section), 1 Mar. 1959.
11. Letter, Graham to cousin Edith Bradley Reeder, 21 Nov. 1954 (OSU RG 40/8/1/25).
12. *Marietta Times*, 7 June 1955. Letter from Sandra B. Neyman, Dawes Memorial Library, Marietta College to authors, 10 May 1983 with photocopy of 118th Commencement Program, Marietta College, 6 June 1955.
13. *Columbus Dispatch*, 28 Aug. 1955, Sec. D, p. 4; *The Ohio Farmer*, Vol. 216, No. 6 (17 Sept. 1955), p. 46; letter and related materials from Mary Lou Pieffer Saunway to authors, 30 May 1983.
14. George M. Barmann, *Springfield Sun*, 17 Aug. 1955, p. 2.
15. *The Ohio Farmer*, Vol. 220, No. 12 (21 Dec. 1957) p. 6.
16. *Ohio Extension Service News*, Vol. 41, No. 1, (Jan 1958), p. 6.
17. *Springfield Daily News*, 12 Dec. 1957, p. 5. Manuscript materials at the Graham High School library include among other items a typescript copy of Graham's dedication address.

18. Letter, Richard Dibert, President, Graham High School F.F.A. to Graham, 25 Mar. 1959 (OSU RG 40/8/1).
19. Editorial, *Columbus Dispatch*, 14 Mar. 1958, Sec. B, p.2.
20. *Columbus Dispatch*, 15 July 1958.
21. (Lebanon) *Western Star*, 14 July 1960, p. 1.
22. *Springfield Sun*, 28 Feb. 1968, p. 33.
23. *The Ohio Farmer*, Vol. 241 (1 June 1968), p. 21.
24. *Ohio Historical Society Echoes*, Vol. 11 (Jan. 1972), p. 2.
25. Dedication ceremony program and photographs, Clark County Cooperative Extension Service. *Springfield News-Sun*, 18 June 1976 and 20 June 1976.
26. "1982 Ohio 4-H Foundation Annual Report," Cooperative Extension Service. The Ohio State University, pp. 4-6. *Springfield News-Sun*, 6 Oct. 1977.
27. *The Ohio Farmer*, Vol. 267 (2 May 1981), p. 12.
28. Ohio 4-H Educational Center, Dedication Program, 20 Nov. 1983; interview, Charles W. Lifer Assistant Director and State Leader, 4-H.
29. News release, 13 April 1984, the Agricultural Hall of Fame and National Center; Agricutural Hall of Fame Induction Ceremonies program, 27 Apr. 1984.

Chapter 12

Footnotes:

1. Letter, Graham to Rev. Lance Webb, 1 Dec. 1954 (OSU RG 40/8/1/25). In retirement Graham often listened to Rev. Webb, of the North Broadway United Methodist Church in Columbus on the radio, and they exchanged many delightful letters inspired by these sermons. Rev. Webb used excerpts from Graham's correspondence in preaching his memorial service.
2. Readers who wish to examine this concept in depth might consult the widely recognized work of Benjamin Bloom and others regarding the cognitive learning domain. Benjamin S. Bloom, ed. *Taxonomy of Educational Objectives: The Classification of Educational Goals, Handbook I: Cognitive Domain* (New York: David McKay Co., 1956).
3. A. B. Graham, "Centralized Schools in Ohio," *The Agricultural College Extension Bulletin*, Vol. I, No. 5 (Feb. 1906), p. 21.
4. O. J. Kern, "The Consolidated School and the New Agriculture," *N.E.A. Proceedings*, 1907, pp. 277-279.
5. Thomas H. Briggs, *The Junior High School* (Boston: Houghton Mifflin Co., 1920).
6. *Ohio 4-H Foundation Report*, 1982, pp. 13-14.
7. Report of Graham speech, 5 Apr. 1937, *The Lena-Conover Searchlight*, Vol. 12, No.5. Photocopy provided to authors by Richard Putnam, St. Paris, Ohio from his personal collection.
8. Letter, Graham to J. P. Schmidt, 17 Mar. 1941 (OSU RG 40/8/4/Ohio).
9. Tombstone inscription, Lot 225, Fletcher Cemetery, Fletcher, Ohio; Details regarding erection of tombstone given by letter, Joseph R. Graham to authors, 18 Sept. 1983.
10. Ralph Waldo Emerson, "Man The Reformer," a lecture read before the Mechanics' Apprentices' Library Association, Boston, 25 Jan. 1841; in *Nature Addresses and Lectures*, Edward W. Emerson, ed. (Boston: Houghton Mifflin & Co., 1904) p. 228.

Index

[#] refers to photograph number rather than page number

Graham Chronology

13 Mar. 1868	Birth, Champaign Co., near Lena, Ohio
1874-79	Student, Carmony School, Champaign Co., Ohio
2 Feb. 1879	Fire destroys Graham home, father fatally burned
1879-84	Student, Allen's School, Miami Co., Ohio
1884-85	Student & graduate, Lena-Conover School,Miami Co., Ohio
1885-87	Teacher, Carmony School, Champaign Co., Ohio
1887-88	Student, National Normal University, Lebanon, Ohio
1888-89	Teacher, Carmony School, Champaign Co., Ohio
1889-90	Student, Ohio State University, Columbus, Ohio
14 Aug. 1890	Marriage to Maud K. Lauer, Miami Co., Ohio
1890-91	Teacher/Principal, Lena-Conover School, Miami Co., Ohio
1891-92	Teacher, Brush School, Shelby Co., Ohio
1892-93	Teacher, New Hope School, Miami Co., Ohio
1893-94	Teacher, Carmony School, Champaign Co., Ohio
1894-96	Teacher, Cook School, Champaign Co., Ohio
1896-1900	Teacher/Principal, Terre Haute School and Superintendent Southern Mad River Twp., Champaign Co., Ohio
1900-04	Superintendent, Springfield Twp., Clark Co., Ohio
15 Jan. 1902	Organized Agricultural Experiment Club, Springfield Twp., Clark Co., Ohio
1904-05	Teacher/Principal, Frey School, Springfield, Ohio
1905-14	Superintendent of Agricultural Extension, Ohio State University, Columbus, Ohio
1914-15	Head of Extension Department, New York School of Agriculture, Long Island, New York
1915-22	Administrative Specialist, States Relations Service, North & West, United States Department of Agriculture, Washington, D.C.
1922-38	In Charge of Subject Matter Specialists, Extension Service, United States Department of Agriculture, Washington, D.C.
12 Mar. 1938	U.S.D.A. retirement
1938-60	Retired educator, Columbus, Ohio
14 Jan. 1960	Death, Franklin Co., Ohio — Burial, Fletcher Cemetery, Miami Co., Ohio

About the Authors

VIRGINIA EVANS McCORMICK was a 4-H member while growing up in Licking County, Ohio. She graduated from Ohio Wesleyan University, completed graduate work in sociology at Pennsylvania State University and received her Ph.D. in education from The Ohio State University.

She has been a high school teacher and extension home economist in Ohio; was a member of the state 4-H staff in Pennsylvania and in Ohio; was an extension home economics administrator at Iowa State and Ohio State Universities.

She is the author of numerous publications in adult education, home economics education, 4-H leadership development and Ohio history.

ROBERT WILLIAM McCORMICK is professor emeritus, agricultural education, from The Ohio State University, retiring as assistant vice president for continuing education.

He was a 4-H member while growing up on a dairy farm in Butler County, Ohio. He graduated from Ohio State University after serving with the medical detachment of the 696th Armored Field Artillery Battalion in World War II. After serving as a vocational agriculture teacher and county extension agent in Ohio he received his Ph.D. in extension education from the University of Wisconsin. He served the Ohio Cooperative Extension Service as leader of training and research and as assistant director for administration.

He is the author of numerous publications in adult and continuing education, vocational education and military history.